# LOST IN THE SHADOW OF FAME

## THE NEGLECTED STORY OF KERMIT ROOSEVELT; A GALLANT AND TRAGIC AMERICAN

## WILLIAM E. LEMANSKI

FIRST SUNBURY PRESS EDITION
*Printed in the United States of America*
January 2012

Trade Paperback ISBN: 978-1-62006-011-7
Mobipocket format (Kindle) ISBN: 978-1- 62006-012-4
ePub format (Nook) ISBN: 978-1-62006-013-1

Published by:
**Sunbury Press**
Camp Hill, PA
www.sunburypress.com

Camp Hill, Pennsylvania    USA

For the vilified yet virtuous, who
wore the uniform many years ago.

# TABLE OF CONTENTS

# Illustrations

# PREFACE

When considering the Roosevelt dynasty, Theodore, Franklin, Eleanor, and even the sharp-witted and acerbic Alice come to mind. However, Theodore's second son, Kermit, both a brilliant and tragic member of the Long Island Roosevelts has generally been neglected from the popular history of that illustrious twentieth-century American family. While all of the Roosevelt boys were exceptional and also forgotten in the public's contemporary memory, Kermit held a special place within the family and perhaps imposed a greater influence on his parents than any other member of the family.

Kermit was the embodiment of a very disparate combination of character traits that encompassed his father's love for adventure, courage and physical vigor along with his mother's sensitivity and intellect. But unfortunately he was afflicted by another Roosevelt trait: severe depression and alcoholism.

Kermit was a multi-lingual intellectual, author, soldier, big-game hunter, explorer, world traveler, writer and corporate executive. Unlike his gruff extroverted father, he was a somewhat moody, introspective and deep thinker who could display the contrasting traits of dreamy sensitivity along with, when necessary, the action of a courageous combat soldier and rugged pursuer of blood sports. In a letter to his daughter Ethel while on safari in 1909 Africa, Theodore commented about his companion Kermit:

> *"It is rare for a boy with his refined tastes and his genuine appreciation of literature - and of so much else - to be also an exceptionally bold and hardy sportsman. He is still altogether too reckless; but by my hen-with-one-chicken attitude, I think I shall get him out of Africa uninjured; and his keenness, cool nerve, horsemanship, hardiness, endurance, and good eyesight make him a really good wilderness hunter."*

On many occasions throughout his life, Kermit displayed great courage in the face of personal danger equal to the many harrowing exploits of his famous father. In fact, during Theodore's famous exploration of the Amazon's "River of Doubt", Kermit actually saved the life of our twenty-sixth president.

Having lived through the first half of the twentieth century, he participated in many of the major events that formed the present day United States. In 1898, the Spanish-American War along with the acquisition of the Philippines and Hawaii established the country as an imperial nation. President Roosevelt's dispatch of the "Great White Fleet" on its around-the-world tour in 1908 and Roosevelt's mediation of the Treaty of Portsmouth in 1905 ending the Russo-Japanese War established the nation as a world power; laying the groundwork for the United States becoming the world's preeminent superpower by the end of the twentieth-century. Kermit had a front row seat to these events as well as participating in both the First and Second World Wars and personally suffering financial loss as a corporate executive in between the wars during the Great Depression.

Despite his many adventurous exploits and achievements, Kermit was unable to cope with the same demons that ended the life of his uncle, Theodore's brother and Eleanor Roosevelt's father, Elliot. He eventually succumbed to the same alcoholic horror ending in middle-age (as officially recorded) in a violent, self inflicted death. After leading a vibrant, adventurous life, Kermit's decline into alcoholism broke his mother's heart. She died in 1948 never learning the true story of his death. Which was also not revealed to the public by the family for another thirty-years following his demise.

My interest in pursuing the writing of this book and selection of the title is based upon two observations. As an admiring student of Theodore Roosevelt for many years, I noticed Kermit continually moving in and out of much of the voluminous material published both by and about Theodore's personal and public life. Kermit's presence and level of influence on his father's life appeared many more times and with a higher level of significance than any of his siblings and arguably anyone else during Roosevelt's life, except perhaps Theodore Senior and his wife, Edith. Of his four male children, Kermit was the one who accompanied Theodore as both companion and protector on lengthy and

2

dangerous expeditions to both Africa and South America. Of the family members, Kermit was his father's confidant. And also his major worry within the family circle.

This frequency of appearance and involvement on the one hand, offset by the limited and almost nonexistent published biographical material on the enigmatic Kermit, puzzled me. The conflicts within the official documents pertaining to Kermit's death and the potential for evil, unscrupulous conduct at the highest levels of government simply add to the mystique of Kermit's story. Having lived a fascinating and complex life while engaged in some of the major events of the first half of the twentieth-century, surely he has been lost in the shadow of his family's fame and was worthy of a dedicated, published story if not a combined Hollywood adventure and mystery drama.

My other reason for pursuing and recording the various exploits of Kermit's life is my fascination with persons in history who have displayed the generally incompatible character traits of both action-oriented and yet sensitive, intellectual lives.

My goal is to introduce the many fascinating and heretofore fragmented details of Kermit's life with the expectation that the reader, once informed about the life of this extraordinary yet tragic American, will also share my fascination and ponder my speculations.

❖

I am indebted to many for the tedious review of the numerous draft versions and subsequent refinements and additions to Kermit's story as it developed. Bob Quinn, editor at the Hudson Valley's Straus Newspaper Company, scrutinized the manuscript as only a skilled professional could. Surely Bob wore-down many pencils addressing my endless struggle with and misuse of commas, apostrophes, and the other quirky little blots of ink that comprise the printed page. Additional thanks to editor, Allyson Gard of the Sunbury Press for many insightful comments during the editing process. My wife Pat provided endless input for the duration with her sharp eye for misspelled words and run-on sentences.

Others who painstakingly picked over and commented on various iterations of the manuscript were Nassau County Police Detective Lieutenant (Ret.) Robert Lucas, Raymond Peretin and Vincent Longo.

Valuable detailed information was gleaned from the following sources: Smithsonian Institution; Explorers Club of New York; the personal diary of George K. Cherrie in the American Museum of Natural History; Harvard University Library; Federal Bureau of Investigation; Franklin Delano Roosevelt Library; Library of Congress; National Archives; the Groton School's Archivist, Douglas V.D. Brown and Robert Alexander, Alan Simcock and Judith Lappin of the United Kingdom who provided historic details on the 14th Light Armoured Motor Battery (LAMB) in World War I Mesopotamia and the Liddell Hart Center for Military Archives at King's College, London.

Any factual errors, omissions or misstatements in this book are solely the fault of the author and whenever or wherever they may exist are published with his deep regret and apology.

Bill Lemanski
Tuxedo Park, New York
October 7, 2010

# INTRODUCTION

He was considered Theodore Roosevelt's most sensitive child, yet it was Kermit who accompanied his father as companion and protector on two dangerous and extraordinary expeditions to remote and uncharted lands at the turn of the Twentieth Century. While in the unknown jungles of Amazonia, braving frightful suffering and starvation, he actually saved the former President's life.

He was a complex combination of character traits. He immersed himself in literature, languages and natural history but he was compelled to engage in adventure and war with an unbridled obsession.

He distinguished himself in World War I, serving with the British in the Middle-East where he skirmished with Arab bandits and Turkish soldiers; on one occasion even liberating a Turkish officer and freeing his harem. His extraordinary language skills were a particular advantage to his British Army superiors.

Kermit's intellect enabled him to complete his education at Harvard in two and a half years; he later developed some of the largest and most important shipping companies in America following the Great War. Even if he were not the son of a remarkable President – or perhaps because of it - while not engaged in international shipping, he traveled the world securing rare and unknown species of animals for America's great natural history museums.

He crossed paths with Lawrence of Arabia and befriended such notable characters as Denys Finch Hatton and Rudyard Kipling. He hobnobbed with international sportsman and high-ranking military officers and maintained a personal friendship with Winston Churchill.

In the days before the Internet and satellites and cable television, intelligence came from personal conversations. With his wealthy friend, William Vincent Astor, Kermit even conducted a clandestine, amateur spy organization during the Fascist's rise to power in Europe and Asia. The group met periodically in a secret New York brownstone with many prominent international travelers where they compiled random intelligence information on world events for Kermit's cousin, President Franklin Delano Roosevelt. Traveling with Astor on his yacht or commiserating with many of the dignitaries he'd met on his journeys, Kermit would provide FDR with an informal, but valuable sense of the world.

However, despite his growing wealth and phenomenal success in the shipping industry during the 1920s, as with many talented business leaders of the period, the 1929 Stock Market crash severely affected his financial stability.

Unable to wait for the United States to enter World War II, he once again volunteered with the British securing a commission from the King. Suffering from his many physical ailments contracted during years of rough wilderness travel, coupled with a severe alcohol affliction, he was cashiered from the British Army after serving valiantly in the debacle of the Norway campaign.

Upon his return to the United States, he would beseech his cousin for a military commission. But concern for Kermit's aberrant behavior led FDR to arrange a posting in the far reaches of Alaska, perhaps to avoid a scandal that would hurt the President and threaten national security.

But for all of Kermit's many gifts, there was a darker side to Kermit Roosevelt. Later, at the behest of FDR, the FBI would watch him for more than a month as he disappeared while he lived in a hotel and carried on an affair with a shady woman. His mounting indiscretions became a major problem for the Roosevelt Administration.

And then there is the manner of his death in 1943 which the New York Times reported the cause and location unknown, although presumably it was natural. For two-decades the circumstances of his death were concealed by the government. Even into the 1970s there were efforts to suppress any information.

Was it suicide, which eventually was released as the official cause of death? Or was there a more sinister reason for his demise? A thorough review of the classified government documents will reveal numerous inconsistencies and improbabilities. One report says he is missing a finger from his left hand; another says it's a missing finger on his right hand. Much conflict exists in the testimony taken from military personnel with no follow-up or corroborating testimony. Even the official time of death conflicts between the autopsy report and the Army's investigation.

The Army rushed to expedite and close the case with no forensics, no ballistics investigation and no follow-up questioning of witnesses. Almost thirty-years later when a general officer requested information on "how he died," the government replied "Died as a result of self inflicted gunshot wound...this information is not to be released."

Who was this multidimensional, brilliant man? Perhaps as Kermit himself wrote: "...it is when men are off in the wilds that they show themselves as they really are."

Sadly, the contemporary memory of this enigmatic and gifted American is as isolated and forgotten as his many achievements. As a member of one of our country's most notable political families, he lived an extraordinary life of great success and accomplishments. His tragic decline and mysterious demise, foreshadowing a possible government cover-up makes his story all the more poignant.

# Chapter I - The Early Years

*"When Nature wants to drill a man*
*And thrill a man,*
*And skill a man,*
*When Nature wants to mould a man*
*To play the noblest part;"*

*"When Nature Wants a Man"* Angela Margan

The latter 19th and early 20th Century, still steeped in Victorian virtue, was an auspicious time to come of age for a person with a romantic character and adventurous spirit. Exploration of the remote regions of the globe was a major endeavor for the western nations as many of the blank map spaces previously depicted as terra incognita were now being filled-in by the courage, sacrifice and endurance of wilderness exploration. The major world powers were locked in a struggle for colonial acquisition and, prior to the awakening horrors of the Great War, were still steeped in boundless confidence, romanticism and greed; spreading tentacles of influence across the wild and isolated regions of the world. The United States was a growing and dynamic nation, fast becoming a world power, having recently spanned the east and west coasts with communications, transportation and settlement.

Science, technology and the advances of the Industrial Revolution were marching ahead as never before. Application of the new internal combustion engine provided a reduction in labor along with dazzling improvements in manufacturing and production. The introduction of the automobile and airplane were reducing both travel distance and time. The expanding usage of electricity in urban areas ended gas lighting in both street and home and enabled the development of many modern homemaking conveniences. International voice communications became a reality with the laying of the transatlantic cable while medicine and the science of physics leaped forward with the discovery of x-ray and the theory of relativity.

Countless other dazzling innovations and discoveries would surface in the span of one or two generations. This was indeed, a breath-taking and exciting period to experience, participate in and savor.

❖

On Thursday, October 10, 1889, Kermit Roosevelt, the second son of then U.S. Civil Service Commissioner, Theodore Roosevelt, was born at Oyster Bay, Long Island, New York. The name Kermit was derived from his mother's maiden name, Edith Kermit Carow, the name originating in honor of her great-aunt's husband, Robert Kermit. Edith was a quiet, serious and studious woman who loved to read. Fortunately for the family, she also had a skill for managing money, which in later years became a critical asset that offset his father's lack of financial acuity and failure in his business enterprises.

Edith was in many respects, the opposite of Kermit's father. She was quiet and demure while Theodore was outspoken and boisterous. Having attended finishing school at Miss Comstock's School1 in New York, she was a feminine and reserved Victorian Lady whereas as a youngster, he was schooled at home and was a bundle of energy, movement, and noise.

Born in Connecticut, Edith grew up on Manhattan's Union Square, a few short blocks from the home where Theodore was born and raised. They were close friends as adolescents, and as children, she was a playmate of both Theodore and his sister Corinne, all sharing family summer outings at Oyster Bay.

As a young man, Theodore was a robust, outspoken and gregarious intellectual, an avid hunter, amateur naturalist and committed family man who worshiped strenuous physical activity. Following graduation from Harvard College, Kermit's father became a prominent New York aristocrat and Republican politician having served as a New York State Assemblyman and Minority Leader. Always in constant motion, he managed at the age of twenty-three to author a voluminous work on the naval war of 1812 while studying the law at Columbia College and simultaneously engaging in New York's seedy political world. However, his idyllic existence came to a tragic end with the demise of both his mother and first wife, twenty-two year old Alice Lee on the same day; Valentine's Day,

9

1884. Ironically, two days before that dark day the relationship produced a daughter named after her mother.

After recovering from his tragic double loss, Theodore rekindled his relationship with Edith Carow, and they married in Europe in 1886. In addition to Kermit's older siblings, Ted Jr., born in 1887 and his half-sister Alice, this union also produced two other brothers and a sister: Archibald in 1894, Quentin in 1897, and Ethel in 1891.

The Roosevelt home on the north shore of Long Island at Oyster Bay where Kermit was born was an imposing Queen Anne-style Victorian mansion of twenty-three rooms2. Located on a hill overlooking the bay, the appearance of the multistory structure could be the venue for a present-day Hollywood murder mystery on the outside while providing the warmth, coziness and clutter of 19th century decor on the inside. Originally built with the expectation of first wife Alice Lee being mistress of the house, the rambling interior was designed by Theodore himself and provided all of the comforts and ambiance reflective of his manly character. Prominent within the house was his large book-lined study which served as both office for his literary pursuits and a comfortable retreat for meetings and contemplation. At the north end of the house was the vaulted-ceiling great room, part trophy room and part museum that contained a growing collection of both animal horns and hides and the varied memorabilia of Theodore's ramblings. The twelve bedrooms he designed into the structure were indicative of his belief in the importance of family, both in the rearing of children and number borne. In emphasizing the value of large families with many offspring, Theodore referred to small families as "*race suicide.*"3 His notion of a large family was both a moral obligation and patriotic duty.

Oyster Bay in the 19th century was a rural and somewhat isolated community on the north shore of Long Island where the terrestrial outdoor activities of the rambling Roosevelt property were enhanced by water sports on the bay and sound; swimming, rowing and shore-line camping were a favored pastime of the Roosevelts. The sprawling 155-acre property provided woodlot and orchard, open field and outbuildings along with the bay access, all the places of mystery and wonderment for a young child to explore. In regard to the family "*They swam, rowed, went barefoot, or camped in the woods or on the beach of Long Island Sound. They learned to shoot-for there was a rifle-range at Sagamore Hill. They made pets of the various animals on the home farm in the summer, and they coasted and skated in the winter.*"[4]

With a gaggle of siblings and the opportunity to ramble about with the largest child of them all, his father Theodore, Kermit was continually exposed to the warmth of a very close and active family life that many considered to be chaotic bordering on the insane. His father had a profound influence on Kermit and his siblings. He was a committed proponent of what he called "*...the strenuous life, the life of toil and effort, of labor and strife*"[5] which embodied continuous, extreme physical activity in all pursuits and shunned slothful ease or half measures. Whether chopping wood, riding to fox hounds, boxing with professional pugilists, single-handedly rowing across the sound in a gale or dictating a letter, he was in a state of perpetual, boisterous motion. Observers of the time likened him to a steam locomotive, others to electrical energy. Having overcome his own youthful frailties through determination and hard labor, Theodore imprinted his action-oriented principles onto his children whether engaged in work or play. Engaging in one of his many frantic physical jaunts, Theodore would lead his string of children, along with numerous cousins, on his rough peregrinations across field and wood, single file and at break-neck speed. The only rule was that everyone must negotiate all obstacles by either climbing over or going through but never around an impediment. During his presidency, Roosevelt even imposed this form of athletic torture upon his cabinet and including visiting dignitaries. On one occasion, with a string of following diplomats stumbling behind, Roosevelt stripped naked to forge the creek in Washington's Rock Creek Park. Along with the others, the French diplomat totally undressed but as a complete gentleman with typical Victorian gallantry and to the amusement of the group, refused to remove his gloves in the event ladies should appear. Negotiating bodies of water, scaling rock cliffs and enduring horseback marathons were typical of Roosevelt's physical pastimes.

Despite his father's emphasis on physical exertion and athletic prowess, personal values, character and academic success were given a much higher priority. In a 1903 letter to Kermit regarding playing football at Groton vs. his studies, Theodore advised:

*"I would rather have a boy of mine stand high in his studies than high in athletics, but I could a great deal rather have him show true manliness of character than show either intellectual or physical prowess...."* 6

The traditional character-building qualities of courage, honesty and devotion to duty, traits that became an obsession with Theodore throughout his life were continually instilled in his children. The lives of Theodore and all his children can best be characterized by his famous speech given at the Sorbonne in Paris upon his return from his African safari:

*"It is not the critic who counts, not the man who points out how the strong man stumbled or where the doer of deeds could have done them better. The credit belongs to the man who is actually in the arena; whose face is marred by dust and sweat and blood; who strives valiantly; who errs...."*

Time and again he would coach and sometimes admonish his children to perform under adversity to their utmost ability in the noblest manner. His continual doting over Kermit's elder brother, actually began to spur a nervous condition that required medical care for a bed-ridden Ted Jr. Once Theodore was informed by the attending physician of his damaging influence, he realized the excessive expectations he imposed on Ted were a subconscious reflection of his own youthful shortcomings. This revelation greatly disturbed him, and he vowed to never pressure the youngster again. However, through his life, Ted Jr. would attempt to emulate his father but never succeed in his own eyes.

A measure of the value and reverence for courage instilled in the Roosevelt boys' is evident in Kermit's diary entry following the loss of the Titanic in April, 1912:

*"Everybody full of the Titanic. Archie Butt\*[1] died like a man; everybody did wonderfully except Ismay\*[2], apparently."*[7]

Qualities that Theodore held perhaps above all others were patriotism and the call to duty in time of war. The notion of military service and, if necessary, personal sacrifice was instilled in all of his children – a concept that would eventually take the life of his youngest son and severely wound both Theodore Jr. and Archie in the Great War. The family's martial tradition resulted in Theodore Sr., for his actions in the Spanish-American War winning the Congressional Medal of Honor and Theodore Jr. for his bravery on D-day. In time son Archie, became severely wounded multiple times being the only American fighting man in history to be twice declared with a one-hundred percent disability across two wars. Service to country and valor in battle almost became a competitive event between the four brothers in World War I as their aging father attempted to raise a volunteer brigade as he had done twenty-years earlier in the war with Spain.

Like Theodore, Kermit's mother Edith also encouraged the children to excel intellectually. Based upon her love of literature and art and her sense of the subtleties of life, she introduced Kermit and his siblings to the more enlightened and cultured pursuits. Unlike Theodore's loud, boisterous and challenging nature, Edith's gentle influence tended to focus on the creative and artistic instilling qualities that the sensitive Kermit displayed throughout his life to a much higher degree than any of his siblings.

As a youngster, Kermit was frail and susceptible to sickness. Spending recuperative time in bed, he enjoyed reading and developed an extraordinary aptitude for languages. In later years his natural literary abilities would result in the authorship and co-authorship of multiple books, a deep interest in poetry and literacy in a

---

1 *Major Archibald Willingham Butt perished on the Titanic. He was a military aide to Theodore Roosevelt and also served as an aide to President Taft. During his White House assignment he became a close friend of the Roosevelt family.

2 *J. Bruce Ismay, a passenger on the Titanic, at the time of the disaster was chairman and managing director of the ship owner, the White Star Line. He received bitter criticism for boarding a life boat and saving himself. He additionally was charged with pursuing a speed record for the ill-fated cruise and with ignoring the warnings that icebergs were crossing their route.

number of foreign languages. Even as a young man, Kermit had a sensitive appreciation for poetry. When he read a poem by an obscure and unknown poet "The Children of the Night" by Edwin Arlington Robinson, he was so impressed with the work that he brought Robinson to his father's attention, and the president arranged for a job at the New York Custom House for the poverty-stricken writer.

Observers sensed that his mother favored Kermit above her other children. Perhaps she recognized that the introverted and dreamy nature of Kermit indicated a vulnerable sensitivity that was not present in the extroverted and hardy character of the other children. Although more adventurous and contemplative, the little blond-headed boy was also moody and sometimes withdrawn. In later years Edith would characterize Kermit as *"the one with the white head and the black heart."*[8] A dark perception which would be sadly verified in later years.

❖

In 1899 the Roosevelt family moved into the governor's mansion in Albany following Theodore's close New York gubernatorial victory. He was riding an enormous wave of public adoration following his exploits in the jungles of Cuba.

From his charge up Kettle Hill and military action in the San Juan heights, to his public criticism of the War Office for ill treatment of the troops, high office in New York was his for the taking. Edith was relieved by the family's move into a higher income bracket, and Theodore was pleased to see his political career advance. Despite having the patrician roots of the Roosevelt name, Kermit was not raised in the 19th century opulence of such notable families as the Astor's or Rockefellers. Although Theodore inherited a modest fortune from his family, most of the money was lost to his ill-considered ranching investments. Besides, he was never concerned with finances. Politics consumed his interests while Edith was burdened with making ends meet. The financial concerns of stretching the family resources continued even into the Roosevelt Presidency and only diminished as Theodore began continuously publishing books and magazine articles following his departure from office.

For the next two years, Kermit's education, along with his brother Ted, shifted from home schooling to the Albany Academy while the other children continued on with private tutoring. Following Kermit's primary schooling in Albany, he entered the elite private boarding school, Groton in Massachusetts, where many of the moneyed Eastern establishment sent their children. While a student at the upscale Groton, his course schedule focused heavily on mathematics and foreign languages specifically designed for entry to Harvard or Yale. While not an exceptional student, he ranked about in the middle of a class of approximately twenty-five students.[9] Even as a young secondary school student, Kermit was following the voracious reading habits of his father, displaying a love of books and reading. While at Groton, he was devouring works such as Thackery's *Pendennis*, the Virginians and Don Quixote and the Pickwick Papers [10]. In later years in his world travels he would search antiquarian book stores for first editions. He would read both the classics and popular novels in German, Spanish and Portuguese and during his life amassed an extensive, eclectic personal library with many first editions.

His athletic skills at Groton were recognized in the Boston Journal[11] when his boxing instructor Fred Bryson, a star in the lightweight class himself, commended Kermit's skill and "scrap" in the ring, commenting *"Strenuous is the only word to describe this youngster in the midst of a fistic mixup..."* He engaged in canoeing, rowing, hockey and ice-skating. Later in Harvard, he would run cross-country track; complaining of one event in his diary entry of October 23, 1911, *"We had a hard five-mile run in the afternoon."* The building of his physical stamina would serve him well in the coming years of big game hunting and wilderness exploration, but would greatly fail him in later years, ultimately leading to his tragic demise.

As a young teenager, Kermit began to display the hunting instincts of his father. In 1905 he embarked on a ten-day bear hunt in South Dakota with his father's friend, the legendary western sheriff and Spanish-American War veteran Seth Bullock. Displaying the typical Roosevelt competitiveness and the desire to emulate his father, a newspaper account of the time[12] quotes sixteen-year old Kermit: *"I want to get a bear"* he said. *"My highest ambition is to beat my father's bear slaying record, but I scarcely expect to do that.* " In 1908 he once again hunted in South Dakota with Bullock who arranged for a buffalo hunt as Theodore had in the bad lands of Dakota Territory many years before. This time, with the later conservation instincts of his father, Kermit refused to hunt the two or three buffalo remaining on the open range. According to Bullock,

*"We had a successful hunt, and the young man is a splendid shot but he declined to kill any buffalo, notwithstanding that it is a rare experience in these days when buffalo are all but extinct."* [13]

Following both his father, older brother Ted and cousin Franklin, Kermit entered Harvard in the fall of 1908. Again, his studies emphasized languages: Latin, Greek, German, French, Spanish and even Slavic. [14] His social standing and engaging personality enabled entry into Harvard's Hasty Pudding club, the Sphinx and the exclusive Porcellian Society, an organization with such restrictive admission requirements that even his cousin and future President, Franklin Roosevelt, was denied entry.

In anticipation of his post-presidency African safari, with the accompaniment of Kermit scheduled to commence in 1909, President Roosevelt wrote to Harvard's Dean, B. S. Hurlbut, requesting a one and a half year leave from study for his son. [15] With approval, Kermit left Harvard in the middle of Freshman year and at the close of mid-year examinations; he did not return until the fall of his Junior year.

Following the African trip, in 1911 the President again wrote requesting a *"three or four day delay"* in Kermit's return for the upcoming semester because *"My son Kermit has been asked by the Smithsonian people to collect for them certain specimens of moose, caribou and beaver in New Brunswick for the National Museum."* [16] Still, after working very hard at his studies, Kermit managed to makeup the absent years and graduate with his class in 1912.

Although a bright student, able to recover and compensate for the extended absence from his studies at Harvard in just two and a half years, Kermit displayed an

*A young, dapper Kermit Roosevelt with his father in 1910.*

independent and recalcitrant nature toward his studies. In 1912, just before his graduation, he was absent without leave from school for one week causing Dean Hurlbut to write 17 to President Roosevelt:

> *"...the members of the Administrative Board feel that Kermit needs a pretty forcible lecture from you on the subject of holding himself up to duty. This second half year his attendance has been decidedly*

*unsatisfactory. He is hurting both himself and the college."*

With graduation so near, Hurlbut and the board overlooked the violation, satisfied with Roosevelt's firm admonition of Kermit. However, this infraction was indicative of his developing rejection of convention and his lack of a serious vision for the future. He would begin to address his future responsibilities with a romantic and dreamy, albeit impractical outlook.

The summer of 1912 began with Kermit attending the Republican National Convention in Chicago, the famous raucous political event in which Theodore was denied the Republican Party nomination for President in favor of William Howard Taft. Although Roosevelt won more delegates to the convention, backroom wheeling and dealing by Taft and his people awarded the majority of the large group of contested delegates to Taft. This forced Roosevelt to request that his delegates abstain from voting.

Roosevelt and his supporters walked out of the convention claiming a stolen nomination and established their splinter-group headquarters at Orchestra Hall, less than a mile from the convention [18]. This was the beginning of Roosevelt's Progressive or Bull Moose Party and the splitting of the Republican Party portended the end of a possible Taft second term in the White House. The Oyster Bay Roosevelt clan was in attendance for this historic event. First daughter Alice spent much time as both cheerleader and advisor to her father. Amid the confusion and riotous affair of the convention, scrappy young Kermit engaged in a scuffle with the delegates while downplaying the incident commenting: a *"Montana man clawed up a Florida delegate; I helped separate them."*[19]

The final result of Roosevelt and his followers bolting the Republican Party enabled Democrat Woodrow Wilson to win the 1912 Presidential election with a plurality of only 42 percent of the popular vote; Roosevelt won 27.5 percent with Taft receiving little more than 23 percent. Although losing the election, Roosevelt denied Taft a second term in the White House and gained the highest number of third-party votes in American history.

Anticipating his graduation from Harvard without any firm plans, Kermit began thinking about pursuing a career.

He had a business lunch with corporate executive, Elon Hooker, in April, 1912 to consider a job with the Hooker Electrochemical Company at Niagara.[*3] [20] Hooker was the Deputy of Public Works under TR when he was Governor of New York. Not surprisingly, the job never materialized. Office work in a corporate environment close to home simply didn't appeal to Kermit's adventurous nature at that time.

In June, prior to the Republican convention, he lunched with a Mr. Hunt to *"...talk over a South American railroad plan that has just come up, and which is a chance I want to take and father wants me to."*[21] The position with the Brazil Railway Company, working as a railroad engineer appealed to Kermit for many reasons. At 23 as a Roosevelt with a number of years traveling around the world as a youth, hunting big game and socializing with the famous explorers, military leaders and sporting personages of the time, he needed to establish his mark in his father's eyes and quench his thirst for solo adventure travel. Besides, laying track in the wilderness jungle of Latin America would be good fun and much preferred over a stuffy office job. His father looked upon this new adventure with guarded support. Eventually he would develop a worrisome yet proud outlook on Kermit's independence and involvement in a dangerous pursuit.

Before beginning his career, Kermit spent the early summer of 1912 at Sagamore Hill developing a relationship and falling in love with Belle Willard, a young, blue-eyed blond haired socialite who would become his future wife. His diary for that period is filled with time spent in outdoor activities with Belle: swimming, playing tennis and rowing; he even taught her to shoot his .38 revolver.

❖

At the end of July, Kermit journeyed to South America via stopovers in Europe where he visited in England with the famous African big game hunter Frederick Courtney Selous and lunched with British author Rudyard Kipling, who became a life-long correspondent and friend. From Spain he boarded the steamer Aragon with one of the railroad executives, a Mr. Egan; the voyage afforded him

---

3 *Many years later the Hooker Chemical Company gained national attention and notoriety for pollution of the Love Canal outside Niagara Falls, New York.

the leisure time to learn Portuguese, the spoken language of Brazil. Kermit was to begin a career in one of the most booming economic and yet inhospitable regions in the early 20th century.

As one of the largest territorial land masses in Latin America, much of central and western Brazil in the early 20th Century was devoid of any transportation infrastructure with the north and western regions being undeveloped and uncharted tropical wilderness. Even the coastal regions contained large tracts of steep, hilly land and steamy tropical bush with minimal railroad development. The majority of interconnecting rail service extended from Rio De Janeiro south through Sao Paulo[22] continuing to Uruguay with only minimal connecting lines extending west.

In the years leading up to 1912, Brazil was experiencing a boom both economically and demographically. Grain and cattle were big business with coffee dominating much of the economy. The nation's commercial center, Sao Paulo, was a growing cosmopolitan city with an immigrant population increasing from 35,000 in 1883 to 350,000 in 1907 [23]. Transporting stock and raw materials from the interior was problematic with coastal shipping the prime method of moving goods north and south. Spurred by the country's growing economy versus the inadequate transportation network through the interior enticed primarily European but also American business enterprises and entrepreneurs to invest; a railroad building boom resulted. Indeed, thanks largely to the savings generated by railroad investments in the early twentieth century Brazil emerged from decades of stagnation to become one of the Western world's fastest growing economies[25]. The key player in Kermit's new employer, the Brazil Railway Company, was American railroad tycoon Percival Farquhar, who was called the South American Harriman[24]. Farquhar was a New Yorker and former Albany politician before entering the world of big business in pursuit of railroad building.

Hardly the position for a Harvard graduate, Kermit's first railroad assignment in Brazil was at Barra Funda near Sao Paulo working on a steam shovel for the construction of a station yard. Living and working conditions were abominable for Kermit. Continuous rain with the resulting mud while difficult to contend with were no match for the incessant mosquitoes. His living accommodations were in a leaking railroad car with his laborer coworkers. One of them came down with tick fever. Kermit was already suffering from malaria contracted in his younger years in Washington where mosquito infested swamps still existed. Kermit's diary of the time records numerous mishaps; derailment and wrecks were a constant danger while causing numerous delays in construction progress.

> 9/12/1912: *"Cook car ran off the rails badly, I was in charge of the dirt car and ran over a horse and just missed some cows which ran ahead on the tracks. Cook car ran off the rails with engine."*[26]
> 9/16/1912: *"Passenger train wreck out at kilometer 117 stopped us getting-in six loads to-day."*[27]
> 9/21/1912: *"The equipment car went off the tracks, but not seriously."*[28]

During the remaining months of 1912, he built a bridge and cribbing in water noting in his diary with typical understatement that the miserable process was only: *"hardwork."* Disaster was their constant companion, *"Four cars off the track"*. On another occasion his shovel car and engine were derailed. On another, a car was *"badly derailed but got it back on the track all right."* On 12/18, *"Lots of work. Four cars off the track..."* Unfriendly Indians in this undeveloped wilderness were another source of concern. In a letter home he wrote *"for the indians are up, and have killed several engineers with their long arrows."*[29] Small wonder any progress was made at all. Despite the hazardous, back-breaking work on the line, Kermit found time to hunt armadillos and take trips to town. Having already developed a taste for alcohol and carousing, on one visit he was requested to referee a barroom prize fight between *"an American and a Jamaican negro."*[30]

Kermit's railroading adventures with the Brazil Railway Company were short lived. In 1913 he gained a more lucrative employment with a bridge-building firm, the Anglo-Brazilian Forging Steel Structural and Importing Company, where he supervised the construction of a large span over the Paranapanema River in Piraju, a small, remote town approximately 340 kilometers west of Sao

Paulo. The danger of his bridge-building activities surpassed even his hair-raising escapades on the railroad when he managed the construction of a bridge across a gorge that collapsed, pitching him forty-feet to the rocks below. His father recorded:

> "...while on top of a long steel span, something went wrong with the derrick, he and the steel span coming down together on the rocky bed beneath. He escaped with two broken ribs, two teeth knocked out, and a knee partially dislocated..."[31]

He was amazingly missed by the collapsing debris as he and the steel mass beneath his feet tumbled into the ravine below. His young, athletic build coupled with a tough Rooseveltian constitution enabled him to quickly recover from the disaster.

However, this incident, coupled with his persistent malaria and many other future cases of physical abuse would eventually waste and ultimately destroy his body in later life.

NOTES:

1  Edith Kermit Carow Roosevelt biography, White House History
2  National Park Service
3  Time Magazine, January 19, 1931
4  Lawrence F. Abbott, Impressions of Theodore Roosevelt, 1920, pg. 303
5  Speech before the Hamilton Club, April 10, 1899
6  Theodore Roosevelt letter to Kermit, White House, Oct. 2, 1903
7  Kermit and Belle Roosevelt Papers, Kermit's 1912 diary, Library of Congress
8  The Lion's Pride, page 106, Edward J. Renehan Jr.
9  Groton School, Douglas V.D. Brown Archivist
10 Kermit and Belle Roosevelt Papers, Kermit's 1906 diary, Library of Congress
11 Groton School, Douglas V.D. Brown Archivist
12 N.Y. Times, August 23, 1905
13 Ibid., September 29, 1905
14 Harvard University Archives, Pusey Library
15 Theodore Roosevelt letter, Oyster Bay N.Y., July 21, 1908
16 Theodore Roosevelt letter, The Outlook, N.Y. September 1, 1911
17 Dean Hurlbut letter to Colonel Roosevelt, Harvard University, May 23, 1912
18 Kermit and Belle Roosevelt Papers, Kermit's 1912 diary, Library of Congress
19 Ibid.
20 The Hooker Chemical Company became a Federal Superfund site in 1983.
21 Ibid.
22 Today, Bras-Roosevelt is the name of a principal commuter Metro-Station near San Paulo, Brazil
23 Britannic.com
24 N.Y. Times, September 22, 1912
25 Government, Foreign Investment, and Railroads in Brazil, 1854-1913, William R. Summerhill III quote, Stanford University Press
26 Kermit and Belle Roosevelt Papers, Kermit's 1912 diary, Library of Congress
27 Ibid.

28 Kermit and Belle Roosevelt Papers, Kermit's 1912 diary, Library of Congress
29 The River of Doubt, pg 43, Candice Millard
30 Kermit and Belle Roosevelt Papers, Kermit's 1912 diary, Library of Congress
31 Through the Brazilian Wilderness, pg 5, Theodore Roosevelt

# CHAPTER II - SAFARI IN AFRICA

*TO*
*KERMIT ROOSEVELT*
*MY SIDE-PARTNER*
*IN OUR*
*"GREAT ADVENTURE"*
*(Theodore Roosevelt's dedication*
*to his son in his account of their African safari:*
*African Game Trails)*

President Theodore Roosevelt left the White House in March, 1909 as the youngest president to serve as the nation's leader; entering private life with the same unbounded gusto he displayed as a charging cavalry colonel or controversial leader of the nation. Following the life of a politician, author, historian, naturalist, cowboy, soldier and hunter, he was not ready to settle into a life of sedentary leisure in early middle age; he craved continual action and embarked on the expedition that he had been contemplating for years.

Mounting a shooting safari to Africa appealed to this fifty-year old human dynamo for many reasons. Two decades before, he withdrew to the western badlands to sooth his devastated emotional condition following his loss of both mother and wife on the same day, along with retreating from the sting of his first political defeats. In Dakota Territory he punched cows and chased bad men, weathered blizzards while hobnobbing with cowboys, sheriffs and ranchmen. In this western wilderness the unique physical activity and social relationships discovered by this eccentric northeastern Harvard dandy calmed his emotions while hardening his muscles. Now once again he needed an escape to organize his post-presidency life and recharge his enormous energy.

He additionally wanted to distance himself from his personally anointed successor to the White House, William Howard Taft, and quell any talk in the newspapers of running again for the presidency. Publicly he wished to avoid upstaging his protégé by not being available to the press during Taft's first year in office. He consciously realized that being isolated in the African wilderness would suppress his natural tendency to critique and second-guess the new president's initial performance and decisions. Publicly grandstanding in the most animated manner was always a known Roosevelt trait. While in Africa he wrote to his sister Corinne, *"I am happy to say that I know nothing whatever of politics at home, and I hope to keep in the same blessed state of ignorance until I return next June."*[1]

Big game hunting on the continent was not a new activity in 1909. In fact, sportsmen, commercial ivory hunters, explorers and adventurers were on the chase in Africa for many years prior to the Roosevelt trip. African legends such as Fredrick Courtenay Selous and William Cornwallis Harris had combined big game hunting with the study of field natural history since the mid-nineteenth century. In 1810, William Burchell, for whom the Burchell's Zebra is named, sailed for Cape Town to begin the first real Safari. The word safari, in Swahili meaning to engage in a trip or travel, is somewhat understated in describing TR and Kermit's nine month journey across central and northern Africa.

In 1909, the East African bush was little changed from the time when the first white explorers ventured to the interior of the Dark Continent, so named from the dark patches on the 19th Century maps denoting the unexplored regions at that time. Zebra still roamed the streets of Nairobi, a small white settlement in British East Africa, now known as Kenya. Settlers on the outskirts of town lost their pet dogs to the occasional leopard. Chasing buffalo from the vegetable garden was a common occurrence. Man-eating lions decimated the work crews and halted the building of a regional railroad just a decade before TR and Kermit rode its rails.

On the outskirts of town spread thousands of square miles of jungle, open savanna, and mountain ranges whose valleys and plains contained enormous herds of elephant, buffalo, antelope, zebra and prides of the ever predatory lion. Rivers teemed with crocodile and hippopotamus. Scattered across this vast wilderness were numerous tribes of natives, many still wandering the huge tracts of land herding cattle and hunting and gathering for their existence as they had been for countless centuries while a few tribes were stationary, engaged in seasonal agriculture. Many of the natives were adorned with slit earlobes containing various trinkets; others went mostly naked and some covered themselves with mud while others filed their teeth to points wearing ostrich feathers, leopard skins and lion mane headdresses, adorned with little or no clothes beyond a blanket. The Masai herded cattle, their most valuable possessions but still hunted lion with spear and sword, their men sustaining horrid injury but gaining the honored title of warrior. Warlike tribes like the Nandi and Sambruru still roamed over portions of the continent. Only thirty years earlier Zulu impis (military units) waged a major war and slaughtered 1,200 British troops at the Battle of Isandlwana in Southern Africa. The Mau Mau uprising in Kenya was still four generations in the future.

Communications, commerce, law enforcement and a justice system were almost nonexistent. However, in British East Africa and other regions under the Union Jack, a marginal degree of civilization was beginning to take hold. Disease, drought and wild animals frequently decimated or forced relocation of entire native villages while tribal war still occurred in many areas. Scattered territorial administrators and missionaries attempted to provide law and order, medical care and religion in a spotty, haphazard manner across the vast bush wilderness. The small trickle of incoming white colonists began clearing and cultivating land only a decade earlier in what was considered "white man's country." Before that, only explorers and hunters braved this threatening land.

Similar to the British in the north, south of the equator the German Empire was penetrating inland into what was called German East Africa or in local vernacular, Tanganyika, now present day Tanzania. Within a few short years, both of these territories would be locked in a bush war as an adjunct to the massive world conflict raging between the European powers farther north. Both Kermit and his African settler friends would later participate in this great struggle in the Middle East and on the African continent.

❖

Pursuing the great animals of Africa in the mysterious regions of this still unknown continent greatly appealed to TR's adventurous nature. He characterized Africa as the *"greatest of the world's great hunting grounds."*2 Since childhood, TR was keenly interested in ornithology, taxidermy and field natural history. His ongoing study of wildlife and frequent hunting travels across the United States enabled him to become one of the most knowledgeable and authoritative persons on the big-game mammals and birds of North America in the nineteenth and early twentieth century.

The prospect of investigating the flora and fauna of the world's greatest wildlife habitat for TR while at the same time being challenged by the world's most dangerous animals was irresistible. However, having reached a rotund middle-age, with poor eyesight and the typical diminishment of strength and stamina most desk-bound men of fifty years experience, TR wisely decided to enlist Kermit as his personal companion. At nineteen, Kermit was lean and tough as whipcord. He was a skilled horseman, fair shot and bubbling with energy, curiosity and courage. He was capable of pursuing the wild game in a manner that TR could not. An example of Kermit's athletic ability was demonstrated when galloping after a giraffe on horseback, his mount became too winded to continue. Kermit jumped off and ran after the giraffe on foot for over a mile until the wounded animal dropped from fatigue. The big drawback and TR's growing concern was Kermit's careless indifference to danger and his willingness to take unnecessary risks. A newspaper in 1908₃ reported an account on Long Island of Kermit risking life and limb to race down on horseback a run-away carriage containing a frightened mother and her two daughters as the driver was pitched out of the vehicle from a mishap:

> *"Young Roosevelt was careful not to swerve the bays from their course into the gutter, where an upset would have been avoidable. Thus they pounded through the streets of the town, while dozens of people rushed out of their houses to watch the sight. Finally the boy's efforts began to tell, and slowly but surely the animals were brought to a standstill."*

*Kermit and his father on African Safari.*

Following this hair-raising stunt, Kermit said little and simply rode away departing in his usual nonchalant manner.

An added advantage to the African expedition was the assignment of Kermit as the expedition's official photographer. His role in this capacity enabled the trip to be recorded for the public and in the many images TR used to illustrate his serialized magazine articles and later his personal account of the trip.

To finance their trip billed as the Smithsonian-Roosevelt Expedition, Roosevelt relied upon funding from the Smithsonian Institution and private sponsors, including Andrew Carnegie also paying the way for himself and Kermit's participation by writing a serialized account of the adventure for *Scribners* magazine. The articles were later consolidated in his voluminous safari account: *African Game Trails*. Typical for the era, the safari was established as a scientific expedition with the goal of supplying game mounts and nature settings for the Smithsonian Institution's National Museum of Natural History in Washington with the prospect also for the American Museum of Natural History in New York. To provide the necessary scientific bench skills, the Smithsonian enlisted three naturalists to accompany the expedition. The skinning and hide preparation of the huge bag of animals was assigned to Edmund Heller of California, a noted explorer and curator of mammals at the Museum of Vertebrate Zoology of the University of California; J. Alden Loring of Oswego, New York, was to have charge of the small mammal collecting and Edgar A. Mearns was selected as head naturalist and bird-collector.[4]

Mearns, a skilled surgeon, also would provide the all-important medical assistance. While TR and Kermit roamed the African bush in pursuit of big game, the trio of scientists, besides providing taxidermy skills, would pursue the trapping of small mammals and birds and make side trips for ornithological and geographic study.

Planning for the Roosevelt's hunting and scientific safari in Africa was akin to organizing the logistics of a major military campaign. Besides TR, Kermit and the three Smithsonian naturalists, the safari entourage included the two African big game hunters and bush experts R.J. Cuninghame and Leslie Tarlton and a support staff consisting of two hundred porters. Additionally, gun-bearers, tent boys, askaris (armed guards) and saises (horse handlers) were enlisted. Supplies included enormous amounts of food and ammunition, four tons of salt for curing animal skins, hundreds of small animal traps and all of the conventional camp gear: tents, lanterns, tables, chairs, etc. TR ensured creature comforts were addressed by packing in each provision box a few cans of Boston baked beans, California peaches and tomatoes. Rounding out the baggage, Roosevelt even packed a private sixty-pound library containing dozens of volumes which he called his 'pigskin library' in regard to the special climate-resistant binding of the books. As

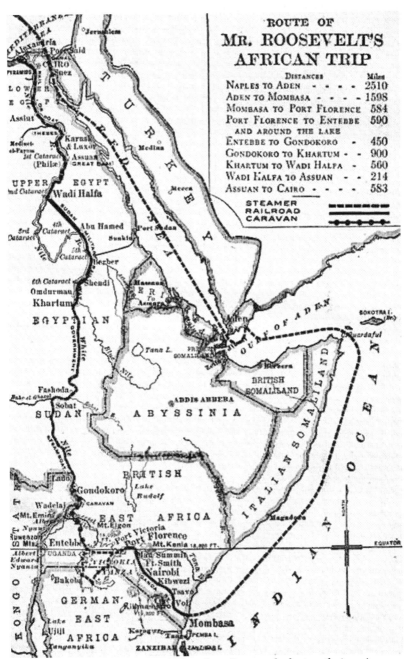

## ROUTE OF MR. ROOSEVELT'S AFRICAN TRIP

| DISTANCES | Miles |
|---|---|
| NAPLES TO ADEN - - - - | 2510 |
| ADEN TO MOMBASA - - - - | 1598 |
| MOMBASA TO PORT FLORENCE | 584 |
| PORT FLORENCE TO ENTEBBE AND AROUND THE LAKE | 590 |
| ENTEBBE TO GONDOKORO - | 450 |
| GONDOKORO TO KHARTUM - - | 900 |
| KHARTUM TO WADI HALFA - | 560 |
| WADI HALFA TO ASSUAN - - | 214 |
| ASSUAN TO CAIRO - - - - | 583 |

STEAMER
RAILROAD
CARAVAN

*Route traveled by Kermit and Theodore Roosevelt during their epic, 1909 African Safari.*

insurance against the rigors of bush travel, he even included ten pairs of eyeglasses.

A portable laboratory was transported to appropriately prepare the animal specimens for packing and shipment. Following the field skinning of TR and Kermit's bag, the head, horns, hide and skeleton of each animal would be carefully prepped for the museum in camp each evening. A male and female pair of each species shot or trapped was desired including their offspring to complete a family setting when available. According to Roosevelt:

> *"...specimens of both sexes of all the species of big game that Kermit and I could shoot, as well as complete series of all the smaller mammals. We believed that our best work of a purely scientific character would be done with the mammals, both large and small."*[5]

Roosevelt considered the trip purely as a scientific expedition, not a sporting event. The great majority of the animals they would harvest were intended to be used for science and feeding the large safari staff, he and Kermit would retain only a few specimens as personal trophies.

The Smithsonian-Roosevelt Expedition arrived in the ancient port city of Mombasa in April, 1909. Following the diplomatic imperatives with the local officials, the party began a trip upcountry on the Uganda Railway, euphemistically known as the 'lunatic line' for its excessive cost and the hardship and danger experienced by the bridge builders and track laying gangs during its construction. During the initial rail trip, Roosevelt and his friend, the world renowned big game hunter, F. C. Selous, rode on the locomotive's cowcatcher on a specially constructed seat where he marveled at the enormous spectacle of wildlife unfolding before them, describing the train experience as a *"...railroad in the Pleistocene."*[6] As the train chugged along over hill and dale, across this prehistoric landscape rising to an elevation of over 7,000 feet, Roosevelt would spot the occasional rhinoceros or antelope crossing the rail line ahead. A hyena ran across the track nearly falling beneath the wheels. Giraffes were particularly vulnerable to entanglement in the telegraph

line strung along the track as large herds of wildebeest and
zebra would stumble across the roadbed. Despite being a
life-long hunter, familiar with almost all of the North
American big game, Roosevelt marveled at Africa's fauna:
*"The land teems with beasts of the chase, infinite in number
and incredible in variety."*[7]   While TR sat on the locomotive
front, Kermit viewed the unfolding spectacle from the roof
of a carriage. Roosevelt's party proceeded to their first
camp on the Kapiti Plains and the formation of his safari.
At the camp, TR and Kermit secured two horses each.

Unlike the hundreds of baggage carrying porters that
would trudge-along on foot, both hunters and their white
colleagues traveled at the head of the safari caravan on
horseback. A newspaper article at the time described the
procession:

> *"Colonel Roosevelt and Kermit with Major Mearns led
> the way on their ponies and then the porters
> followed in one long line headed by a gunbearer
> carrying the Stars and Stripes. The column extended
> for a quarter of a mile."*[8]

Besides a means of basic transportation, horses were at
that time also de rigueur for sport hunting by chasing and
running-down game prior to making the shot. Great sport
was enjoyed by many and many lives were lost when this
dubious technique was applied to the hunting of lions.
Kermit became particularly adept at bringing game animals
to bay by riding long distances on the chase at a dangerous
breakneck speed over broken ground. Roosevelt later
recorded an incident when Kermit chased-down a hyena:

> *"... and though the brute had a long start he galloped
> after it and succeeded in running it down. The chase
> was a long one, for twice the hyena got in such rocky
> country that he almost distanced his pursuer; but at
> last, after covering nearly ten miles, Kermit closed
> with the animal  in the open, shooting it from the
> saddle as it shambled along at a canter growling
> with rage and terror."*[9]

In another incident, Kermit shot a warthog:

*"...from the saddle as he galloped nearly alongside, holding his rifle as the old buffalo-runners used to hold theirs, that is, not bringing it to his shoulder."*[10]

However, not all of the hunting was on horseback. TR and Kermit also walked many miles through the African bush in pursuit of game.

Roosevelt's warm personal relationship with hunter-naturalist Selous, who would later fall to a German sniper's bullet in Tanganyika, and the influential Edward North Buxton, both of whom planned the safari details during the last days of TR's Presidency, enabled the establishment of an itinerary that would combine both wilderness hunting and hunting on various farms (which in the United States would be called ranches). Along with farm hunting, their two thousand mile journey trekked open savanna, woodland and water passages from Mombasa on the Indian Ocean to Khartoum in the north.

Their first prolonged stop was for a two-week stray at the farm of Sir Alfred Pease in the Kitanga Hills. A New York Times article of April 27, 1909 reported TR and Kermit were *"...resting from their fatigue at the ranch"* and their trip from the Kapiti Plains. The Kitanga Hills were so named by the natives in honor of an Englishman killed by a lion and buried locally; a very frequent occurrence in the African bush.

Sir Alfred was a former member of parliament and a big game hunter notable for authoring the *Book of the Lion.* He and his wife entertained their illustrious guests for two weeks. TR noting *"...they took a keen interest, untinged by the slightest nervousness, in every kind of wild creature from lions and leopards down."*[11] Describing the farm he said *"The game was in sight from the veranda of the house almost every hour of the day."*[12] And, neither he nor Kermit missed the opportunity to pursue this ubiquitous game.

With Mount Kilimanjaro as a backdrop, the Kitanga Hills sentimentally reminded Roosevelt of his own ranching days and peregrinations in the far West. The rolling landscape of withered grass resembled the cattle country of the Great Plains and he compared the courageous efforts of the British settlers to the western migration across America.

Roosevelt would continually comment on the fecundity of central Africa while characterizing it as *"a white man's country."* Similar to buffalo, wolf and pronghorn on the Great Plains, the open savanna of Pease's farm provided excellent habitat for the vast herds of Africa's common plains game: various antelope, zebra and the predatory lion along with a great variety of birds and small mammals. Both TR and Kermit spent days galloping across the land in pursuit of the herds, while occasionally using native beaters to stampede stray animals from the security of a ravine or dry creek-bed.

However, consistent with his enormous ego and lifelong sense of self-righteousness, Roosevelt passionately required dangerous challenges equal to his aggressive and competitive nature. Kermit, on the other hand, had a natural and careless attraction to hazardous pursuits often without consideration or concern for the outcome. Whether storming jungle covered hills in Cuba under withering rifle fire or dueling with robber barons in the White House, pursuing a benign, unequal quarry was second rate and beneath TR's character. But bagging a lion, as king of the jungle and the most feared predator of all Africa's big game, was closer to Roosevelt's notion of an equal challenge. In his account *African Game Trails* he recounts numerous instances where men were mauled and killed by lions and statements by noted big-game hunters classifying the lion as the most dangerous of the African big game. These tales stimulated Roosevelt, and he also adopted this viewpoint of their relative danger. His and Kermit's first hunting encounter with the king of the beasts was a great disappointment as both blindly fired into bushes and shot two cubs that Roosevelt embarrassingly pronounced were *"the size of mastiffs."*[14] This failure did not deter them from the goal of shooting one good lion; TR expected to harvest the first between he and Kermit and as luck would have, he did. In fact he shot two large cats on the return to the farm house that day. Within a few days, both were once again on the hunt for lion. The game was so abundant in this region, the hunting resembled the shooting gallery in a penny arcade. Three days following the cub shooting incident, Kermit shot a male cheetah where *"...he bowled it over in good style."*[15] Immediately following this, Kermit killed a reedbuck and a steinbuck with TR bagging another lion albeit "...*not much of a trophy*"16 being a half-grown male. Before the day ended, Roosevelt managed to shoot two additional lions. Their total safari bag for the king of beasts was nine for TR and eight for Kermit.

In one hair-raising incident Kermit almost fell prey to a wounded leopard. Kermit and the wealthy American, William N. McMillan, later Sir William*4, the owner of Juja Farm on the edge of the Kapiti Plains went hunting together during a week's visit following Sir Alfred's farm. As Kermit and McMillan tracked a cat into a large thicket, their native beaters attempted to drive the feline into the open just as the beast unexpectedly came charging straight at Kermit. He charged to within six yards before being turned by Kermit's first bullet. After being severely wounded from Kermit's second shot on the run, the leopard returned to the safety of the thicket once again.

The excited and overzealous natives, impressed with the charge and the manner in which Kermit turned the animal, ventured too close to the cat's lair and he came charging on once again. The wounded animal chased one of the beaters, seized him and began with the fury of a buzz-saw to maul with teeth and claws. Due to the injured cat's weakness, the native wrenched free whereupon McMillan successfully hit the cat once more sending it back into the long grass. In a short time the leopard returned and again charged Kermit before finally dropping to another shot from his rifle.

Upon returning from the safari adventure the following year, his naturalist companion, J. Alden Loring would comment:

> "*I do not think that the Colonel gives his readers a fair impression of the very great danger that he and Kermit so often met. After we had said good-bye to four or five settlers with whom we had become acquainted and met them again several weeks later to find one with a badly injured arm chewed by a*

---

4 *McMillan was an enormously overweight American (at approximately 300 pounds) who hailed originally from Canada. During World War I he distinguished himself with the famous Legion of Frontiersman in Africa and was knighted by the Queen in 1918 for his exploits.

*leopard, a second in the hospital at the point of death from a lion mauling, and a third who exhibited a rent in a shirt made by the tusks of a charging elephant that killed his gun bearer...."*

He continued:

*"... we began to realize that hunting African big game was not altogether a one-sided affair."* 13

The tenacity and strength displayed by this beast is not unusual for the animals of Africa. Unlike wounded deer or mountain lion of North America, the wildlife of Africa have always been considered to be especially hard to stop when hit. Numerous stories tell of wounded lion or buffalo or even antelope charging and often killing the unwary hunter. Some African hunters theorize that due to the extreme predation and hard existence experienced by these animals over the eons, unlike the wild animals elsewhere, an unnatural toughness and tenacity has evolved which Kermit and TR experienced on numerous occasions.

❖

The Juja Farm was another one of a number of stopover visits for TR and Kermit with local settlers and missionaries during their circuitous trek across east and central Africa. TR's established fame as both former president of the new emerging world power and eclectic reputation of being an eccentric cowboy, intellectual, soldier and naturalist enabled him to rely on influential contacts in Europe for trip planning and support. A measure of Roosevelt's international popularity was expressed in the gift of a unique 500-450 Holland & Holland double rifle that he used as his heavy gun on the safari. The custom-made rifle was dedicated by such 19th century British notables as Sir Reginald Wingate, Lord Curzon and G. O. Trevelyan prior to the African trip.

Despite long, hot days covering many miles on foot and horseback, with the frequent insect bites and minor bruises, safari life for the Roosevelt party was very pleasant and enjoyable. When on the move, camp was dismantled as early as possible in the morning with tents, bedding and equipment packaged into fifty to sixty pound bundles, the maximum load permitted for carry by each porter. Once under way, the sinuous, single-file line of march created a very picturesque and loud column extending for a considerable distance to the rear.  At the head was TR and Kermit riding ponies along with the white safari members followed by the camp staff in order of job importance. Horns, tom-toms and whistles would serenade the column along with occasional native chants.  The American flag was carried at or near the head.  As the miles passed under foot, they traversed scrub brush, forest and savanna under the burning African sun.

The marchers were attired in a colorful show of big-game hunter fashion.  The white safari members wore the traditional khaki-colored outfit with puttees or leggings and sun helmets with puggarees or slouch hat while the native porters were adorned in a hodgepodge of clothing; a blouse and drawers with blanket and even the occasional umbrella, open or closed, as momentary fashion impulse dictated.  Some were bareheaded with others wearing a fez or for the Moslems, a skullcap.  TR commented one wore "...*the skin of the top of a zebra's head, with the two ears. Another was made of the skins of squirrels, with the tails both sticking up and hanging down.*"17  During the course of the long safari, TR and Kermit became attached to their camp staff, particularly their gun bearers and trackers and were quite saddened upon leaving them when the adventure came to an end.  The natives in return also developed a friendly attachment to the hunters and naturalists, giving them Swahili names, indicative of their appearance or mannerisms.  Kermit was dubbed "Bwana Maridari," Mr. Fancy-Pants for his slim, neat appearance. TR was "Bwana Mkubwa," Great Master, but behind his back he was called, "Bwana Tumbo," Mr. Big Belly.  The naturalist Heller was the "Bwana Who Skinned"; Loring, the collector of small mammals was named "Bwana Pania," the Mouse Master.

Following the day's march, a camp ground would be selected with tents being organized on the order of a military installation with a central "main street."  Each shelter was designated for a specific purpose: cooking, dinning, sleeping, skinning and provision tents, and so forth.  Firewood would be gathered for the many camp and cooking fires.  Following an evening meal that generally consisted of wild game, the safari would gather around their respective camp fires, the native staff huddled within their separate groups according to job function and rank with the hunters relaxing around a huge, separate blaze. Roosevelt would religiously devote time to writing the day's account for his serialized magazine articles. Kermit would occasionally strum tunes on his banjo or tend to his photographic equipment. Sometimes he would steal away to engage in his literary interest of reading. The natives would often breakout into a wild chanting African melody while competing with the occasional eerily whoop and wail of hyenas or throaty grunts of lion from beyond the campfire light. Camp guard and order was maintained by armed Askaris, native soldiers who had no other duties besides policing the line of march in the day and securing the camp at night.

When camping in fertile hunting grounds for prolonged periods, TR and Kermit, along with their white hunters, would spend long hours of the day roaming the African bush while carrying a light noontime lunch, usually consumed far from camp. Similar to safaris today, a mid-day siesta was taken during the hot hours of high noon by all members except TR, who would read in the shade of a tree or bush from books he carried in his saddlebags.

If any game was taken, a runner was sent to camp to alert the naturalists who would return and setup station near the kill until the skin, horns and head were removed and carried back for fleshing and salting. For large animals, this became a major operation, sometimes requiring the naturalists to camp overnight in the bush with the carcass to complete the skinning. The heat of the day and roving wild animals, hungry for the opportunity of an easy meal were a continual problem for the preparation of hides. Large animals such as rhino and elephant were a particular problem due to their enormous size and weight. Timing was always urgent and the large quantities of meat were always a welcome sight though burdensome load for the natives. When not on safari, the native diet consisted mainly of a mealy-like porridge made from maize. The opportunity to eat meat compensated for their protein deficiency enabling them while on safari to consume over ten pounds of meat each per day; calorie loss throughout the rigors of safari life was great.

❖

Even prior to their game collecting expedition in Africa, both TR and Kermit were avid and frequent hunters across North America. History has credited TR as a great American hunter, but aside from the advantages of being younger, Kermit was both the better hunter and sportsman. Besides, never having good eyesight, in his adult life, TR became totally blind in one eye with diminished sight in the other. Unlike the African hunting technique most favored today, the patient stalk to gain an in-close, accurate killing shot at the animal, TR continually stretched both his shooting skills and the rifle ballistics of the day on very long range shooting. His extremely poor eyesight only added to the problem, and his numerous misses along with the loss of wounded game didn't seem to deter him from taking extreme potshots at distant targets. While encountering a large herd of topi one day, four to six hundred yards away on the open plains and unable to accurately range the distance, he said *"...I fired more time than I care to mention before I finally got my topi – at just five hundred and twenty yards."*[18] Another time he expended sixty-five cartridges at fourteen different animals with the average shot at a little over two hundred and twenty yards. On this occasion, one wounded animal got away. When hunting the Guaso Nyero, a river in equatorial Africa, after wounding and losing two Oryx Roosevelt fired at six others at four hundred yards and missing the shots exclaimed:

> *"By this time I felt rather desperate, and decided for once to abandon legitimate proceedings and act on the Ciceronian theory, that abandon legitimate proceedings and act on the Ciceronian theory he mark some time. Accordingly I emptied the magazines of both of my rifles at the Oryx, as they ran across my front, and broke the neck of a fine cow, at four hundred and fifty yards."*[19]

Besides ineffectually shooting at targets considerably beyond his skill level, TR was not averse to losing wounded game if tracking was inconvenient. When his hunting companion R. J. Cunningham wounded a bull elephant immediately following the shooting of another great, tusked beast, TR casually discounted any effort to secure the second animal commenting, *"If we had been only after ivory we should have followed him at once; but there was no telling how long a chase he might lead us...."*[20] For the modern hunter, losing an elephant, or any game animal in this manner would be a sacrilege. Kermit was more apt to rely on his horse or the stealth of stalking in close to bag his quarry. Being very fleet of foot with much stamina as a former long-distance runner, he would on some occasions actually run down a wounded animal. He was a good shot with the benefit of youthful eyesight. The game was so prolific and the shooting opportunities were so great that when his right arm and shoulder were sore from shooting, he would fire left-handed and even took a gazelle and three topi with his left-hand.

❖

The Roosevelt safari trekked an enormous, circuitous route across British East Africa, Uganda, Sudan and up the Nile into Egypt. On foot, horseback and even boat when they crossed Lake Victoria Nyanza, they traversed savanna, dense scrub, desert, swamp and river sometimes doubling back on their track but always traveling north-northwest. While in the no-man's land of the Lado enclave, TR and Kermit met with the professional elephant hunters who became notoriously famous for the short period of their ivory poaching and their evasion of border officials before this region was claimed as sovereign territory. TR noted:

*"They are a hard-bit set, these elephant poachers; there are few careers more adventurous, or fraught with more peril, or which make heavier demands upon the daring, the endurance, and the physical hardihood of those who follow them."*[21]

The many months of wilderness travel began to take a toll on the white hunters and naturalists who, unlike the natives, were not accustomed to either the rigor of continuous bush travel or the many tropical diseases. Upon arriving in Gondokoro in January, 1910, Mearns, Loring and even the local district commissioner were seriously ill. A German missionary who dined with the party one evening died the next day of black water fever. Mearns treated an English sportsman who was close to death. Almost all were suffering from either fever or dysentery or a combination of both. Although TR bragged about his and Kermit's robust health, Kermit was laid up for three days with tick fever and TR for five days with a recurrence of malaria that he contracted years before in Cuba.

When the wilderness adventure finally came to a close, TR and Kermit met with Edith and Kermit's sister, Ethel, at Khartoum in March 1910 and continued on a months-long diplomatic excursion across Europe, meeting with heads of state and royalty. The time was spent with TR giving speeches, revisiting old sights from his former wanderings and representing the United States at the state funeral for the death of Great Britain's King. When in England, he even spent time bird watching.

Kermit had the unique opportunity to travel across Europe with the world's leading and first international superstar a mere four years before that continent become embroiled in the great conflagration of World War I. While in Germany, he would ironically accompany on horseback, his father and Kaiser Wilhelm II to review the very troops that he would meet in combat a mere seven years later.

The total bag of animals resulting from this famous hunting and natural history expedition resulted in an enormous collection of both large and small game, common birds, small furbearing mammals and reptiles. The final tally of animals numbered 296 for TR and 216 for Kermit, the numbers including multiples of some species for family group settings in the museum displays. They additionally collected Egyptian geese, yellow-billed mallards, spurfowl, and sand grouse *"for the pot, and certain other birds for specimens."*[22] The field naturalists harvested many hundreds of additional small animals and birds.*[5]

---

5 *The entire collection of roughly 4400 mammal specimens procured in East Africa (1909-1910) by Edgar A. Mearns, Edmund Heller, J. Alden Loring, Theodore Roosevelt, and Kermit Roosevelt has been cataloged and incorporated into the research collection in the Division of Mammals at the Smithsonian Institution. Researchers studying African mammals have used these specimens for almost 100 years; many scientific publications have cited specimens from this expedition. While the Roosevelts were interested in the big game species, Mearns, Heller, and Loring, as professional mammalogists, actively collected small mammals such as rodents, bats, and shrews, and these groups comprise a major part of the Smithsonian collection. Only a small portion of the collection has been exhibited to the public, mainly large game specimens taken by the Roosevelts. The Division of

Much to the chagrin of TR a majority of the animals ultimately ended up out of sight in museum storage with only a small number ever being placed on display. TR and Kermit kept a few of the animal mounts as personal trophies. Anticipating public criticism for the huge number of animals he and Kermit had hunted, TR justified the killing by claiming the trip was based upon scientific need: *"I can be condemned only if the existence of the National Museum, the American Museum of Natural History, and all similar zoological institutions are to be condemned."*[23] A major critic of the Roosevelt approach to hunting was a clergyman and amateur naturalist and author from Connecticut, Dr. William J. Long who called TR a "game killer." As both men jousted heatedly in the papers of the day on the habits and characteristics of various wild animals, TR retorted to Long's name-calling by describing Long as a "nature faker," a term that could be appropriately applied to many today.

The federal land acquisition and the conservation efforts of President Roosevelt are well known. However, despite the enormous number of animals TR shot in his lifetime, he is also known as a modern supporter of managed game hunting during an era of huge waste in the commercial game market. He railed against the excesses of game slaughter and was the founder of the Boone and Crockett Club.[24]

Following their prolonged shooting extravaganza, safari hunting changed forever. In the fifty to seventy-five years following this well-publicized adventure came many wealthy and famous personages who patterned their trip on the Roosevelt model: an extended shooting adventure requiring numerous support staff, complicated logistics and plush living in a harsh environment. From American business tycoons and movie stars to the royalty and aristocrats of Europe, Africa served up her magnificent

---

Mammals currently has about 400 specimens on public exhibition, out of a collection of over half a million specimens. In addition to public education via exhibits, the National Museum of Natural History (and all other large museums) maintains its collections in perpetuity to support scholarly research. -Craig Ludwig, Scientific Data Manager, Division of Birds and Mammals, Smithsonian Institution, In a letter to the author, 2008

wildlife and exotic ambiance in a seemingly endless supply. While on their trip, TR and Kermit's acquaintances later became the genesis for a century of big-game sport hunting in Africa. Their friends, Leslie Tarlton, the Hills and Philip Percival, who 30 years later would guide British royalty and Ernest Hemingway and become the hero model in one of Hemingway's novels, all crossed paths with the Roosevelt's in Africa. Other famous hunter/explorer/naturalists of the 20th century who link back to the Roosevelt safari are Carl Akeley of museum fame and the married film duo Osa and Martin Johnson.

As his father's age and declining health in the years following Africa and their Brazilian expedition in 1914 along with the rigors of his ill fated campaign reduced TR's ability to hunt in wild places, Kermit continued to engage in sport hunting and game collecting. The African adventure wetted his appetite for distant romantic places and adventurous travel. His future ramblings would merge exploration, hunting and the pursuit of natural history for many years to come and similar to his father, provide new information[6] on game animals, geography and the customs of indigenous people in some of the most remote regions of the world.

Beginning in 1914, Kermit would once again accompany his father on a long and momentous adventure into unknown and dangerous territory. The experience will change and diminish the former President for the remainder of his relatively short life while evoking an even higher degree of courage and endurance in both, beyond either war, politics or charging wild animals had in the past. Their new adventure would also alter the map of South America.

---

6 *Among the animals that carry the famous Roosevelt name today are the Hippotragus niger roosevelti, a rare form of Sable Antelope; the Muntiacus rooseveltorum Roosevelt's Muntjac or Roosevelt's barking deer and the Roosevelt Elk also known as Olympic Elk. This form is the largest animal within the Elk family.

NOTES:

1   My Brother Theodore Roosevelt, pg. 256, Corinne
    Roosevelt
2   African Game Trails Forward, Theodore Roosevelt
3   New York Times, August 28, 1908
4   Edmund Heller papers, Smithsonian Institution
    Archives
5   African Game Trails, pg. 5, Theodore Roosevelt
6   Ibid., pg. 17
7   African Game Trails Forward, Theodore Roosevelt
8   New York Times, July 19, 1909
9   African Game Trails, pg. 62, Theodore Roosevelt
10  Ibid., pg. 129
11  Ibid., pg. 42
12  Ibid., pg. 42
13  New York Times, August 25, 1910
14  African Game Trails, pg. 84, Theodore Roosevelt
15  Ibid., pg. 90
16  Ibid., pg. 78,
17  Ibid., pg. 84
18  Ibid., pg. 161
19  Ibid., pg. 275
20  Ibid., pg. 252
21  Ibid., pg. 395
22  Ibid., pa. 468
24  TR was not the only Roosevelt to defend the nation's
    wildlife by founding the Boone & Crockett Club; the
    first game conservation organization in the United
    States.  His uncle, Robert Barnhill Roosevelt was an
    early hunter-naturalist and conservationist and
    beginning in 1862, published three books on the topic:
    *Game Fish of the Northern States of America and British
    Provinces, Superior Fishing* and *The Game Birds of the
    Coasts and Lakes of the Northern States of America.*
    TR's nephew and future President of the United States,
    Franklin Roosevelt, when a state senator in New York
    was chairman of the state's Forest, Fish and Game
    Committee.

# CHAPTER III -
# STUMBLING THROUGH MISERY
# ON THE RIVER OF DOUBT

*"My last chance to be a boy"*
*(Theodore Roosevelt commenting on*
*his expedition to the Rio Da Duvida)*

Living a life of loneliness and isolation in a land far from home may have been praying on Kermit's sensitive emotions and innate sense of despair. During his months of railroading and bridge building in Argentina, Kermit maintained a flirtatious correspondence with his former acquaintance from the Sagamore Hill summer of 1912, culminating in a written marriage proposal to Belle Willard in October 1913. A more inopportune time from a more inconvenient and distant location could not have been chosen for proposing a life commitment to a person he hardly knew beyond a summer's jaunt. Now, a new emerging commitment to his father with the possibility of unknown dangers coupled with yet additional isolation for the coming months may have imposed on him a sense of foreboding and desperate urgency. Despite Belle's immediate acceptance of the long-distance proposal, a new adventure for Kermit along with his father would further delay and ultimately threaten any plans of a marriage ceremony.

The emerging Roosevelt-Zahm Expedition later metamorphosized into an adventure that was potentially destined for doom long before the twenty-two man party[1] dipped their first paddle into the dark, threatening waters of the Rio Da Duvida, the River of Doubt. This threatening-jungle enclosed water course so named because of its extreme isolation and unknown length or end. The unmapped, mysterious body of water was located in remote jungle in the Amazon basin so far from any settlement that at that time its existence had only been recently discovered and was unmapped and un-travelled by any white man. In the words of the expedition's originator, *"For, strange as it may seem, South America is still more of a terra incognita than darkest Africa, and many parts of it are today less known than they were three hundred years ago."*[2] The ill-selected and poorly provisioned crew was surprisingly imbalanced in knowledge and experience for this wilderness trip by having the greatest Amazonian explorer teamed with an aged, inexperienced Catholic priest and a former failed Arctic explorer. This poorly staffed eclectic group, separated by different languages and backgrounds entered one of the most inhospitable and least known regions of the world. Added to this was the questionable safety of the world's most famous leader, who in middle age was suffering poor health.

*The Genesis of the Adventure*

The idea for a South American journey began percolating in Roosevelt's mind during his presidency in 1908 by a suggestion from an old friend, Father John Augustine Zahm. Zahm piqued Roosevelt's eclectic curiosity from his publication of, "Evolution and Dogma" a theological work arguing a compatibility between the opposing views of religion and evolution. He and Roosevelt also shared a keen interest in the works of Dante and the field of science. Short and slight of build, the scholarly Zahm was a Catholic official at Notre Dame University and amateur scientist. He was also known as an explorer but in reality, he explored more as a sightseeing tourist with a penchant for comfort rather than a hardened wilderness traveler inured to danger and privation.

Just prior to his initial meeting at the White House with Roosevelt, Zahm had recently returned from a trip through the Andes Mountains and a journey down the Amazon River. He excitedly proposed the idea of mounting a joint expedition with the President into the interior of South America. However, at that time, Roosevelt had his sights set on an African shooting safari and delayed any future consideration of the idea. Zahm left the nation's Capitol disappointed but decided to bide his time for a future South American trip with Roosevelt.

❖

*American members of the ill-fated expedition to explore the River of Doubt: (left to right) Anthony Fiala, George Cherrie, Father John Augustine Zahm, Theodore Roosevelt, Kermit Roosevelt, Frank Harper, and Leo Miller.*

Years after his meeting with Zahm, following the doomed Progressive Party primary loss and his disastrous presidential election loss of 1912, Roosevelt aimlessly drifted into seclusion at Sagamore Hill and once again slumped into a restless despair. He knew that his election loss to Wilson coupled with his cleaving of the Republican Party by the Bull Moose debacle may be his last opportunity to once again gain the White House. His wife Edith and his close associates knew that he needed travel and preferably another dangerous and exotic adventure to steady his mind and clear his emotions of the recent embarrassment and disappointment of his political losses.

Fate provided this opportunity as the South American adventure began to develop anew in the spring of 1913 when the governments' of Argentina, Brazil and Chile invited the restless ex-president to give a series of lectures at their institutions of learning. Specifically, he received an invitation from the Museo Social in Buenos Aires to lecture before it on the topic of Progressive Democracy.3 The offers enabled Roosevelt to garner a handsome honorarium with the additional advantage of embarking on another adventure. Naturally, stepping again into the public spotlight would provide the opportunity to expound on his notion of democracy in the Western Hemisphere, and besides, this also would provide him an opportunity to visit in South America with his long-absent son Kermit and survey a portion of the world only vaguely familiar to him.

His initial plan was typical of Roosevelt's life-long interest in natural history; following his academic and political commitments to the Latin American governments then conduct a leisurely specimen collecting expedition through the middle of the continent north into the Amazon. In the beginning of the twentieth-century, the huge land mass of the Amazon basin in central South America with its endless miles of dense jungle, scrub plains and winding rivers were little known and vast regions were barely explored and generally unmapped. The trip would provide for a perfect Rooseveltian excursion:

> *"...it occurred to me that, instead of making the conventional tourist trip purely by sea round South America, after I had finished my lectures I would come north through the middle of the continent into the valley of the Amazon...."* 4

The American Museum of Natural History in New York City would be his choice for sponsoring the expedition. Roosevelt had a longstanding personal relationship with the institution. His father was one of the original founders of the museum in the 1860s and he was a personal friend of museum head, Henry Fairfield Osborn. The museum was at that time the preeminent natural history and exploratory institution in the world. Despite his prodigious knowledge of natural history, as an amateur Roosevelt knew he would need the specialized skills of trained scientists to study and document the expedition's findings. He also recognized that any trip into a distant wild land, even a somewhat benign and previously traveled region required the knowledge of experienced hands.

As fate would dictate, when attending a luncheon meeting at the museum with ornithology curator Frank Chapman to begin planning the venture, Zahm arrived at the same time with the same intentions. The result was a collecting trip up the 1,500 mile long Paraguay River through the Mato Grasso region into the valley of the Amazon. As concept originator of the South American expedition many years before and his previous sojourn down the Amazon, Zahm became the unofficial trip coordinator and logistician. This assumed role would later prove to be a disastrous oversight by Roosevelt when a major change in both the trip itinerary and level of effort transformed into a dangerous enterprise of enormous proportions.

For the specimen-gathering project, the museum recommended two recognized and seasoned professionals to support the scientific goals of the team. George K. Cherrie was an experienced wilderness traveler and naturalist, specializing in ornithology. Having spent nearly two-decades in South America collecting birds, he spoke Spanish fluently and he was accustomed to facing hardship and danger in foreign lands. His other attributes were courage and physical toughness despite his advancing age of forty-seven. The other member enlisted by the museum was a young twenty-six year old museum mammalogist, Leo Miller. Miller was already a veteran of South American exploration and despite his young age was a highly respected scientist at the museum.

The first planning error, besides teaming with Zahm and which would result in much of the trip's later problems, began with the recruitment of Anthony Fiala. Fiala was a discredited ex-arctic explorer ending his career as a salesman in the Rogers Peet & Company clothing store on 5th Avenue in New York; a far distance and fall from the frozen wastes of the North. He met Zahm's acquaintance when the good father was shopping for the expedition's supplies in the city. Never one to assume a troublesome burden he couldn't pass off to another, Zahm was immediately taken with the man's background and hired him on the spot to join and outfit the expedition. Fiala jumped at the chance to once again engage in exploration and redeem his discredited reputation. No concern was wasted on consideration that the frozen region of the arctic is somewhat removed from the steaming jungles of the Amazon.

In addition to his total ignorance of the survival requirements of travel through tropical wilderness, Fiala's resume cataloged a questionable if not varied career of adventure. Besides his current store clerking occupation, Fiala was a former lithographic designer, photographer, chemist, cartoonist, head of the art and engraving department of the Brooklyn Daily Eagle and a trooper in the Spanish-American War. His later arctic adventures were a study in multiple failures in the early 20th century's age of competition to reach the North Pole. In 1901 he was employed as expedition photographer and second in-command[5] for the Baldwin-Ziegler Expedition to be the first at the North Pole which ended in failure. His next journey to the far north, the Fiala-Ziegler Expedition in 1903, with Fiala as commander, also ended in failure when poor selection of anchorage, unexpected ice pressure resulting in the sinking his ship and a prolonged two-year stay on the ice nearly caused a mutiny. The expedition's chief surgeon, Dr. George Shorkley, scathingly remarked:

*"Although the large, splendidly equipped expedition had some bad luck, its failure was mostly due to Fiala's inexperience and ineffective leadership, which allowed indifference and dissension to spread among the many bored and idle men."*[6]

This negligent oversight in the critical selection and responsibility of two of the expedition's key members was the result of Roosevelt's disinterest in the planning details of the trip. Although typically he was game for any possible emergence of danger, his initial belief was the expedition would be more of a pleasant excursion rather than what was to become a major undertaking. Consequently, Roosevelt's agreement to relegate the logistics to Zahm, and Zahm's careless enlistment of Fiala as the chief quartermaster ensured that the wrong equipment and supplies would be procured. Numerous supplies of unnecessary luxuries were purchased. A debate ensued between the team over the type of boats to be used indicating ignorance of the type of terrain and climate that would be encountered. Aside from food supplies, watercraft was the most essential addition to the expedition's needs as the great majority of the distance being traversed would be on water. Fiala favored light, Canadian freighter-type canoes while Zahm insisted on and purchased two large, bulky and extremely heavy steel-hulled motorboats. In the end, the expedition was forced to abandon the unusable steel boats due to their weight and unsuitability for jungle portage and settle for extremely tipsy and difficult to paddle native-built dugout canoes.

Fiala wasn't the only team member newly enlisted by Zahm to relieve the priest of any troublesome exertion, inconvenience or responsibility. A self proclaimed "handyman" seemingly walked through the door and was immediately hired by Zahm to serve as his personal attendant for the expedition. Jacob Sigg, similar to Fiala, had a varied and questionably checkered past and even Zahm considered him to be "absolutely unique." Having served as an army nurse and cook, he also claimed he was a:

> "courier and interpreter for an Indian princess, had
> sailed before the mast in many parts of the world,
> had mined for gold on the eastern slopes of the
> Andes, and had charge of a gang of men in the
> construction of a railroad in Bolivia."7

He was also a chief engineer in a power plant, operated steam engines in Manitoba, could operate a motorboat, drive a car, use firearms and spoke Spanish and Portuguese. Zahm appeared to have had questionable skills and insight in conducting job interviews for perspective wilderness travel companions. With his trio of rogues, the former President of the United States would embark, along with his son on the most dangerous mission of his life since receiving fire from Spanish mausers in Cuba many years before.

Frank Harper, Roosevelt's British private secretary, also was expected to accompany the expedition. However, with a spark of prescience returned home partway into the unexpected and previously unplanned new journey. Dangerous exploration in unchartered wilderness regions was not the forte of the deskbound assistant, accustomed to the soft environment of public affairs and administrative work.

*A Change in Plans; the Roosevelt-Rondon Scientific Expedition emerges:*

The newly formed team of would be explorers steamed out of Manhattan's East River on October 4, 1913, aboard the steamship Vandyck with Roosevelt impatiently spending the weeklong trip contemplating the adventures ahead. During their long trip south, Edith, who accompanied the group along with her young cousin for the first leg of the journey, spoke of Roosevelt in a letter to his sister Bamie, *"I think he feels like Christian in Pilgrims Progress when the bundle falls from his back, in this case it was not made of sins but of the Progressive Party."* 8

Before embarking on their great wilderness adventure, Roosevelt linked up with Kermit in Bahia, Brazil, and then continued on his six-week speaking tour through Brazil, Uruguay, Argentina and Chile as his team continued up the Paraguay to Corumba to organize the packing of the enormous stock of supplies and await his arrival. Kermit left his construction job to accompany his father with a heavy heart having just received a delayed letter from Belle who was many miles across the Atlantic in Europe. Belle had accepted his marriage proposal, leaving him torn between his overwhelming desire to speed to her but frustrated by his responsibility to look after his father's safety. Aside from his advancing age and expanding waistline, Roosevelt was not in the type of health necessary for an arduous trip into the unknown. During his presidency, he sustained gunshot wounds from a would-be assassin, a near fatal carriage disaster that left him with a seriously chronic leg wound9 and he was deaf in one ear from a wrestling bout in the White House with a Japanese judo expert. Besides all this, he suffered with poor eyesight since his childhood. Edith's worries for the safety of her husband and words of concern to Kermit, along with his own worry and devotion to his father, impelled Kermit to participate in the long journey delaying his betrothal and compounding his usually deep and downcast emotions.

As Roosevelt began his prolonged speaking tour, the Brazilian minister of foreign affairs, Mr. Lauro Muller, offered to assist the expedition. Encouraged by the positive publicity that would emerge from the former American President and his entourage traveling throughout his country, Muller was also aware of the potential advantages a well-provisioned scientific expedition could provide by investigating and documenting some of the unknown regions of the country. Muller proposed two offers that would change the entire nature of the adventure.

His first suggestion was a change in the course of the expedition's route from a fairly comfortable collecting excursion through previously traveled territory to a major exploration undertaking in the unknown regions of the western Matto Grosso. The focus of the trip would be the descent of a wild river whose course, origin and ending were unknown to geographers and was not even depicted on any maps.[10] The second suggestion was the enlistment of a Brazilian Army officer who first discovered the isolated river as a seasoned explorer knowing more of this remote region than any other living person, excepting the wild Indians who roamed its dark interior.

The enlistment of Colonel Candido Rondon was an outstanding but somewhat contrary choice to partner with Roosevelt. His stiff, stern military demeanor was the antithesis of Roosevelt's easygoing, gregarious personality. Part Indian, he was already a legend in Brazil, having spent many years in the wilderness supervising the installation of a telegraph line across much of the barren interior. His travels were not only notable for surveying and mapping vast areas of the wilderness, but also for his tolerance and humane treatment of many of the warlike tribes of Indians. The addition of a proven leader and wilderness veteran like Rondon provided a much needed balance to the haphazard collection of team members. Roosevelt immediately agreed to the plan alterations and Rondon's addition, noting:

*"I eagerly and gladly accepted, for I felt that with such help the trip could be made of much scientific value, and that a substantial addition could be made to the geographical knowledge of one of the least-known parts of South America."* [11]

*The Adventure Begins:*
Changing the expedition's route from a mainly benign collecting trip along various known waterways to a serious exploration project into the unknown meant traversing an enormous stretch of barren land across the Brazilian highlands even before reaching the mysterious river. The Roosevelts began their expedition by river steamer on December 9th at the city of Asuncion in Paraguay for a three-day cruise up the Paraguay River later to meet with Rondon at the confluence of the Apa River on Brazil's southern border. This initial leg of the journey provided a

pleasant, leisurely opportunity to loll in the sun on deck and view the occasional settlement or cultivated farm. Fishing from the boat, Roosevelt marveled at one species of wildlife that would be an ever-present danger to the expedition in the coming months. Even beyond the vicious South American alligator, the caiman, the piranha imposed a threat to any man or beast that ventured into the countless waterways of much of South America. Although enjoying the diversion of catching these fish, a serious respect was held for the threat they represented. The ubiquitous piranha or cannibal fish infested the freshwater rivers the expedition would travel and according to Roosevelt will *"snap a finger off a hand incautiously trailed in the water; they mutilate swimmers"* and *"will rend and devour alive any wounded man or beast; for blood in the water excites them to madness. I never witnessed an exhibition of such impotent, savage fury as was shown by the piranhas as they flapped on deck."* 12 Rondon had lost a toe to one of these vile creatures on a previous expedition, and one of his men was severely bitten on his tongue when fishing. Even the naturalist Miller had recently been bitten by one. This preliminary exhibition of savagery portended only one of the many dangers the future would impose on the men.

❖

After linking-up and first meeting with Rondon and his officers, Roosevelt's confidence in the trip increased:

> *"It was evident that he knows his business thoroughly, and it was equally evident that he would be a pleasant companion. Colonel Rondon has spent the last twenty-four years in exploring the western highlands of Brazil, pioneering the way for telegraph-lines and railroads."* 13

Besides Rondon and his enlisted men, his team consisted of three army officers and a Brazilian doctor who would accompany the expedition on the wild river.

The combined team steamed up the Paraguay to the frontier town of Corumba arriving on December 15 where they met Cherrie and Miller, Sigg and Fiala some six-hundred miles distant from Roosevelt's original embarkation point. The two naturalists had already independently collected eight hundred specimens of mammals and birds. Their stay at Corumba enabled the assessment and organization of the huge store of supplies that Fiala had procured for the expedition and provided a few days of hunting opportunities for Kermit and his father. Roosevelt, contrary to his background of conservation, killed many of the detested caimans on the trip. The pair also killed anteaters, marsh deer and capybara with Kermit taking a large jaguar with his .405 Winchester.

Their technique of jaguar hunting used dogs for scenting and following the track with the hunters tagging along behind on horseback. Leaving well before sunup, Roosevelt, Kermit and a string of their Brazilian military party began fording rivers and wading through bog and swamp while traversing jungle lowland. The water-soaked column continued on into the steaming heat of the day, hour after hour they proceeded through island-like stretches of tree-covered land and thorn thicket sometimes swimming the horses and dogs across deep water. The hunters were not deterred by the ever-present swarms of mosquitoes and various stinging insects or caimans lurking on the river banks, nor the danger of schools of piranha being agitated by the horse hooves and the possibility of tangling with an anaconda or poisonous viper. The trip was so arduous that even the dogs were giving out, requiring Kermit to refresh one by throwing water over him. Finally, Roosevelt dispatched a jaguar, high in the forked branches of a tree that was brought to bay by the howling, maddened dogs. On another occasion Kermit went hunting for tapir despite being down with a case of fever. When fording a river, two of his dogs lost the tips of their tails to the ever-present piranhas.

Another notable episode of their side hunting trips exhibited Roosevelt's still remarkable stamina, even at the advanced age of 55. They embarked on another early morning jaguar hunt through the stifling jungle on foot, torn by the spines of small palms, bitten by the numerous swarming insects and fire ants, they waded through marshes hip deep. The day-long trek proceeded without any food and produced no game. Fiala later recounted a remarkable sight. Having remained on board their boat, in

the late afternoon Fiala heard an Indian call from the
jungle depths:

> *"'Burroo-gurra-harru,' he muttered, fell into a corner,
> and went to sleep. Twenty minutes later another
> Indian stumbled out of the forest. 'Plenty work-tired,'
> he cried, and fell and also went to sleep. A third
> Indian came and dropped on the deck."*

Worried for the safety of the hunters and thinking some
major disaster had befallen the group, Fiala organized a
relief party as the sun was setting. In a clearing a short
distance from the river he came upon one of the Brazilian
officers, lying exhausted on the ground, his clothes torn,
his face and neck covered with dust and blood.[14] He was
sent back to the boat in the care of some Indians.

Continuing on, the rescue party came upon Roosevelt
and Kermit dragging another of the Brazilian officers
through the jungle. Roosevelt and Kermit's clothes were in
shreds but Fiala noted Roosevelt's countenance *"on his
grimy face was a look of warlike determination. All right,
Colonel?"* asked Fiala, *"I'm bully"* answered Roosevelt.
Although the Brazilians were laid up for days following the
ordeal,

Roosevelt and Kermit continued in a nonchalant
manner as if nothing untoward occurred.

On Christmas Day, the entire expedition, food,
equipment, specimens and even K-9 mascots pushed off
into the Paraguay for their continuing trip upriver into the
Mato Grosso. The comfortable security of civilization
waned as the evidence of human settlement became more
infrequent and began to fade; as each mile of the turbid
waters passed below their keel the dark, foreboding
wilderness thickened and insidiously encroached around
them.

❖

Following various detours along minor river tributaries
for specimen collecting, hunting and visits to the
increasingly sparse ranches, the expedition ended their
river journey at Tapirapoan on January 16, the
headquarters of Rondon's Telegraphic Commission. This
would begin their long overland journey to the River of
Doubt. The country ahead would be traversed by a long

pack-train of mules and pack-oxen, similar to Roosevelt and Kermit's previous safari in Africa.

The land was highland wilderness that Rondon had pioneered in past years as he and his men laboriously and at great danger installed his telegraph lines. Heat, insects, starvation and hostile Indians claimed many of the construction crews during the building of the line. Many men were lost and many more simply rejected the danger and privation associated with his command. For Rondon, contact with the Indians and attempting to bring civilization to the warring tribes was equal to the importance of bringing communication to this wild country and even exceeded the safety and comfort of his men. His courage and doggedness within this region over many years established him as one of the preeminent explorers of the Brazilian wilderness but also defined him as an unrelenting driver of his men.

At the Tapirapoan camp, Fiala and Sigg were charged with the task of sorting the numerous supplies and organizing the near 250 pack-animals. Days were spent in heavy, humid, 91 to 104 degree heat engaged in the onerous process of not only packing but in some cases breaking the half wild live stock that would be their conveyance for the coming weeks. Kermit, anxious to return to his recently betrothed and impatient with any delays, was *"ready to kill the whole lot (of pack animals) and all the members of the expedition."*15 Ever the naturalist, Roosevelt observed with amazement the predatory habits of the local wildlife. *"We were now in the land of the bloodsucking bats, the vampire bats that suck the blood of living creatures...."*16 Ticks, poisonous ants, wasps, biting flies and gnats were in abundance outside of the camp compound, however the army-ants, insects that he characterized as the most dangerous and aggressive lower-life creatures, drew his special attention. While at Tapirapoan, Cherrie and Miller continued to collect various mammal and bird specimens and up to now, their scientific bag contained about a thousand birds and two-hundred and fifty mammals. As usual, Kermit indulged in his local hunting trips securing an occasional armadillo, coati or agouti to contribute to the scientific enterprise. To expedite the already delayed trip, the baggage was divided and an advance party with Rondon's subordinate,

Captain Amilcar leaving ahead of Roosevelt, Kermit and the main expedition members. The previously collected specimens along with unnecessary baggage would return back down the Paraguay to New York with Harper.

The expedition had travelled almost two-thousand miles since entering the Mato Grasso on the Paraguay. On January 21st the Roosevelt team began the long overland trek northwestward to the Rio da Duvida. Their route of march led at times through thick tropical forest requiring a bushwhack with machetes opening a trail for the long string of pack-mules. Noted Zahm:

*"Our second day's journey was through a dense forest composed of trees and shrubs of all sizes and innumerable species. The branches of the larger trees interlaced overhead in such wise that at times we seemed to be passing through a dimly lighted vegetable tunnel"*

At other times they traversed many miles on open, hot, rolling plains of sand on the high Parecis plateau.*[7] Travelling in the rainy season, they would often ride into a heavy downpour of rain, soaking everyone to the skin and turning the loose soil into slippery mud, making conditions difficult for the mules. The tiny sand-flies required everyone to use head nets and gloves; one bite would leave a mark on the skin lasting weeks.

On one occasion, Kermit, always the hunter, broke from the line of march to hunt, returning later with two buck deer. At night, the group would gather around the camp fire seated on ox skins, in some cases, eating their only meal of the day, and end telling stories of their various past adventures. Rondon would relate many incidents of hardship and struggle during his years of building the telegraph line through the very country they now traveled; one time near starvation forcing him and his men to subsist for many weeks on wild fruit. He explained how when blazing the trail for his communication line they had once lost every one of their one-hundred and sixty mules which they began with.[17] Fiala recounted his frozen years

---

7 * The mountains in this remote region formed the basis for Arthur Conan Doyle's "Lost World."

in the arctic with Cherrie holding the group spellbound with his reminisces about holding-off a cavalry charge in Venezuela while he and five comrades were on foot with only rifles as defense against mounted lancers.

❖

Although still many miles from beginning their descent of the Duvida, the trip was starting to wear on both man and beast. Despite the enormous stock of supplies Fiala organized, much of it was useless on this type of journey and either was sent back with Harper or discarded when the pack-animals began to give out and buck off the increasingly heavy loads. Ample food and water for both man and beast became a problem. In anticipation of challenges and hardship on the Duvida, Roosevelt took a dark, philosophical view,

> *"If our canoe voyage was prosperous we would gradually lighten the loads by eating the provisions. If we met with accidents, such as losing canoes and men in the rapids, or losing men in encounters with Indians, or if we encountered overmuch fever and dysentery, the loads would lighten themselves."*[18]

An ominous sign greeting the column of march:

> *"...was shown in the numerous skeletons of oxen and mules which littered both sides of the road. Besides these bleached skeletons, we saw a number of boxes scattered here and there bearing the inscription, 'Roosevelt South American Expedition.'"*[19]

Evidence of the difficulty Captain Amilcar's advance party experienced just days before. To conserve food, meals were becoming less frequent and less filling.

The long hot and monotonous days of trudging across the barren wilderness of the highlands also began to undermine the men's morale. With growing apprehension as they followed the trail of the telegraph line, pole after pole, mile after endless mile, the men were aware of the former hardships endured in this region before even reaching the unexplored river with its unknown dangers. At one of the villages, Rondon learned one of his subordinates died from beriberi ahead on the expedition's line of march. He was also informed that three other of his men had recently drowned ascending the Gy-Parana attempting to deliver provisions to part of the expedition that would be descending that river later on.[20]

Roosevelt and Kermit both knew that when the comfort and amenities of civilization are removed, the hardship and danger of the wilderness trail tends to expose both the best and worst in men; great bravery is sometimes stimulated, but frequently treachery expressed with self-serving disregard for others will be exposed. The seeds of this dangerous human frailty would surface to a murderous degree as the trip continued.

Besides Rondon and his party of officers, Captain Amilcar, Lieutenants Lyra and Filho and Doctor Cajazeira, he enlisted a group of Brazilian porters known as camaradas for handling the pack-animals on the first leg of the journey and later as paddlers for the river passage. One of his enlistees, a surly character named Julio de Lima of Portuguese descent was a large and muscular individual whose devious and violent nature became apparent early in the trip when he attacked another camarada with a knife during an altercation. As the trip progressed, Julio would present himself as an increasing problem just as an insidious, chronic disease slowly immerges with devastating effect.

Besides fatigue, jangled nerves and a diminishing food supply, Kermit's chronic malaria flared-up and Father Zahm was becoming a continual nuisance to the expedition. With the apprehension and foresight of a soft office worker caught trudging through a wilderness and his recent contraction of malaria, Harper assessed the situation early on and had already departed. But the other weak link in the group was Zahm. Having led the soft life of an academic and cleric, Zahm's stubborn constant pursuit of comfort in the face of growing adversity angered his comrades. He displayed an arrogant, elitist attitude toward the Brazilians that incensed Rondon who spent a life of suffering and deprivation in the wilderness with these very same people that Zahm denigrated. The inability to communicate clearly across the varying languages no doubt also added to the tensions. Although Rondon spoke many Indian dialects as well as French and Portuguese, Kermit became the intermediary translating in French between Rondon and Roosevelt. With the camaradas, hand signals, gestures and facial expressions were all they could use.

Despite the growing hardships, the expedition was travelling through a beautiful wilderness of extraordinary foliage, wild rivers and magnificent waterfalls. One of the last vestiges of civilization on their journey through this picturesque land was at the villages of the Parecis Indians. The Parecis were an indigenous group Rondon had been cultivating by providing employment for patrol of his telegraphic line. The diversion of the Indian villages provided a few days respite and the opportunity for the naturalists to collect additional specimens.

While at one of the villages, a measure of the exhaustion that was overtaking the expedition was indicated when a pack-ox wandered into the tent in which Roosevelt and Kermit were sleeping, entering one end and exiting the other without waking either of the human occupants. While stumbling through the tent, the ox ate their shirts, socks and underclothes without waking the exhausted travelers.

On February 3rd the expedition was once again on the move, however, major changes were made in who would continue on. Thus far it was becoming quite clear that if the party was to continue and descend the Duvida successfully, a reduction would have to be made in the number of members making the attempt. Thinning the ranks was essential; both the consumption of limited resources and the human risk were too great to continue on the increasingly difficult journey into the unknown with anyone who was not absolutely essential or up to the task.

Father Zahm was physically unsuitable and besides his age and frailty, he was too much of a social burden to continue so both he and his attendant, Jacob Sigg were forced to turn back. This rejection for the one who was the originator of entire enterprise must have been a big disappointment to Zahm. The remaining party members were relieved with the departure of this arrogant, cranky cleric. Fiala and one of the Brazilian officers were assigned to return via canoe descent of the Papagaio, Juruena and Tapajos, also wild rivers that were perhaps just as dangerous as the Duvida, a trip which Roosevelt considered a necessary part of the expedition's work.

Ultimately, Fiala would come close to losing his life in rapids*[8] on this altered route. In the rapids of the Papagaio two of Fiala's canoes were upset, half of their provisions and all of his baggage were lost and he almost drowned.

Roosevelt weighed the dual and in some respects duplicate scientific skills of Cherrie and Miller against the need to thin the group and Miller reluctantly volunteered to withdraw leaving the elder Cherrie to continue with Roosevelt as the expedition's naturalist.

As difficult as the previous 150 miles or so had been, the trail ahead presented even a higher degree of danger and hardship for the men. The land was wilder and more remote and was the territory of the Nhambiquara Indians,[21] a group of primitive forest people and only recently had Rondon won their tentative trust. The Nhambiquara were a stone-age people, fierce and wild which Roosevelt characterized as *"light-hearted robbers and murderers."* They went entirely naked carrying seven-foot long bows and five-foot long arrows tipped with curare. Their short stature belied their warlike habits and were a continual scourge to the Parecis and always a potential threat to Rondon's men working on the telegraph line. The poor condition of the pack-animals now compelled each member of the expedition to discard everything above the basic necessities. Oxen were so weak from lack of good forage they could no longer pull the carts, nine of their mules were already left behind on the road. On they rode through the heat, swarms of insects and the alternating weather of soaking down pours and humid sunshine.

*"One afternoon we pitched camp by a tiny rivulet, in the midst of the scrubby upland forest; a camp, by the way, where the piums, the small, biting flies, were a torment during the hours of daylight, while after dark their places were more than taken by the diminutive gnats which the Brazilians expressively term 'polvora,' or powder, and which get through the smallest meshes of a mosquito-net."*[22]

---

8 *The rapids are known as Isl do Diablo or "rapids of the Devil"

They waded rivers and crossed swollen bodies of water on crude bridges or makeshift log ferries. *"...many hours might be consumed in getting the mule-train, the loose bullocks and the ox-cart over."*[23]

On February 15, at a place called Campos Novos (new camp), Roosevelt's column met with Captain Amilcar's advance party nearly a month following their separation. The ox-cart was left behind and the combined expedition continued on the trail only with pack-animals. Kermit, wandering a few miles from camp one day stumbled upon an encampment of Nhambiquaras. They were stark naked, some had long reeds thrust through holes in their lips. Although savage and dangerous, they did not molest Kermit and accompanied him back to camp where they entertained the expedition members with primitive dancing around the campfire. In the morning, one of the Nhambiquara women attempted to steal a fork but it was retrieved before they departed.

After a day's march, the column visited a village of these Indians then proceeded a number of miles where Amilcar along with Miller and two of the Brazilian officers once again would separate from the main group and backtrack. Their plan was to march to the Gy-Parana where they would follow that river, down the Madeira onto Manaos. Roosevelt would continue with Kermit, Cherrie, Rondon, Lyra and the doctor along with sixteen paddlers to challenge the Duvida.

### On to the River of Doubt

On February 27, Roosevelt, Kermit and the remaining group of explorers arrived at the river's edge. After traveling overland for over a month, the expedition finally arrived at the beginning of their goal. The trip until now had been an endurance test that had worn the men physically and frayed their recently established, delicate relationships. Natural selection had reduced the size of the expedition, hard travel and the need to lighten the load had frayed and diminished their supplies, and yet the most serious and dangerous leg of the journey was still before them.

Despite all of the preplanning and past debate by Zahm and Fiala, the only watercraft available to them ultimately were seven dugout canoes hand-hewn from large trees

*River of Doubt expedition members share evening meal while in the Matto Grosso. Father Zahm is on left with Colonel Candido to his left. Kermit is sitting on makeshift hide blanket on left with Theodore Roosevelt sitting on chair on right.*

which had a tendency to ride very low in the water, had a limited capacity and were difficult to steer. The primitive craft were also very heavy and being made of raw wood eventually became waterlogged unlike the light Canadian freighter-canoes that Fiala originally wanted to use. According to Roosevelt, *"One was small, one was cranky, and two were old, waterlogged and leaky. The other three were good."*[24] Having already discarded all unessential baggage, the only items carried were the necessities required for survival, surveying instruments and a few books. The provisions were not full rations but were expected to last about fifty-days if combined with a plan of living partially off of the land by hunting, fishing and gathering nuts and palm-tops.

Shortly after noon, the small flotilla dipped their paddles into the dark swift waters of the rain-swollen Duvida. At their embarkation point where the river was narrow, Amilcar, Miller and others of their party bid them farewell from a makeshift log bridge constructed by Rondon's men on a previous trip. A feeling of unspoken foreboding overcame all as the small group disappeared around a bend in the river. All understood the questionable survival chances Roosevelt's group faced on a river of unknown length through uncharted wilderness and now, with no chance of turning back.

The fast running water of the unmapped river tracked a course through dense, overhanging jungle foliage that frequently would create a watery tunnel through which the men paddled:

> "The lofty and matted forest rose like a green wall on either hand. The trees were stately and beautiful. The looped and twisted vines hung from them like great ropes. Masses of epiphytes grew both on the dead trees and the living; some had huge leaves like elephants' ears."[25]

The strange stillness of the jungle, devoid of any animal life raised both curiosity and dread in the men. Due to the wet season's enormous rainfall, the high water covered many submerged snags that were a constant threat to the limited steerage of their unwieldy craft. The dugout canoes, laden with men and supplies had very limited freeboard with the waterline just inches below the sides; two pair were lashed together for stability, further reducing their steerage. An upset in this swift water flowing past river banks concealed beneath the dense overgrowth could be disastrous with no easy location to beach, turnaround and then return upriver for a rescue. Then again for anyone in the swift current, there was always the concern for encountering schools of the piranha or the hungry jaws of a caiman.

Fortunately the sixteen camarada paddlers in the group were up to the task and greatly impressed Roosevelt:

> "They were expert river-men and men of the forest, skilled veterans in wilderness work. They were lithe as panthers and brawny as bears. They swam like water-dogs. They were equally at home with pole and paddle, with axe and machete."[26]

A major goal for the expedition besides locating the end of this mysterious river was to detail survey its course. To achieve this, Rondon adopted the meticulous and time consuming method of sighting a straight line along each section of the river while documenting its distance and compass direction. The process consisted of Kermit paddling ahead in his small tipsy canoe with a sighting-rod and stopping at a station point on the river with a long unobstructed view to the following canoes where he would plant the rod while holding onto the foliage along the river bank. From behind, Rondon and Lieutenant Lyra would site Kermit's target and record the data. They would then move on to the next location and repeat the process. Over and over, the slow, tedious routine required Kermit to post a position nearly a hundred times in the first half-day while the group covered only nine and a third kilometers. Kermit, paddling in the survey's target canoe was also the most exposed to dangers of the unforeseen both on the river negotiating its current and on its banks each time he would halt to set his sighting rod. The tropical rainforest was notorious as the home for poisonous snakes. Each time Kermit stopped while holding onto the overhanging plants and vines steadying his canoe he ran the risk of stumbling onto a snake. Or at the least, barging into a swarm of stinging wasps or receiving a shower of stinging ants from the green canopy above. Many times he would have to hack into the foliage from the canoe to present a clear line of sight. Roosevelt, always concerned for the safety of his son, did not appreciate either the danger to Kermit or the slow arduous process. With limited supplies to sustain the group on a passage of unknown duration, the expedition could ill afford to dally. However, Rondon's overriding interest in documenting his watercourse and as the expedition's military leader, Roosevelt had little choice but to defer to Rondon's plan. Tensions between the two strong and determined personalities would continue to grow.

On the third day after traveling barely 46 kilometers on the river, they encountered the remnants of an abandoned Indian village. The Indians of this region were totally unknown. Although the Nhambiquara were primitive and unpredictable, they were a know entity that Rondon had managed to tame, to a degree. However, the indigenous populations of this region were not only a puzzle to the expedition, but the strange new white travelers on their river would not be seen as just temporary passersby but strange invaders to the Indians. Although no visual sightings of the unknown jungle inhabitants had been made, the expedition members had the constant uneasy feeling of being watched themselves from the jungle depths and discovery of this village only heightened their apprehensions.

❖

For a period of time they paddled on placid water that due to the heavy rains extended over large areas of the forest. However, as the river course continually dropped in elevation, the current began to accelerate. This increasing decline in the river's flow began to present serious problems in both the speed and type of current and the nature of the river bottom. Although generally following a circuitous northerly direction, the river continued to drop, sometimes gently but they also began to encounter serious waterfalls. As the river narrowed and descended, dangerous currents, swirls and eddies would form, creating a turbulent maelstrom sometimes above, and sometimes below a falls. The fast current would water-wash the river bottom exposing rocks around which the water would violently swirl. This combined with the natural turns in the wild river made paddling the crude canoes difficult and sometimes impossible to maneuver without mishap. The river was so erratic that at one point it was over a hundred yards wide, then in less than two miles as it cascaded over rapids it narrowed to a width of less than six-feet.

At this point the violence of the rapids were too much for the canoes to negotiate so a long portage was required. Moving the canoes around dangerous sections of the river on land was a backbreaking and time consuming project and became a frequent occurrence. The initial portage consumed the first three days in March as the men chopped a road through the forest and hauled the heavy, water soaked canoes around the rapids on log rollers. The men were harnessed two by two and with block and tackle dragged each while a man behind pried with a cut log. Up steep embankments from the shore the men labored, bouncing and pulling the log craft weighing close to a ton each, in stifling humidity and the occasional pouring rain. Slipping in the mud while being scrapped by the dense foliage, bitten and stung by insects the men toiled. Kermit participated in the slave-like labor along with the camaradas. The rough treatment of the canoes during the overland journey to bypass the rapids was not without mishap. Roosevelt's canoe was split and another sank when being re-launched, requiring additional effort just to raise it.

On the afternoon of March 5 the expedition again took to the river. The men were beginning to suffer from insect bites and stings they received while on land. Kermit was stung by a giant, inch and a half-long ant which Roosevelt said was like the sting of a small scorpion. The group was barely on the water one day when they again detected the roar of fast water ahead. They beached their canoes and after a reconnoiter of the river ahead once again made camp in preparation for a long, time consuming portage. *"...the rapids continued for a long distance, with falls and steep pitches of broken water, and that the portage would take several days."*[27] The next three days were spent in unpacking, hauling and repacking the canoes. After eleven days on the river and despite the expenditure of food, exhausting labor and time, the expedition only progressed a mere fifty-five kilometers north of their original starting point. Besides burning body fat and calories, exposure to wild animals and wild Indians and disease carrying insects, the potential for starvation never left their minds.

Riding the river for short distances to the next set of rapids or falls, then portaging continued for days. The rough and ready Kermit, with the strength and exuberance of youth, worked alongside the camaradas in the water and on the heavy overland drags. His clothes became tattered rags and his body was scored with numerous blisters and the bites of stinging ants. The camaradas fared even worse while going barefoot or wearing only sandals. Two or three camaradas were so crippled from biting gnats they could hardly walk.[28] One morning after camping at the foot of rapids, the men awoke to discover the river had risen during the night and swamped two of their seven canoes. The carelessness in their mooring was the cause and their loss was a disaster – they could ill afford any unnecessary delays. The only course of action was to establish a camp and prepare to construct new canoes. The preparation of a dugout canoe is a specialized and difficult task. Before beginning the labor of hollowing-out the center of a huge tree trunk with axe and adze, the appropriate tree must be found. Following that it must be cut down, trimmed and laboriously hauled to the camp even before the axe work begins. They worked day and night sometimes in the pouring rain and other times by candlelight. Roosevelt, Kermit and Lyra scoured the immediate forest for game to supplement their diminishing food supply. Kermit killed two monkeys, Lyra a curassow, Roosevelt bagged nothing.

On March 14th their work was finally completed, and they took to the river covering close to sixteen kilometers. To attempt running minor rapids to make up lost time, they lashed bundles of burity-palm branches to the gunnels of the canoes for additional buoyancy which ran only inches above the water. The next day began with a short progress of six kilometers and then serious trouble befell the group. When men are exhausted and living on short rations in wretched conditions, both caution and judgment begin to fade.

*Death on the River*

Rounding a bend, the river widened into a series of dangerous rapids extending for about six-hundred yards with a small island splitting the river at the head end. Kermit was in the lead canoe, a small, tender craft with his dog and two camaradas, Joao and Simplicio. They were also carrying a week's provisions along with some tools. Kermit beached the canoe above the rapids as others reconnoitered the river ahead on foot. Impulsively and foolishly, Kermit decided to paddle to the island to investigate a possible route on the other side. Deciding against either passage, Kermit and the camaradas turned about in the current and attempted to head up-stream while being turned sideways they became captive to a whirlpool of horrific flow. Although almost reaching shore by enormous effort, the canoe became swamped, and they were uncontrollably swept through the rapids into another whirlpool. The strength of the current flung the small craft back into midstream where the canoe capsized spilling the men and its cargo into the swirling water. Roosevelt would write later:

*"Poor Simplicio must have been pulled under at once and his life beaten out on the bowlders beneath the*

70

*racing torrent. He never rose again, nor did we ever
recover his body."*29

Kermit managed to climb on top of the over turned
canoe clutching his Winchester rifle when he again hit
rough water. He was pitched into the current and
continued to be swept through the rapids and pounded in
the river's fury.

Having lost his rifle and having almost drowned, he was
fortunate to have grasped an overhanging branch and
pulled himself to shore. Joal, the other camarada with
Kermit, and Kermit's dog managed to swim ashore. The
submerged canoe and rifle were never found but they did
retrieve the provisions along with a paddle. In memory of
the disaster at this spot on the river, the expedition erected
a memorial sign: *"In These Rapids Died Poor Simplicio"*.30

Shortly after leaving this tragic location, Kermit
reconnoitered a few miles further down the river and once
again spotted a set of rapids more treacherous than those
that previously caused such havoc. A channel that
bypassed the worst of the kilometer-long rapids was
located. On the morning of the 16th, in blinding rain, the
canoes were let down the channel on ropes the men walked
from the river bank. While the men struggled with the
canoes, Rondon and one of the expedition's dogs, Lobo,
began to explore the river ahead. While walking through
the dense jungle, Rondon heard a strange howling noise
that he mistook for the wailing of monkeys. Lobo ran
ahead and when out of sight, Rondon heard the dog yelp
with pain as the howling sound began coming closer. Lobo
yelped once again and then there was silence convincing
Rondon that the dog was dead, the victim of Indians.
Rondon fired his rifle into the air to discourage any attack
by Indians who probably had never come into contact with
white men and then he quickly returned to the portage.

Rondon and Kermit, in the company of two men
returned to the site of the Indian contact and discovered
Lobo's body pierced with two arrows. Now the expedition
was directly confronted with the reality of hostile Indians
who probably had been lurking in the forest observing the
small flotilla throughout their passage. This realization
now imposed upon the group a heightened need for armed
security. Although bearing firearms would be a great

advantage to the expedition in any open, pitched battle, the forest Indians technique for hunting and in battle was to rely on the concealment of the jungle, attacking from stealth while silently employing poison-tipped arrows with deadly accuracy. The disadvantage of focusing on navigating the difficult river in unprotected canoes while on the open water and camping in the total darkness of the jungle at night exposed the expedition to the very type of warfare that the Indians excelled at. Portages would now have to be guarded with every man on alert.

As the drama of the Indian attack was unfolding, the rest of the men were struggling to skid the canoes around the latest set of rapids. While lowering their new canoe into the swift water on pulleys and rope, one of the lines broke sending both the canoe and the irreplaceable tackle into the river. This new disaster compounded the numerous problems the expedition already faced. Besides the loss of the new canoe, now any future rough water they encountered requiring a portage would not be able to be bypassed without the critical block and tackle gear. Besides, they only had four canoes remaining; not enough to carry the men. The expedition, lasting eighteen days, was on the river and used over one third of their food supply. The group had travelled only 125 kilometers. Wasting additional days in cutting and building a new dugout was also out of the question. Their desperate decision was to lash the four remaining canoes in pairs and float them down the river while thirteen men walked the river bank alongside. With the overgrowth of jungle foliage bordering the river bank, this would be a difficult task indeed. Their hopes were to travel for a few days without encountering any dangerous rapids or falls, gaining enough distance to enable the delay of building yet additional canoes. Again, they were forced to abandon some of their remaining equipment. The torment of the incessant[31] biting and stinging insects were also taking a serious toll on the scantily-clad camaradas. Roosevelt later wrote:

> "They wrapped their legs and feet in pieces of
> canvas or hide; and the feet of three of them became
> so swollen that they were crippled and could not
> walk any distance."[32]

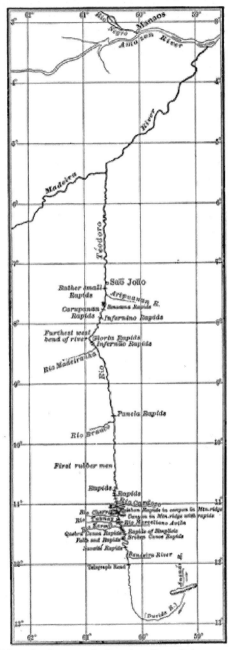

*Map the Roosevelt-Rondon Expedition
traveled exploring the River of Doubt.*

To relieve their suffering, the doctor administered medication daily. The next day was spent combining walking and portaging and occasionally risking a run through a set of dangerous, hair-raising rapids which fortunately, the group negotiated without mishap.

At their next camp, after travelling almost seven kilometers, they came upon a small river entering the Duvida. The new body of water contained a small waterfall just before the junction and Rondon named the new flow after Kermit. The Rio Kermit was rich in fish. Besides feasting on their catch, the expedition's hopes were raised when one of the camaradas claimed these fish never came up heavy rapids, thereby believing the trip ahead would be milder then that passed. He was mistaken; the worst rapids were yet to be encountered.

Rondon, as a spit and polish military officer, was also keenly aware of the importance of the discipline of ceremony and daily routine for the morale of the troops especially when under stress. Although his men were clad in tatters, half starved and worked almost beyond endurance, he required the expedition to stand in military formation each morning as he officiously read the orders of the day. The discovery and naming of a new river was an event worthy of formal recognition. So the next morning, Rondon organized the men into ranks, read the orders of the day in front of a post he had erected bearing a board with "Rio Kermit" inscribed, commemorating the new stream. As part of his recitation, Rondon surprised Roosevelt when recognizing the Duvida as a great river, and by order of the Brazilian Government, he formally named their mysterious river of doubt, the Rio Roosevelt. Contrary to the Roosevelt's disagreement with this honor, Rondon insisted and the men all cheered the event which raised everyone's spirits. To this day, contemporary maps of Amazonia depict this lengthy river, still enshrouded in wilderness jungle as either the Rio Roosevelt or the Rio Teodoro.

After spending hours with some of the group paddling half-loaded canoes down fairly gentle rapids as others marched along carrying the balance of their supplies, they established a campsite and decided to build new canoes once again. The continuous delays were becoming critical;

always the specter of starvation haunted the men. In his diary for March 13, Cherrie recorded:

*"We went over provisions today. The men have sufficient for thirty-five and we have enough for about fifty days. It is estimated that we have about 600 kilometers to go. During the past fifteen days since starting we have averaged about 7 kilometers! (Due north we have only averaged about 2 ½ miles out of a possible 400!) At that rate we will be shy about 35 days food! There may be very serious times ahead of us."*[33]

On March 19th the work began on two dugouts. Despite the insects being fought with fire, the camp site was rife with swarms of carregadores and foraging ants which continued taking a toll on the expedition's meager supplies. Besides building the new craft, the three-day stay enabled the men to swim in the river while also catching the dreaded piranhas in the same water. During their three-weeks on the Rio Duvida, Roosevelt estimated the river's elevation had dropped approximately 124 meters over a run of about 140 kilometers, which would account for the high incidence of fast water. Many of the rapids the expedition encountered would today be classified as dangerous whitewater for even modern canoes and rubber rafts managed by experts. While continuing in a generally northerly direction, the constantly looping river had consumed a disproportionate amount of time for distance covered, *"The river had wound so that we had gone two miles for every one we made northward."*[34]

Over the next few days the expedition alternated between walking the river bank while running the canoes empty, sometimes on ropes, sometimes empty with just paddlers, sometimes with a full portage. The weather alternated between incessant downpours, drenching everyone through, then miraculously sunshine appeared that steamed the water from their tattered clothes until the next downpour within an hour or two. They discovered abandoned Indian villages, and Cherrie shot the occasional bird for their collection. They dined twice a day drawing from their meager rations supplemented with palm-tops or rarely having the good fortune to shoot a monkey or catch a fish. The low caloric intake combined with the constant physical exertion in the harsh environment was reducing the men to walking skeletons.[35]

*Murder on the River*

After the many days of hard travel, at the end of March the expedition was departing the high plateau and entering a region of low mountain ranges as the river continued to fall. From passage through jungle covered land as the water stepped down in stages, it now began to cut through the hills in deep gorges. Their next challenge was a three-kilometer passage through a gorge with sheer rocky walls. The ground was too rough and the distance too great to consider a portage up the mountain and around this new obstacle; the only remaining possibility was to attempt to rope the canoes through the long defile. Against the opinions of both Rondon and Roosevelt, Kermit believed he could rope the empty canoes down the falls and through the gorge while he and a few of the deft-footed camaradas clung to the narrow shelves bordering the gorge. The daring work of handling the ropes and restraining the heavy canoes against the current below while climbing across the rocky sides and stepping through the numerous shrubs dotting the narrow ledge was both laborious and dangerous. Despite their best efforts, one of their six canoes was lost. As the rope-men negotiated the canoes down, the rest of the men cut a trail over the mountain and hauled the supplies up and down the steep, forest-clad slopes. In desperation to lighten their load, the men once again reduced their baggage.

The next few days were a repeat of the harrowing experience in the gorge: running the canoes down the river empty while hauling the baggage on foot over a high, broken jungle trail. Roosevelt's strength was giving out as he was able, only with difficulty to carry his rifle and cartridge bag while the men carried the remaining baggage. On this occasion, Rondon climbed a mountain bordering the river to possibly find a route suitable for hauling the baggage but his effort was to no avail; a struggle along the cliff face was the only alternative. Kermit exercised his rope skills with the assistance of Cherrie, Lyra and with a group of camaradas on the narrow cliff ledge. They were constantly wet with rotten shoes from their boat handling, their bodies were spotted with insect bites and festering wounds. Despite their best efforts, another canoe was lost.

❖

As the last of the loads were being brought into their camp at the foot of the rapids, a shot rang out on the trail behind, shattering the jungle silence. Within a moment a group of the men came running into camp stating that Julio de Lima had just shot one of the Brazilian officers dead. As a whining complainer who shirked his work, Julio was reprimanded recently by the officer for stealing food. Roosevelt characterized him as: *"... a fellow of powerful frame, was utterly worthless, being an inborn, lazy shirk with the heart of a ferocious cur in the body of a bullock."*36 When he saw his chance, the crazed Julio picked up a rifle and shot the man dead before retreating into the forest.

Upon hearing of the killing, a shocked Roosevelt, Doctor Cajazeira and a couple of camaradas immediately began pursuing the murderer through the forest. Although armed with a rifle, when considering his poor eyesight, the ever-ready ex-President deferred to the doctor in leading the manhunt. They tracked the fleeing killer some distance after finding the rifle Julio dropped in his haste and then decided to let the jungle impose its justice on the criminal - if starvation didn't take its toll, the wild savages might. The expedition was not in any condition to share its meager rations with a coldblooded killer while at the same time sparing men to guard him against the risk of additional killing. After scraping out a shallow grave at the murder site, the men placed the poor soldier's body to rest and conducted a small ceremony over the grave. Roosevelt recorded *"Then we left him forever, under the great trees beside the lonely river"*.37 Three days later as the canoes continued downriver, Julio appeared on the riverbank pleading to surrender. Roosevelt, Rondon and the rest of the expedition passed him by ignoring his pleas. After consultation with Roosevelt at their next camp, Rondon decided to send two men back on foot to bring Julio in but they failed to find him. Whether the jungle consumed him or he fell to Indian arrows or found a tribe and became adopted was never determined.

*Sickness and Delirium*

As the expedition's slow, harrowing movement down the river progressed, the men continued to weaken under the backbreaking exertion and physical abuse the jungle imposed. All were in an emaciated state and Kermit had recurrence of his fever. His condition was so serious, he was barely able to stand. His temperature had spiked to 104 degrees and the doctor was administering quinine to relieve his suffering. Cherrie and Lyra developed dysentery.

Roosevelt had spent much of his life on wilderness excursions and was always sensitive to contributing his share of labor and hardship in the bush. This trip was no different for him and despite his age and physical disabilities, he was adamant about shouldering his portion of the burden. While working in the water alongside of the men to upturn a canoe, he bruised his leg against a boulder. The wound became inflamed and within a day he came down with fever and was unable to walk. For forty-eight hours he lay in his tent while slipping in and out of delirium with an abnormally elevated temperature. As he lay in rags, burning with fever and perspiration, the doctor administered as best as he could in the fetid jungle environment laboring under the absence of any medical facilities. Kermit, who had partially recovered from his own disability, along with Cherrie and the doctor stood watch over the sick patient, fearful that he was close to death. Roosevelt's stern and unforgiving wilderness ethics and military nature demanded all members of any expedition to bear an equal measure of burden and hardship and not present a danger to his comrades in any way. His stated opinion was:

> *"No man has any business to go on such a trip as ours unless he will refuse to jeopardize the welfare of his associates by any delay caused by a weakness or ailment of his. It is his duty to go forward, if necessary on all fours, until he drops*[38]

If one is unable and becomes a threat to the lives of others he must be sacrificed to save all. Consequently, during his intermittent periods of being conscious, he implored Cherrie and Kermit to leave him behind stating:

*"Boys I realize that some of us are not going to finish this journey and I know that I am only a burden to the rest of you. Cherrie, I want you and Kermit to go on, I want you to get out – I shall stop here."* 39

Naturally, neither Cherrie nor Kermit would leave Roosevelt. He no doubt correctly realized that he would never be abandoned and from a practical standpoint, if he did expire he would impose a greater risk to the expedition as Kermit would never leave his body to the appetite of the jungle. This realization may have had a great effect in spurring him on. Within a couple of days, both Roosevelt and Kermit recovered enough to continue. All of the men were considerably emaciated from the lack of food, exertion and the jungle's toll with Roosevelt losing close to one quarter of his body weight and much of his stamina. His strength and robust constitution never fully recovered and some speculate, may have hastened his early death in just a few short years.

*Deliverance*
    At long last conditions on the river began to slightly improve as the men were close to reaching the limit of their endurance; their emaciated bodies racked with fever and numerous bruising. The mountainous jungle began to level in elevation as the river widened portending a possible end of the treacherous rapids and debilitating portaging. Even their diet began to slightly improve when Cherrie and Kermit were able to secure some monkey and turtle and the men caught a large river catfish. The next few days were a disheartening repetition of encountering rapids and the arduous task of handling the canoes. Some of the comaradas were becoming so weak and unfit they were unable to man the canoes and Kermit began the task of fulltime paddling.
    On April 15th, just a day following the discovery of tree cuttings suspected of being made by rubber-men (harvesters of rubber), the expedition came upon a crude sign on the left bank of the river with the initials, J.A. In

view of the hostile Indians and impassable river cataracts, the rubber collectors had been working the river upstream as far as their courage and endurance would permit and this was the limit of their assent. After seven weeks on the river, the claim marker confirmed the expedition was finally approaching the fringes of civilization and touched-off a euphoria within the group; evidence that their long jungle nightmare was reaching an end.

Throughout the day the expedition passed evidence of civilized habitation: clearings, unoccupied thatched huts and even a couple of barking pet dogs. Due to the total isolation and wildness of this region of the river and fearing a possible Indian raid, the inhabitants fled at their approach, believing that no civilized white man could be venturing down this far from upriver. Finally they returned and the bone-weary and bedraggled men were able to sleep their first night since embarking on the river under a firm roof.

From here on the trip conditions became an amazing contrast compared to what the men had endured on the Rio Duvida. Roosevelt was still sick and spent much of the remainder of the trip sheltered from the blazing sun and occasional downpour, prostrate under a canopy rigged over his canoe. The men spent nights indoors at borrowed thatched houses and ate fresh meat and vegetables. The river trip also became easier as they were now traveling along a well-known waterway with established portage trails around the rapids they continued to encounter. Some provisions were available at the houses of the rubber-men and at one makeshift wilderness store, Cherrie and Kermit being drinking men, even procured a bottle of Italian Vermouth.

On April 26th the expedition arrived at the confluence of the Rio Duvida and the Aripuanan where Rondon had previously sent one of his lieutenants ahead with provisions for the expedition on the off chance that the Duvida may converge with the Aripuanan. Lieutenant Pyrineus had been encamped there for over a month with flags flying as the flotilla of small canoes came into view. Rondon's instincts proved correct. Up until this time, whether they would ultimately meet and from which body of water they would emerge, if they were to emerge at all, was only a guess. Always the military traditionalist, the next day Rondon officiated over the last "orders of the day" ceremony as the men gathered around a monument he hastily erected to commemorate the long journey and the amazing contribution the expedition made and the sacrifices they endured.

*History's Disbelief and Modernity's Shallow Memory*
The Roosevelt-Rondon Expedition should clearly be classified as one of the greatest explorations of the 20th century in both geographical importance and for human courage and endurance. With meager provisions and by using primitive equipment, instruments and techniques, a small group of men charted and placed on the map of South America a wilderness body of water the length of the Rhine River in Europe. During their almost six-thousand miles of travel, the expedition collected approximately 3,000 bird and mammal skins, 1,500 photographs including some birds, eggs and nests not yet known to science. Perhaps the most notable aspect of the adventure is that it was lead by a middle-aged ex-President of the United States along with his son.

Today, many Americans are probably unaware of this extraordinary historical drama. Theodore Roosevelt is perhaps best known in the contemporary mind as a Mount Rushmore icon and remembered as a trust buster displaying a large set of grinning bicuspids; Kermit being not known at all. However, equal to today's historical ignorance, following the expedition's return, even with the facts before them, many prominent explorers and leading scientific institutions were in disbelief of Roosevelt's South American claims. Perhaps from the jealousy of believing South America was the scientific domain of the British Empire, much of the criticism and doubt originated with the British. Sir Clements Markham, former President of the Royal Geographic Society thought the expedition explored a different, known river. Other British geographers and some overseas newspapers criticized Roosevelt as having mistakenly explored the Tapajos instead of a tributary of the Madeira. Particularly vicious accusations against Roosevelt came from Henry Savage Landor, a well known British explorer of the time. Eventually, the discoveries and claims of the expedition were verified and accepted by the scientific community, placing the Roosevelt's, Rondon and the other expedition members in history as some of the great explorers of the twentieth-century.

NOTES:

1  Theodore Roosevelt, Through the Brazilian Wilderness, 1914, pg. 247
2  John Augustine Zahm, Following the Conquistadores, 1916, pg. 5
3  Ibid., pg. 9
4  Theodore Roosevelt, Through the Brazilian Wilderness, 1914, pg. 2
5  William James Mills, Exploring Polar Frontiers: A Historical Encyclopedia, 2003, pg. 222
6  Darthmouth College Library, the papers of Dr. George Shorkley (1871-1945). According to the library listing: *"among Shorkley's papers there is a little booklet titled 'Fialaisms,' in which he collected what he considered Fiala's ridiculous remarks. Shorkley also kept a journal titled 'Medical Records,' that he used as a personal journal as well, recording his view of events and frequently criticizing Fiala and others."*
7  John Augustine Zahm, Through South America's Southland, 1916, pg. 13 and 14
8  Nathan Miller, Theodore Roosevelt, 1993, pg. 535
9  Kermit later recorded "In September, 1908, he wrote me from Washington: *'I have never gotten over the effects of the trolley-car accident six years ago, when as you will remember, they had to cut down to the shin bone. The shock permanently damaged the bone and, if anything happens, there is always a chance of trouble which would be serious.'* Kermit Roosevelt, The Long Trail, 1921, pg. 37
10 Viewing a modern satellite image of the Amazon basin hydroshed resembles the nearly uncountable web of arteries, veins and capillaries in the human body. Numerous branches and tributaries that ultimately link into the mighty Amazon are arrayed over hundreds of thousands of square miles of this tropical wilderness basin. The Rio Roosevelt (aka Rio Teodoro) is still a remote, isolated waterway and tracks a frenetically circuitous route, continuously circling almost back into itself and dropping at numerous falls until merging in the north with the Madeira and ultimately emptying its conjoined waters into the Amazon.
11 Theodore Roosevelt, Through the Brazilian Wilderness, 1914, pg. 9

12 Ibid.. pa. 42 and 43
13 Ibid., pa. 51
14 Hermann Hagedorn, The Boys Life of Theodore Roosevelt, 1918, pg. 355
15 Quoted in Stringing Together a Nation, Todd A. Diacon, 2004, pg. 36
16 Theodore Roosevelt, Through the Brazilian Wilderness, 1914, pg. 172
17 Ibid., pa. 184
18 Ibid., pa.247 & 248
19 John Augustine Zahm, Following the Conquistadores, 1916, pg. 480
20 Theodore Roosevelt, Through the Brazilian Wilderness, 1914, pg. 159
21 Arthur Tylee, his daughter Marian, and nurse Mildred Kratz, were killed on Nov. 3, 1930, together with three other missionaries by these tribesmen. As recently as January, 1951 adventurer Dave Yarwood was found dead with four turkey-feathered arrows in him within Nhambiquara country.
22 Theodore Roosevelt, Through the Brazilian Wilderness, 1914, pg. 231
23 Ibid., pg. 229
24 Ibid., pg. 249
25 Ibid., pg. 252
26 Ibid., pg. 250
27 Ibid., pg. 265
28 The American Museum Journal, volume 15, 1915, pg. 39
29 Theodore Roosevelt, Through the Brazilian Wilderness, pg. 276
30 Ibid., pg. 277
31 Ibid., pa. 256. At one of the campsites, carregadores ants devoured the doctor's undershirt, ate holes in his mosquito-net and consumed the strap on Lyra's gun case. One morning Roosevelt awoke in his tent to witness a procession of red and green leaf-bearing ants carrying away sections of his handkerchief and hat. They also devoured sections of his socks and underclothes; all necessary garments since his kit was already greatly reduced to lighten the load. Pg. 40
32 Ibid., pg. 282
33 George K. Cherrie Diary, Oct. 13 to May 14, pg.54

34 Ibid., pg. 292
35 Ibid., pg. 297, *"One day more would complete a month since we had embarked on the Duvida-as we had started in February, the lunar and calendar months coincided. We had used up over half our provisions. We had come only a trifle over 160 kilometers, thanks to the character and number of rapids."*
36 Ibid., pg. 298
37 Ibid., pg. 317
38 Theodore Roosevelt, Through the Brazilian Wilderness, 1914, pg. 328
39 George K. Cherrie Diary, Oct. 13 to May 14; from a speech written by Cherrie, found in the diary. Document dated May 26, 1927

# Chapter IV - Settling Down in Civilization

*Ye have followed fast, ye have followed far,*
*And where did the wandering lead?*
*From the day that ye praised the spoken word*
*To the day ye must gloss the deed.*
*Rudyard Kipling "The Ballad of the Red Earl"*

During the many months of Kermit's jungle wilderness trek in 1914, his mind and heart were continuously occupied with his fiancée, Belle Willard. Now, he was finally free of any commitments to his father and anxious to marry and continue on with his life.

Belle Wyatt Willard was a young, vivacious socialite from a wealthy and prominent southern family. Belle's father, Joseph E. Willard of Fairfax Virginia was ambassador to Spain and a former lieutenant governor of Virginia. The family built and maintained the famous Willard Hotel on Pennsylvania Avenue in Washington, DC, where presidents and potentates frequently lodged. During the 19th and first half of the 20th Centuries, such notables as Abe Lincoln, U.S. Grant and even Martin Luther King stayed at this Washington institution.*[9] In later years, Kermit served on the hotel's board.

During the Civil War, Belle's grandmother, Antonia Ford, became a hero for the south as a spy for the famed Confederate Cavalry officer, JEB Stuart. Prior to the Battle of Second Manassas in August 1862, she saved Confederate troops by driving twenty-miles through Union lines to personally deliver intelligence information to Stuart on Union troop activities.

In recognition of her service, she was awarded a commission as "honorary aide-de-camp" by Stuart. As the war progressed, she continued to spy for Stuart and the guerrilla commander, John Singleton Mosby, until her

---

9 * The Willard family retained ownership of the upscale hostelry until 1946.

capture and confinement by Union troops. In the tradition of a romance novel, she ended up marrying one of the Union officers charged with guarding her following her capture: Major Joseph Willard.

*Marriage at Last*

Following Spanish civil law, the wedding civil ceremony on June 10, 1914, was held in Madrid at the office of the Chief of Police with a later Episcopal ceremony in the chapel of the British Embassy. Afterwards, a reception was held at the United States Embassy by Ambassador Willard. Among the many guests, the King of Spain was represented by his cousin, Don Alfonso of Orleans, and his wife, Princess Beatrice of Saxe-Coburg. The couple spent their honeymoon in the south of Spain. Even the wedding celebration of a president's son could not deter Roosevelt's detractors from criticizing their recently completed trip. By happenstance, Dr. Hamilton Rice, an American explorer who publically denounced the Rio Divuda discoveries, travelled on the same train as some of the wedding guests, raising concerns about a possible violent encounter between Rice and Roosevelt. During their stay in Spain they avoided each other and eventually, as details of the exploration became accepted within the scientific community, Rice apologized to the Roosevelts.

Following their European honeymoon, the newlyweds settled into a conventional lifestyle in Argentina where Kermit secured employment as assistant manager for the National City Bank in Buenos Aires. In 1914, National City became the first foreign branch of any U.S. national bank (National City eventually became Citi Bank, one of the leading financial institutions in the United States today). This mid-level office position enabled Kermit to gain white collar experience in a managerial role that would later serve him in various executive level positions in the shipping industry. The Kermit Roosevelts lived a middle class lifestyle in Argentina through 1916 until he departed for the war in the Middle East. While in Argentina, Kermit's first child, also named Kermit and nicknamed Kim, was born. Kim was later to become a high-level World War II operative in the OSS, forerunner of the Central Intelligence Agency. He was also credited with the over-through of the Iranian Government in 1953 that placed the Shah in power.

Kermit and Belle's family continued to grow with the birth of Joseph Willard in 1918, Belle Wyatt in 1919 and Dirck in 1925.

*The Interference of War*

The belligerent Kaiser Wilhelm II had been increasing Germany's land and naval forces for years, precipitating an arms race with Britain that even troubled TR when he was President.

Tensions continued to rise among the major powers and the assassination of Archduke Franz Ferdinand in June 1914 set the fuse of the European powder keg that had been forming for a number of years. Due to nationalism, militarism and distrust, various alliances were formed between the European powers. France, the British Empire, Germany, Russia and the lesser countries of Belgium, Serbia and Austria-Hungary along with Japan, engaged the entire European continent in a major conflict that began the following August. In November 1914, the Ottoman Empire, allied with Germany declared a holy war (jihad) against France and Great Britain. As the maelstrom grew, in May 1915 even Italy joined the fray. The "Great War" eventually became

> *"the most widespread and costly conflict man had yet known, one that eventually would put under arms sixty-five million men from thirty countries representing every continent, and one that would involve sea battles around the globe and major land campaigns not only in Europe but in parts of Africa and Asia Minor."*[1]

Although the United States didn't declare war against Germany until late in the war, many prominent Americans foresaw the need to prepare for the possibility of armed conflict. Despite President Woodrow Wilson's stubborn policy of neutrality, Theodore Roosevelt leading other influential citizens argued strenuously in the press for military preparedness. When the United States finally entered the war, Roosevelt even offered to raise and command a division. In 1915, Major General Leonard

Wood who was Roosevelt's commanding officer during his Rough Rider days and continued as his personal friend, created a summer camp for reserve officer military training in Plattsburg, New York, for professional and business men. Many prominent athletes, businessmen and members of society attended the training and would later become junior army officers when the United States entered the war. Theodore Roosevelt Jr., Archie and Quentin attended the Plattsburg training.

Kermit, because of his established business career in South America, missed out for the most part on the Plattsburgh summer camp. In 1917, just as he was to be transferred to a newly anticipated Russian branch of the National City Bank in Petrograd (now Saint Petersburg), the United States declared war on Germany. True to the Roosevelt ethic of patriotism and military obligation, Kermit immediately decided to enter the war. Although the United States officially declared war on Germany in April, General Pershing did not engage troops until the spring offensive of 1918, and then they were initially intermingled with French troops.

In July, 1917, Kermit, not waiting for U. S. forces to enter the fray, pursued a commission from the King of England. He was granted an honorary commission in the British Army[2] and offered a position on the staff of General Maud operating against the Turks in Mesopotamia.

Major Theodore Roosevelt Jr. and Second Lieutenant Archibald Roosevelt left Plattsburgh and sailed for Europe to join Pershing's command as young Quentin began training at Long Island, for service in the newly formed air corps. As family members donned uniforms, TR approached Wilson with a plan to organize and command a volunteer fighting force as he did in Cuba two decades earlier. However, Wilson, ever the politician and angered by Roosevelt's years of venomous public badgering of his administration for his delaying U. S. entry into the war, denied Roosevelt's request. Roosevelt and Wilson were at odds both philosophically and politically since the 1912 election, and Wilson certainly did not want to provide Roosevelt with any added fame that could possibly impact in Roosevelt's favor for a potential 1920 presidential election campaign.

William E. Lemanski

Notes

1   Office of the Chief of Military History, United States
    Army; World War I, The First Three Years, Chapter 17
2   From a note dated July 31, 1917 from Royal Pavilion
    Aldershot Camp signed by Lord Stamfordham, King
    George V's Private Secretary, British Military Archives

# CHAPTER V- ACTION IN THE GREAT WAR

*Once more we hear the word*
*That sickened earth of old: --*
*"No law except the Sword*
*Unsheathed and uncontrolled."*
*Once more it knits mankind,*
*Once more the nations go*
*To meet and break and bind*
*A crazed and driven foe.*
*"For All We Have And Are" Rudyard Kipling*

*Mesopotamia*

Small, wispy vortices of extremely fine, powdery sand danced across the hot, sun-baked flatland gaining speed and the momentum to continually grow, enabling each to transform on the erratic wind into large wavering phantom-like funnels. At other times, a more stable and consistent wind would scoop enormous volumes of the abrasive mix into a wall of stinging particles that would enter every crack, crevice, seam and orifice of both man and machine. From mid-June to mid-September, a steady wind, the "shamal", blowing from the north and northwest, would usher in sand storms rising to several thousand feet.

Combining with this abrasive mix, the searing temperatures of July and August would reach 120 degrees Fahrenheit, baking the shifting desert sand similar to the burning coals of a kiln. During the wet season, torrential rains would turn the dry water-courses into a raging maelstrom, flatland and roads into a sea of glutinous mud. Adding to the misery of these extremes were the occasional swarms of desert flies.

In 1914, within the hostile and ancient cradle of civilization of Mesopotamia, the British Army deployed. The Middle-East regions of Arabia and Mesopotamia*[10] were strategically critical to both the British and French

---

10 *Present day Iraq, named so by the British, based upon the June 1919 mandate under the League of Nations

even before the outbreak of World War I. This was primarily for the same reason the United States and the West have a major interest in Iraq and the surrounding Arab countries today: oil.*[11] However, at the beginning of the 20th century, this land was under the control of the Ottoman Empire dating back to 1534 when Mesopotamia was taken from Persia. As the war progressed, British military forces were beginning campaigns throughout the Middle-east while simultaneously scheming in Cairo and Whitehall against the French for post-war domination of this entire region. Colonel T.E. Lawrence was organizing the Arab Revolt as General Allenby planned the Palestine Campaign while further north in Turkey, thousands of allies were dying on the beaches at Gallipoli.

The Standard Oil Company of America already had a foothold in Persia to the north. Anglo-Indian Army Forces landed in Mesopotamia in November 1914, capturing the southern port city of Basra with the goal of thwarting the Ottoman Turk allies of Germany. The plan was to open access to the oil fields and pipeline near Basra which would provide a much needed commodity to the Imperial British Navy as the fleets of the world's major powers had recently converted from coal to oil.

The capturing of the seaport of Basra and securing the oil-rich region for large scale troop disembarkation was only the first step in a three-year struggle in the drive north to Baghdad and domination of Mesopotamia. Numerous skirmishes and major battles ensued during the next two years, testing both the British forces on the ground and the politicians in London.

In 1915, the British failure at the Battle of Ctesiphon and the retreat along with the subsequent siege and surrender at Kut-al-Amara*[12], coupled with the losses at Gallipoli*[13] simply added to the dire military position of the Empire. However, this situation soon changed in early

---

11 *Similar to the United States in the twenty-first century, the British also applied the same level of diplomatic condescension and subterfuge by the 1917 Proclamation of Baghdad of Major General Sir Stanley Maude: "but our armies do not come into your cities and lands as conquerors or enemies, but as liberators." President George Bush's claim was that Democracy was the goal.

12 *Of the 11,800 men who left Kut-al-Amara with their captors on 6 May 1916, 4,250 died either on their way to captivity or in the camps that awaited them at the journey's end.

1917 with the addition of troop reinforcements and a command change to General F S Maude. This began a major troop incursion north.

Captain Kermit Roosevelt, volunteer with the British Expeditionary Forces, arrived in Basra in 1917, beginning his Middle-East odyssey from England by train through France and then to the Italian seaport of Taranto. Following his training in the Reserve Officer Training Camp in Plattsburg, New York, during the early summer of 1917, Kermit was offered a commission and service on General Maude's staff in Mesopotamia. At Taranto, he boarded a troop transport and began a long and tedious sea voyage through the Suez Canal, south down the Red Sea, through the Indian Ocean and the Persian Gulf.

There was no overnight flight for a VIP Roosevelt aboard a plane or first-class accommodations aboard a steam ship as a former President's son. Despite the discomfort of travel as an ordinary junior grade British officer, Kermit was conditioned to both rugged travel and the anticipation and even welcome expectation of danger. The combined qualities of duty and patriotism expressed through military combat service had been a family tradition since Kermit's maternal uncles, James and Irvine Bulloch, served in the Civil War on the Confederate side: James served as a confederate agent and Irvine on the CSS Alabama which sank in the Atlantic off the coast of France following a naval battle.

Kermit's grandfather, Theodore Senior, avoided military service in that conflict which may have been the underlying basis for Rough Rider and San Juan Hill hero, Colonel Theodore Roosevelt, to obsess over the Cuban revolution in 1898. He ultimately was awarded the Congressional Medal of Honor for his conduct in the resulting Spanish-American War.

Kermit's brothers also distinguished themselves under arms. Youngest of the clan, twenty-one year old Quentin would be killed in action as an aviator over France on July 14, 1918. Brother Archie, serving with the 26th US Infantry, was severely wounded in March 1918 and was

---

13 *The British had 205,000 casualties, the French 47,000 and more than 33,600 ANZAC losses.

awarded the Croix de Guerre. Ted Jr. was gassed at
Cantigny and, like his father, was later awarded the
Congressional Medal of Honor posthumously for his service
as a WWII general.

As a member of this vocally patriotic family with a
legacy of hyper-martial tendencies, Kermit's natural
impulse was to enlist in the center of the storm. Great
Britain's military force was his choice as his own country
was hurriedly mobilizing after equivocating and marking
time in a neutral posture for the previous three years.

❖

The searing Middle-East August heat burned the decks
of the twin-stack Union Castle troopship Saxon and
shimmered like a mirage as she cut through the swell of
the Red Sea. Below decks, the un-ventilated vessel was a
veritable oven.

Discomfort and danger lurked for Kermit and his
British colleagues on this voyage even before hearing the
first enemy fire on land. To secure the ship from predatory
German submarines that were prowling the Adriatic and
Mediterranean, taking a toll on allied shipping, two
Japanese destroyers were assigned to convoy the vessel.
The combination of evasive zig-zag nighttime cruising in
blackout darkness added to the difficulty of coordinating
multiple vessels in two languages within that difficult
pattern and ended in a collision. Fortunately, the breach
in the Saxon's hull was above the waterline and after a
two-day repair, continued on its way to Basra.

It was within the searing heat of the ship's engine room
when Kermit decided to exercise his dormant muscles and
shovel coal with his new friend, the British aristocrat
Denys Finch Hatton. Finch Hatton had been serving as a
lieutenant after initially fighting the war against the
German Schutztruppe*[14] as a bush scout in his chosen
home of Africa. While exercising his bush craft skills and
keen intellect, he quickly gained notice of the British
commanders and was assigned as aide-de-camp to the
former Inspector General to the Kings African Rifles,
Lieutenant General Reginald Hoskins. He later was a

---

14 *Schutztruppe was the colonial armed force of the German Government in
Africa from the late 19th Century to the end of World War I in 1918 when Germany
lost her colonial possessions.

prominent character in British East Africa (now Kenya) during the Happy Valley days of the 1920s and was the lifelong love of writer Karen Blixen, author of the bestselling autobiography, and later motion picture, Out of Africa. Finch Hatton also became a world famous big-game hunter and, due to the kinship of similar personality traits, became a life-long intimate and friend of Kermit's*[15]. Finch Hatton was also a loner and dreamy intellectual who valued a solitary, adventurous lifestyle. For the remainder of his life, he and Kermit would share frequent correspondence and Kermit would visit with him when in England. He was not the only prominent Brit that Kermit would befriend in the Middle-East.

As the British began to aggressively build railways, roads and communication lines, attempting to travel north from Basra during war became exceedingly difficult for the traveler, and typical for any large military movement, a major project. Hence, moving upcountry to Baghdad and the northern action required Kermit to rely on a hodge-podge of paddleboats, rail and flat cars for his transportation ultimately arriving in Samarra, approximately one-hundred miles north of Baghdad.

In Samarra, he was assigned to the Royal Engineers where he engaged in motorized reconnaissance work. In true Desert Fox fashion, he skirmished with Turkish forces in the region between Samarra and Daur in a four-ton Armored Rolls Royce car. However, despite being in His Majesty's Army and assigned to a motor unit in a war zone, in typical Victorian fashion he found the time and wherewithal to privately secure two horses and retain both a Dervish syce (horse handler) and a Kurdish servant boy.

While moving through Daur and advancing on Tekrit, Kermit's unit engaged the enemy and in one day suffered casualties of about two thousand. Besides attack by ground troops, artillery and assault by Turkish aircraft, the Anglo-Indian army fell victim to heat stroke and sand fly fever. Even the British Commander, General Maude, was not immune to the dangers of this desert campaign and succumbed to cholera and died in November 1917.

---

15 *Similar to Kermit, Finch Hatton suffered an untimely death in middle-age when the Gypsy Moth plane he was piloting crashed in the African bushveld in the 1930's.

Following these engagements, Kermit was transferred to the Motor Machine-Gun Corps, Fourteenth Battery[1] of light-armored motorcars (LAMB) and was employed in raiding Turkish forces, quelling Arab uprisings and operating with mounted cavalry during attacks. The Rolls Royce armored car[2] provided mobility with a marginal degree of protection behind light armored bodywork while carrying a single turret for a Vickers machine gun, but the vehicles were stiflingly hot death boxes. Kermit's war chariot, the armored motorcar was similar to the airplane as a new innovation in military technology. The motorcar was constructed on a standard RR Silver Ghost chassis with a steel superstructure and revolving turret. The four-ton vehicles had twin rear wheels compensating for the additional weight and provided a high degree of mobility for both reconnaissance and skirmishing; the disadvantages being mechanical repairs, fuel supply requirements, traction on mud and the hot, sandy desert environment. When under fire, Kermit said:

> "the crew would pull the steel doors shut. The slits through which the driver and the man next to him looked (through) could be made still smaller when the firing was heavy, and the peep-holes at either side and in the rear had slides which could be closed. The largest aperture was that around the tube of the gun."[3]

He said "splinters of lead came in continuously, and sometimes chance directed a bullet to an opening. One of our drivers was shot straight through the head near Ramadie." He complained of temperatures within the steel coffins, "During the great heat of the summer the inside of the turret was a veritable fiery furnace, with the pedals so hot that they scorched the feet." Through the rainy season of 1917 his unit fought their way northwest battling Turks, raging rivers and muddy bogs all the way to the Kurdish hills in the northeast.

In March, Kermit participated in a major attack on the Euphrates front.[4] While pushing on through the towns of Khan Baghdadi, Haditha and Ana, the British forces captured three-thousand Turkish prisoners along with German officers, liberated captured British officers and even mounted an expedition to capture a gold convoy. Describing the operation, a New York Times article of the period reported *"In addition 10 guns, 2,000 rifles, many machine guns, 600 animals, and a quantity of other booty have been taken."*

Shortly after his return to Baghdad and following his adventures on the Euphrates front, Kermit volunteered to participate in the attack on the Persian front at Kifri, in what is now Iraqi Kurdistan. Throughout the campaign he traversed many miles of barren desert where he engaged in numerous skirmishes, witnessed a sword-wielding Indian cavalry charge that rendered six-hundred Turkish prisoners and he even personally liberated a Turkish General's "field harem."

Besides conducting military operations against the enemy, Kermit spent much time and energy maintaining the finicky machinery of the primitive armored vehicles, searching for petrol dumps to fuel their endless appetite and fording or bridging swollen rivers and creeks. Aside from the enemy and the practical problems of day to day mechanized desert movement, Kermit and his comrades had to contend with some of the world's most severe and extreme weather conditions. On one occasion he noted:

> *"The wind blew so hard that I thought the car would be toppled over. What made us more gloomy than anything else was the thought of all the dry river courses that would be roaring floods by morning, and probably hold up the ration supply indefinitely."*5

On another occasion he recorded:

> *"...the river had risen so rapidly that many of the tents and a few ambulances were washed away. By morning it had settled down into a steady, businesslike downpour.*6 *We found that we were inextricably caught in among some low hills. There was not the slightest chance of moving the fighting cars; they were bogged down to the axle. There was no alternative other than to wait until the rain stopped and the mud dried. Fortunately our emergency rations were still untouched."*

Supply lines were always an intermittent, unreliable affair forcing the troops to sometimes forage for food, sometimes barter or buy from any local villages as they passed through.

❖

In the spring of 1918 Kermit finally received his desired transfer from the British to the American Army in France. After reaching Kirkuk with his armored car detachment, he decided to return to Baghdad and prepare for the long journey to Europe and a new conflict, thus ending his Mid-East adventure.

During his months in the Middle East besides befriending and living with the common British Tommy, he had the opportunity to meet and associate with many notable British officers. In Egypt, he met the famous Colonel T.E. Lawrence (Lawrence of Arabia). He described Lawrence as:

> *"Scarcely more than thirty years of age, with a clean-shaven, boyish face, short and slender in build, if one met him casually among a lot of other officers it would not have been easy to single him out as the great power among Arabs that he on every occasion proved himself to be."*[7]

Kermit spent his first night in Baghdad in General Maude's house. During his return from Mesopotamia while waiting to sail from Egypt, he stayed at the residence of Sir Reginald Wingate. Kermit's friendly, easygoing personality (similar to his father's and perhaps developed from years of associating with people ranging from indigenous natives in Africa, Indians in South America to heads of state at the White House) enabled him to naturally be at ease in all circles. He was equally at ease sleeping in the desert sand with the common soldier or dining with Arab potentates. His ability to gain fluency in languages enabled him to quickly learn Arabic and integrate into the culture of common Arab merchants or high-ranking officials and desert sheiks. His communication skills as an interpreter were used by the British command on a number of occasions.

Despite the harsh and dangerous conditions of the desert campaign, he managed to continually pursue his intellectual interests. During the months while serving in Mesopotamia, he managed to engulf himself in Xenophons's *Anabasis*, Plutarch's *Lives*, Voltaire's *Charles XII*, two volumes of Layard's *Early Adventures*, Disraeli's *Tancred*, Camoens' *Lusiad and David Harum*, and a copy of the *Lusiads* – all a form of traveling "pigskin library" similar to his father's library when on safari in Africa seven years before.

In his own semi-autobiography of his Mideast experiences, "War in the Garden of Eden," Kermit alternates between his war experiences, conditions in the British Army and a running monolog on the biblical history of the region including glimpses into Arab and Turkish customs and culture.

For his efforts as a volunteer officer in the British Army in Mesopotamia, during the months of 1917 and early 1918, Kermit was awarded the Military Cross*[16]. On June 1, 1918, TR wrote to Kermit's brother Ted, *"He has received the British War Cross for gallantry in action in command of a light armored battery; he is to report to Pershing...it is a load off my mind to have him transferred."*

Although considered a secondary effort in relation to the war in Europe by the British High Command, the campaign in Mesopotamia was a costly exercise for the British people. *"Between the armistice and 1922, the cost of Iraq to the taxpayer was in the region of £100 million."*[8]

*The War in Europe*

In the spring of 1918, TR wrote to General March, the Chief of Staff, requesting Kermit to be transferred to the U.S. forces in France. Upon arriving in France following his service in the British Army, Captain Kermit Roosevelt was ordered to attend the Artillery School at Saumur. His wife Belle joined him and his surviving siblings who were also stationed in Europe. Each serving the war effort in various capacities; Major Theodore Roosevelt Jr. was commanding a battalion in the 26th Infantry Regiment, with

---

16 *The British Military Cross was instituted on 28 December 1914 as a means of formally recognizing the courage of junior officers during wartime (officially for "gallantry in the field" for the rank of Captain and below).

Ted's wife Eleanor supporting the troops working as a full-time volunteer with the Y.M.C.A. Brother Archie was commanding a company under Ted.

Eleanor's state-side aunt, Mrs. Hoffman, owned a large house in Paris which enabled Eleanor to live in very comfortable quarters and the home became a base for the occasional visiting family member. Besides her immediate in-laws, her brother-in-law, Dr. Richard Derby, his brother Lloyd, Ted's cousin's George, Philip and Nicholas Roosevelt all passed through from time to time. Although enjoying the warmth and camaraderie of the occasional family gatherings at the Paris house, thoughts of the war constantly weighed on the minds of the Roosevelt clan. Young Quentin was gone. Archie was recovering from a severely damaged kneecap and fractured arm*[17], Ted was suffering from a gun shot through his leg, a wound which bothered him for the rest of his life and Kermit was once again, being thrown into the breach of war.

At the end of July, Kermit and his wife stopped off at the Paris house prior to his reporting to the artillery school. Their spirits were running very low on this occasion with the anticipation of this perhaps being their last family gathering. The war appeared to be an endless conflict, slowly consuming the family.

To bolster morale, Kermit, Ted, and their wives decided to dine at a local restaurant - the Roosevelt ethos would never display fear, cynicism or dread. Having consumed too much wine himself, Kermit concluded Belle needed some "good red wine" to improve her complexion and against her will, began to force feed her from the bottle. As Belle and Eleanor rose to leave, embarrassed and complaining about being "conspicuous", Ted whispered to Archie, *"Let's show them what being conspicuous is!"*9 During their rushed walk home, Belle and Eleanor were followed by the raucous band of Kermit in uniform, Archie

---

17 *This was the first wound Archibald Roosevelt was to suffer in defense of his country which classified as a 100 percent disability. After he imposed upon his cousin, President Franklin Roosevelt for entry into the Second World War, he was severely wounded again, gaining him the unique distinction of being the only American to ever be classified with two 100 percent disabilities in two different wars.

wearing his plaster cast, Ted on crutches singing and shouting *"En avant, mes braves!"* Before long, a large crowd gathered to watch the three American officers chasing the two dreadfully embarrassed women. The cheering group formed up a noisy parade of strangers including an entourage of hobbling, wounded French soldiers and proceeded to march through the streets of Paris.

The outward good cheer would be short lived. The Roosevelt family once again returned to war as TR Jr's wounds healed he was temporarily assigned as an instructor and attended the General Staff College then returned to the 26th Infantry.

Following his training, Kermit was assigned to the Seventh Field Artillery[10] in the 1st Expeditionary Division later re-designated as the 1st Infantry Division.*[18]

At the timing of his emergence into the European war, the conflict was near to its end. He was engaged in the Meuse-Argonne campaign*[19] beginning in October and participated in the attack on the city of Sedan shortly before the armistice was signed on November 11, 1918. The remainder of his service was in a dull and uneventful series of occupation and troop movements through Europe. In January, 1919 Kermit was assigned to duty with the American Commission to Negotiate Peace and War Damages in regard to the Treaty of Versailles. Despite his short combat service in Europe, the postings enabled him to be reunited with family members during the conflict who also were contributing to the war effort.

---

18 * The 1st Infantry, the Big Red 1 is the oldest division in the United States Army and has seen continuous service since its organization in 1917

19 *The Meuse-Argonne was the greatest battle yet fought by the U.S. Army. Almost 1,250,000 American troops had participated during the course of the offensive. Casualties were high—120,000 total.

William E. Lemanski

*To Camoes in Mesopotamia*[20]
*Two small black tomes that first saw light*
*In Lisbon scores of years ago,*
*Have been my comfort and delight*
*Amid the desert and snow.*

*When first I turned the yellowed leaves*
*'Twas' mong the palm trees of Brazil*
*Now in the caliphs land I find*
*Their magic unabated still.*

*And when the sweltering troopship steamed*
*Through Ormuz Strait neath molten sky*
*The sea worn galleons of Camoens*
*Seemed there at anchor riding high.*

*Upon the house tops of Baghdad*
*I've read of Inez' luckless fate,*
*And midst the scorching desert dust*
*Heard stout daGama's sailors prate.*

*In long sea watches, of the bout*
*That was held in London town,*
*Twixt twelve of England's sturdy knights*
*And Portuguese of far renown.*

*Now in pursuit of cautious Turk*
*With kit reduced to the absurd,*
*One volume still I've brought*
*And read, Among the mountains of the Kurd.*

*And so I've scrawled these vagrant lines*
*To offer thanks where they are due,*
*For many a weary moment cheered*
*By these companions tried and true.*

The armistice treaty, marking the end of hostilities was in effect at 11am, November 11, 1918. The war had taken

20 *Authored by Kermit Roosevelt describing his service in Mesopotamia. Published in New York shortly upon his return to the United States.

102

the lives of 10 million people and changed international boundaries and politics in Europe and the Middle East forever. Unforeseen at the time, the war's outcome and the conduct of the victorious nations in the years following the armistice laid the groundwork for yet again another world conflict within two decades. As the defeated and cowed loser, Germany sank into a spiral of enormous inflation and economic distress, the allied nations began a binge of celebration and growth. Following a post war recession, the 1920s were a decade of reckless euphoria and flourishing economic growth.

Notes:

1   Machine Gun Corp Old Comrades Association, Alan
    Simcock report: "14 LAMB was equipped with eight RR
    armored cars divided into four sections of two cars each
    with motorcycle mounted scouts. The LAMBs in
    Mesopotamia were Army troops and were used for
    patrolling roads, reconnaissance, often with cavalry and
    in support of flanking attacks. Their main base was in
    Baghdad."

2   Ibid. "The Rolls-Royce armored cars had originally been
    designed by the Royal Naval Armored Car Division and
    were based on the Rolls-Royce Alpine Tourer version
    with a Silver Ghost chasis and six-cylinder, 7428cc
    engine developing about 80hp. A four-speed gearbox
    was fitted and the top speed was about 45mph. The
    armor was 4mm thick."

3   War in the Garden of Eden, 1919, Kermit Roosevelt pg.
    120

4   As observed by Lieutenant Colonel Edward Davis, U.S.
    Cavalry, in a report to the American War Department,
    1918: "During this round-up of the 50th Division, a
    very creditable piece of work was done by an American,
    who held at that time a commission in the British
    army, to wit: Captain Kermit Roosevelt, of the Light
    Armoured Motor Car Brigade. These armoured motor
    cars made a successful effort to recapture two British
    officers of considerable rank who had been taken
    prisoners by the Turks when they had been forced to
    descend during an aeroplane flight over the Turkish
    lines, and who were being sent under escort to Aleppo
    at the time of the battle of Khan-Bagdadie. Learning the
    whereabouts of these officers after the battle, the
    British division commander sent the armoured car
    brigade up the Euphrates, which they followed to a
    point 75 miles about Ana, or just about half way from
    Baghdad to Aleppo. During this push up the
    Euphrates, a part of the British forces chanced to
    encounter a very important German agent. They
    captured him, but left most of his baggage, together
    with a lot of papers, scattered about the bivouac where
    they had captured him. Later, Captain Roosevelt came
    along in his car, saw these papers, recognized the

importance of them, gathered them up, and later turned them over to the appropriate staff officer. Upon careful examination, the papers proved to be of the very greatest importance and Captain Roosevelt was, for this act and for other instances of admirable conduct, suitably rewarded. I might add appropriately, that Captain Roosevelt by his work with the armoured cars, as well as by his generally admirable conduct, made a very favourable impression on the officers of the British Mesopotamian Expeditionary Force, all of whom spoke of him in terms of the greatest praise."

5  War in the Garden of Eden, 1919, Kermit Roosevelt pg. 174

6  Ibid. pg. 179

7  Ibid. pg. 203

8  Too Close to the Sun, Sara Wheeler, pg. 123

9  Day Before Yesterday, The Reminiscences of Mrs. Theodore Roosevelt, Jr., Eleanor Roosevelt pg. 106

10 In a letter dated July 23, 1921 to Colonel Fred Feigl, editor of the Tammany Times, Kermit's brother Ted as Assistant Secretary of the Navy wrote: "Nothing pleases me more than to be able to testify to the splendid efficiency of the 7th Field Artillery. Our artillery supported us at all junctures with dash, devotion and intelligence. I have seen battalions wheel into action when needed in a rapture attack not more than two or three hundred yards behind the attacking lines. My own brother Kermit served as a battery commander in the 7th Field Artillery." Letter received by the author from the Andrew E. Woods, Research Historian, Colonel Robert R. McCormick Research Center, Cantigny First Division Foundation

# CHAPTER VI - CONDUCTING POSTWAR BUSINESS

*Cities and Thrones and Powers*
*Stand in Time's eye,*
*Almost as long as flowers,*
*Which daily die:*
*But, as new buds put forth*
*To glad new men,*
*Out of the spent and unconsidered Earth*
*The Cities rise again.*

"*Cities and Thrones and Powers*"
*Rudyard Kipling*

In 1919 the US economy began a downward spiral into recession as many thousands of returning Doughboys shed their uniforms for work clothes and business suits and began to flood the job market. Simultaneously, the end of wartime production depressed job availability in this country as Europe began experiencing hyperinflation. Race riots broke out across many American cities as the great migration of Southern blacks began to move to the Northern cities looking for work and a better quality of life. Adding to the worldwide economic problems, as the war was ending, an influenza epidemic began spreading across the globe and before ending in 1919 would eventually claim more than fifty-million lives exceeding even the death toll of the Great War. Kermit returned to this tumultuous environment to once again begin his life anew.

In 1919 he entered the business world pursuing two diverse projects: the shipping industry, which was to become a lifelong career in various management and ownership positions, and a sideline interest in a family partnership in the restaurant business in New York. Long before Starbucks ever became a national trademark, Kermit, with brothers Theodore and Archibald, their brother-in-law Dr. Richard Derby along with their cousin Philip Roosevelt began a company to operate a chain of coffee houses in New York.[1] Perhaps the first of its type in the country. The initial establishment, named the "Brazilian Coffee House" was located on West 44th Street in the theater district. The family members all retained an equal share in the ownership. Kermit originated the idea based upon coffee shops that he frequented in Brazil years before. Keeping true to Kermit's literary taste, *"Upon entering the long narrow shop, a patron saw portraits' of Voltaire and Shakespeare on opposite sides of the room."*[2] In 1921 the coffee house name was changed to the "Double R" (for Roosevelt and Robinson) and relocated to a new location on 45th Street. Before long, another store was opened on Lexington Avenue.

However, by 1927 the business was experiencing heavy losses and the family decided to sell the operation. Kermit began negotiations with the Maxwell House Coffee Company and considered selling a fifty-one percent share for a firm price of $15,000. Maxwell House expressed interest primarily in the advertising opportunity for their product realizing the revenue would amount to little but no deal was struck. The family continued managing the business until it was sold completely in 1928.

❖

By the beginning of the 20th Century, American shipping was transporting only a small fraction of the country's foreign trade but the Great War proved the need for a substantial merchant fleet. Few today realize that at the outbreak of World War I and the years following that conflict, the United States Government literally confiscated the American maritime industry. This move can be compared to the 21st century banking and auto industry takeover.

As the war progressed, German submarine warfare began taking a tremendous toll on allied shipping. In 1917 there was a great need for cargo and troop ships to support the transport of American troops to France, and the U.S. fleet was inadequate. Recognizing this deficiency, the United States Shipping Board and the Emergency Fleet Corporation was signed into law by Congress in September, 1916 enabling the government to manage the U.S. shipping industry. Between 1917 and 1922 the government built more than 2000 ships. According to the wartime shipping board chairman, Edward N. Hurley:

*"Considering the program as a whole, the
accomplishments in the number of ships constructed,
the tonnage secured and the time within which the
ships were completed and delivered, constitute the
most remarkable achievement in ship building that
the world has ever seen".*4

Following WWI, the American maritime industry was
recovering from years of neglect, and the government was
inappropriately in possession of thousands of ships no
longer required for combat duty. The Merchant Marine Act
of 1920₃ codified the importance of maintaining a strong
maritime capability for both commerce and national
defense. At the end of the war the government began
selling the ships to U.S. firms and engaging in a
partnership with private operators to manage the
remaining government-owned vessels.

A number of civilians, including William Averell
Harriman, son of railroad magnate, E.H. Harriman foresaw
the importance of a growing U.S. shipping industry and
focused his attention not on rail but on commercial
shipping noting in 1916: *"The most important matter
connected with the growth and well-being of the U. S. was
shipping."*5 The Harrimans would play a major role in the
shipping industry in the post WW1 era along with a few
other wealthy entrepreneurs, including William Vincent
Astor.

With shrewd foresight in seeing a potential business
opportunity, Kermit also pursued involvement in this new
enterprise along with his friend Astor. Coincidently,
Kermit's forebears on his mother's side also were engaged
in the shipping industry. His mother Edith's grandfather,
Isaac, and her great aunt's husband, Robert Kermit owned
the fleet of Kermit & Carow clipper ships in 19ᵗʰ Century
New York.

During the turbulent business years following the Great
War (through Prohibition, the Roaring 20s and into the
Great Depression), Kermit participated in a myriad of
maritime business ventures, and he became one of the
leading shipping-men in the country managing some of the
largest maritime concerns in the nation. His involvement
included both cargo and passenger ocean liners.

❖

In September 1919 Kermit was appointed secretary of the American Ship and Commerce Corporation, a holding company of the Cramps Shipbuilding Company and the Kerr Navigation Company. However, this initial foray into the world of international shipping was short lived.

In 1920, Kermit formed the Roosevelt Lines for the U.S. Shipping Board to compete in the competitive jute trade from India to the Atlantic coast. He held 520 shares of

*Kermit as a successful businessman in 1926.*

stock, being the largest shareholder of the initial 1000 shares issued. In 1921 the Roosevelt Steamship Company was approved by the United States Shipping Board to be a Shipping Board operator of vessels. Also in that year, Kermit, W. Averill Harriman and Emmett McCormack (of Moore & McCormack ship operators) were selected by the shipping board to operate vessels under a new firm called the United States Line. In later years, the company would operate many famous steam ships worldwide, including the *Manhattan*, *President Harding*, *President Roosevelt*, seven merchant ships, and the *Leviathan*. In 1924 Kermit held the title of President of the Roosevelt Steamship Company and Vice President of the Kerr Steamship Company. Kerr operated vessels for the Shipping Board from New York to India. Kermit also established a joint service with Kawasaki of Japan in 1924 called the "Kawasaki-Roosevelt Line" to provide around the world service. Initially, his Japanese partners named the organization the KKK-Roosevelt Line (Kawasaki-Kisen-Kaisha). Kermit quickly informed the Japanese of a needed change to the company title when he became deluged with complaints as the Ku Klux Klan was extremely agitating at this time.

In 1926 he partnered with John M. Franklin whose father was head of the International Mercantile Marine (IMM) and Basil Harris, two well known shipping executives. Kermit's personal friend and wealthy financier, William Vincent Astor provided the capital to secure a substantial interest in the company.

In 1927 when Kermit's company was being denied fair access to India's jute cargo, his competitive nature and aggressive business style triggered a rate war with the US Steel Company's shipping subsidiary, Isthmian Line. Kermit, as president and his vice president, Philip Albright Small Franklin, pursued sixteen ship loads from Indian jute shippers claiming his organization was losing out to a disproportionate share of the business. When undermined by the entrenched companies, Kermit offered a greatly reduced rate of $4 per ton for jute shipment from Calcutta to New York while the going rate had been $7.90 per ton[6] His competitors reduced their rate to $4.50 per ton and the rate war began. In 1928 a settlement was finally reached with both shipping organizations sharing an agreed upon volume of cargo. Kermit distrusted Isthmian's willingness to adhere to the agreement, and in 1929 a New York-India conference was formed to discuss concerns. The Great Depression, however, emerged and severely affected world shipping and undermined any hope for the conference.

In 1928 Kermit and his business partner and friend, Vincent Astor, placed an initial bid on the West Africa Line for approximately $600,000 and a bid for purchase of American Merchant Lines. Other business acquisitions in 1931 were the Baltimore Mail Steamship Company to operate a Hamburg-Baltimore service where Kermit served as Vice President and control of IMM[7] where he was titled as Director. Simultaneous to this flurry of shipping activity in his role as the head of the Roosevelt Steamship Company, he invested in the Deep Bay Lumber Company in Panama to ship lumber from Central America to Baltimore to offset the light loads of his vessels returning from Australia.

In 1933 he was elevated to President of Baltimore Mail. At that time, the Roosevelt Lines managed a fleet of 18 ships owned by the government operating to Australia, India, the Philippines and the Far East. Additionally, they managed under IMM a fleet of 46 steamers. By that year he was titled as Director of eight steam ship companies. In 1938 he was elected Director at the Atlantic Transport Company. Another business involvement of Kermit's in this period was with the American Pioneer Line which provided service from New York to Havre and Hamburg.

❖

Despite his extraordinary business schedule and world travel on distant expeditions in the 1920s and 30s, Kermit found time to serve on numerous boards and committees and maintain a hectic social and club schedule.

In 1921 he sat on the Managing Operators Committee of the United States Shipping Board with W. Averill Harriman and other major players in the US shipping industry.[8] Not surprisingly considering his penchant for alcohol, in 1924 he sat on the advisory committee of the Association Against the Prohibition Amendment, an organization dedicated to repeal the Volstead Law which prohibited the sale and consumption of alcoholic beverages. Kermit was Vice President of the New York State Division and was active primarily in gaining new membership. From 1933 to 1938 he was on the boards of the Aberchrombie & Fitch Company, the Northern Dock Company, and the American Trust Company. Between 1933 and 1935 he sat on the board of the Atlas Tack Corporation of Fairhaven Massachusetts, and from 1935 to 1937 he was President of the National Audubon Society.[9]

His club activities define a mind boggling variety of organizations: the Harvard, Knickerbocker and Piping Rock clubs, the Missouri Pacific St. Louis Chess Club, the Seawanhaka Corinthian Yacht Club, the Porcellian Club of Harvard University and Hartford Hunt Club, the Tennis and Racquet Club, the American Society of Mammalogists and Wilderness Club. He also served on the board of the Boone & Crockett Club, an organization which his father started many years earlier. In the mid 1920s he was also a Director at the élite Explorer's Club in New York. Other affiliations were the New York Zoological Society, the National Geographic Society, the Saint Nicholas Society, and the Reptile Society of America.

Perhaps his most enigmatic involvement that would portend his son Kermit Jr.'s involvement in espionage a generation later was his membership in a mysterious group known as "The Room." The Room was an exclusive, secret organization that centered around monthly luncheons and dinner meetings in a rented townhouse in New York City. To remain completely anonymous, the apartment even contained an unlisted telephone number and mail drop.[10] Both Kermit and Vincent Astor were charter members and general organizers since the club's inception in 1927 with Astor being the prime mover. William Vincent Astor was a remarkably wealthy and socially active member of upper crust New York society. A descendent of the legendary 18th Century fur trader, John Jacob Astor, William (generally referred to as Vincent) inherited the family fortune at the tender age of 21 when his father perished on the Titanic. A New York Times article in 1912 listed his wealth at the tidy sum of $150,000,000 – mostly in New York real estate including the posh Waldorf Astoria Hotel. Astor's fortune enabled him to *"...control more millions than any man of his age in the country."*[11]

Kermit and Astor's The Room, was partly a social gathering for like minded upper-class Brahmins and doubled as a meeting place where the members, as amateur spies, could exchange intelligence information on topics of note from international finance to foreign relations.

*"At their monthly meetings, ROOM members gathered for dinner and conversation. When members returned from their continual series of world travels, they reported observations to The ROOM. 'It is hoped to learn from Suydam [Cutting] what he has been doing in China,' Kermit noted before one session. Indeed, the entire atmosphere surrounding The ROOM resembled that of an intelligence office, albeit in an informal and somewhat romanticized manner."*12

The group was also notable for its prominent membership. In 1927 charter members included Kermit's brother, Theodore Jr.; world traveler, Sydam Cutting; business magnate and wealthy benefactor, Marshall Field; yachtsman and inheritor of the Astor fortune, William Vincent Astor and other leaders of society, commerce and the sporting world. In later years, publisher Nelson Doubleday; wealthy Wall Street investor, George Mason Grant; British sportsman and member of the Fourth Hussars, Captain H. Nugent Head and others would socialize and share experiences over lunch or dinner. Occasionally guests would be invited to recount their interesting adventures and perhaps secretly disclose their personal observations of world affairs. In 1928 a dinner was held to honor and wish good luck to Richard E. Byrd for his upcoming expedition to explore Antarctica:

*"The visit to The ROOM of British author and veteran intelligence officer Somerset Maugham evoked the most enthusiasm, because many members had themselves worked for Allied intelligence during the first world war. (sic)"*13

Although not directly involved in the secret society's activities, Kermit's cousin, Franklin Roosevelt was frequently an interested and grateful recipient of information gathered by the members. As world travelers, bankers and heads of business and industry, the like-minded and politically conservative members of The Room would coordinate any facts, figures or fantasy gained via their privileged positions and report back to FDR whose appetite for both rumor and factual secrets knew no bounds.

Vincent Astor*[21] with his 264-foot yacht Nourmahal would occasionally entertain Room members and FDR on board the Nourmahal. Kermit was a frequent guest of his friend. With support from the U.S. Navy, Astor and Kermit even cruised to the Pacific with the intent of spying on the Japanese in the Marshall Islands. Kermit's ongoing drinking problem was temporary curtailed during the cruise, prompting Astor to inform cousin, FDR : *"He has had hardly anything to drink – and then only beer and sherry - and is in the best shape in years. When you see him, I think you will agree."*[14]

Upon returning from the trip FDR was amazed at Kermit's improvement. In a letter to Astor he commented, *"He looks infinitely better than before he left and I do hope the result will be permanent."* This was not to be; following the cruise, Kermit once again began his excessive alcohol consumption. Despite Kermit's light libations, the motive for the trip was not for pleasure. Astor and Kermit planned to visit the Marshalls and gather intelligence for both FDR and the Office of Naval Intelligence reporting on any military buildup. The Japanese Government denied the Nourmahal any access to their Marshall Island territories. The two seagoing amateur spies cruised to Bikini, Eniwetok, Wotje and Jaluit. Astor relayed information back to FDR about the island's dock facilities, fresh water availability, permanent structures, etc. Upon returning to the states, Kermit met to debrief his cousin at the White House and hear the President voice his concern that they

---

21  *Astor was an avid yachtsman with a penchant for philanthropy, social concerns and the drama of cloak and dagger intrigue. In 1917, after planning with his friend, Assistant Secretary of the Navy, Franklin Roosevelt for the creation of a new flotilla of yachts to assist in the war effort, he loaned his own 262 foot yacht, the Noma to the Navy and volunteered himself as a young ensign. Astor saw action on the vessel off the coast of France and the flotilla concept eventually became the United States Naval Reserve. Later, during the Second World War, Astor donated his new yacht, the Nourmahal, to the war effort and became a Lieutenant Commander serving as a clandestine intelligence operative in New York for President Franklin Roosevelt.

may have "touched at the Marshalls."[15] Although without any documented evidence, some speculate that they may also have been searching for the fate of Amelia Earhart who disappeared a couple of years before over the Pacific.

❖

Use of the plush yacht was not confined to surreptitious voyages, however. On occasion, the civic-minded Astor would cruise to distant locales with Kermit such as the Galapagos Islands for scientific research on behalf of museums and often would invite his friends, Kermit and FDR on other pleasure cruises. On these occasions alcohol would flow freely and locker room high jinks would prevail. Indicative of the close relationship between Kermit and Astor is demonstrated by a humorous five page list in 1934 of "fees owed" by Kermit for indiscretions he supposedly committed on one cruise:

> *"Loss of tennis balls through knocking into water - . 50; Damage to tennis balls - $6.00; Damage to outer edge of court - $10.00; Ordinary services of Gwendolyn – no charge; Unusual services of Gwendolyn – ($25.00 per day for 7 days) - $175.00.*[16]

In 1933, Kermit, Astor, President-elect, Franklin Delano Roosevelt, and a group of friends were in Miami and planning to board the Nourmahal when Roosevelt stopped to make a speech from the back seat of his car. Kermit was riding a few cars back in the entourage when shots rang out and a deranged unemployed construction worker attempted to end the life of the President-elect. The shots missed Roosevelt. However, Chicago's Mayor Anton Cermak, who was shaking hands with the President-elect, was struck by one bullet and died shortly after. In the late 1930s, as the Japanese Empire spread across the Pacific, Southeast Asia and into China, FDR and Room members became more worrisome, even changing the organization's name to the Club with some members stepping-up their worldwide snooping operations. Before the Central Intelligence Agency and even before the OSS, Astor envisioned himself organizing a formal national spy service under FDR. Although never rising to official status, during the war he eventually managed to have FDR assign him certain formal intelligence tasks within the New York area.

Kermit's participation in the clubbish and otherwise questionable activities of The Room and other organizations were not his only social and entertainment focus. Throughout the 1920s and 30s he engaged frequently in many upper-class athletic activities: squash, tennis, polo and bridge. He maintained a close friendship and corresponded with many influential persons, worldwide. In 1927 he dined with the King of Spain. On another occasion, he dined with Bertrand Russell and Priscilla Auchincloss. Some of his lunch guests of 1928 were the writer Ford Madox Ford; the humorist Will Rogers and the architect, Grant La Farge. He maintained a long standing correspondence and friendship with the British writer, Rudyard Kipling. Kermit was continually besieged to endorse products or speak on behalf of various causes – many he declined. Since returning from his many adventures, he became a considerable public celebrity. In 1929 he dined with Gilbert Grosvenor and lectured to an audience of 5000 at the National Geographic Society.

Kermit's personal magnetism was one of his greatest assets. With a flair for adventure and an articulate manner of speech, he could entrance a group of friends or acquaintances with his stories of distant, exotic travel. Similar to his father, his adventurous peregrinations enabled him to relate an endless repertoire of danger derring-do and knowledge of arcane facts on indigenous tribes or man-eating carnivores. When visiting family, he would keep younger members of the Roosevelt clan enthralled with his stories and present little gifts of unique trinkets from far-off places.

The boom years of the 1920s enabled Kermit and Belle to enjoy a high lifestyle and amass a considerable amount of financial independence. Both enjoyed world travel and maintained servants. They lived in a large home, Mohannes, in Oyster Bay, not far from Sagamore Hill and the property where brother Ted's mansion would be built. In 1930 Kermit even purchased a 1920 Rolls Royce Touring Car from Vincent Astor. During the 1920s his continual cash deposits totaled many tens of thousands of dollars in the Bank of America in New York. On one occasion in 1928 he deposited the lump-sum amount of $30,000. This was at a time, even during the prosperous "roaring twenties" when the average yearly net income was

$6,078.93[17] Kermit's investment portfolio in this prosperous decade held many shares of stock with Carter & Company of New York representing a significant holding in the maritime industry along with other investments. However, the stock market crash of 1929 and the ensuing economic depression of the 30s began to take an insidious toll on Kermit and Belle's financial wellbeing. Many of their investments began to suffer devaluation as the economic debacle spread through the nation and across the world.

The decade of the 20s was a period of unbridled enthusiasm, prosperity and development leading many people to believe the good times would never end. The euphoric sense of wellbeing and wealth lead many to engage in excessive spending, much of it haphazard and careless. Many new technical innovations were being developed such as radio, new home appliances, improvements in automobiles and an endless variety of modern luxuries providing outlets for people to part with their money. The belief that financial investments in the stock market were a sure method of gaining financial independence increasingly encouraged a large segment of the population to cash in their savings, mortgage their houses or borrow money to buy stocks. Between 1922 and 1929 the Dow Jones Industrial Index Average increased from 91.0 to 290.0[18] – an astonishing 300 percent rise. Unfortunately, much of the overpriced stock acquisitions were based upon margin buying enabling a very small down payment on the purchase with the expectation of gaining a windfall profit on the stock to finance the initial cost. In the end when the value of many of these stocks plummeted the buyer was obligated to cover the full purchase price. This unanticipated development in speculation forced many into bankruptcy who could not make good on the purchase.

A second probable cause of the market crash was the great expansion of investment trusts and public utility holding companies.[19] As utility regulation increased, the value of their highly inflated and leveraged stocks dropped drastically. The combination of these events precipitated a selling panic and in 1929 on October 24th and 29th, "Black Thursday" and "Black Tuesday," the stock market crashed under a massive selloff. *"By the time the crash was*

117

*completed in 1932, following an unprecedentedly large economic depression, stocks had lost nearly 90 percent of their value.*"[20] During the decade of the 1930s following the Wall Street debacle, many banks across the nation failed in the era before the Federal Deposit Insurance Corporation, leaving their depositors penniless. Bank loans were extremely scarce, money was tight or non-existent, with an unemployment rate reaching 25 percent people were losing their homes and businesses, manufacturing ground to a halt and jobs in many areas were scarce or non-existent – the nation was suffering deeply.

This dreadful set of events cascaded around the world and severely affected the world shipping industry. Although gainfully employed through this difficult period, Kermit's investments and general economic condition began to fail precipitately requiring a major change to his lifestyle and retrenchment of his spending habits.

Between 1929 and 1933 his investment portfolio showed a flurry of investment activity for International Mercantile Marine. Following the October market crash he held a highly leveraged account (at 30 percent) of 7500 shares of IMM with a debit balance of $144,440. The account listed a credit balance of only $1,024.21.[21] In 1933 he suffered a net loss of $27, 424.50 for IMM. His 1929 purchase of Aviation Corporation of Delaware, purchased for $2000 was sold in 1933 for $1200. Between September and December, 1930 the Roosevelt's received dunning letters for numerous small, household bills in arrears totaling over $16,000.[22] Checks were written for $884.34 but not sent due to a lack of funds in their Fifth Avenue Bank account. Throughout 1930, their account was overdrawn on many occasions totaling thousands of dollars. Even his son, Kermit Jr. was informed of an overdue payment to B. Altman for a $33 charge on a new suit.

By the early 1930s, Kermit and Belle were *"cutting their budget drastically"*[23] as many others across the nation were desperate for jobs and resorting to soup kitchens for their meals. Although continually employed throughout the decade of the depression and still earning a sizeable salary in the shipping industry, Kermit and Belle were forced to balance their investment losses and living expenses against his income. In 1930 Belle discontinued her membership in the Child Study Association of America for a yearly savings of $20.00 as the Book of the Month Club was complaining about unpaid bills.  Kermit resigned his membership in the Explorers Club in 1931 and began to curtail unnecessary expenses.  In 1937 Kermit cancelled his subscription to the New York Times and resigned from the Tennis and Racquet Club.

The economic pressures following his investment losses after the stock market crash, mounting expenses and problems with the shipping industry severely affected Kermit's already fragile temperament and greatly contributed to his lifelong predisposition of severe mental depression.  He began to purge his demons in alcoholism and social carousing with his friends leading to a decline in both his mental stability and his once splendidly strong and athletic physical condition.  Despite the diminishment of his finances and growing personal problems, he left a legacy in American shipping and commerce that is equaled by few if any others.  His efforts and those of a few others enabled the United States to recover from the virtual absence of a national shipping industry prior to the First World War and play a major role in economic development following the war.  A measure of his contribution to the world of shipping is represented by the honor bestowed by the United States Navy.  In May, 1945 the navy commissioned a 411 foot Luzon Class repair ship the USS Kermit Roosevelt.

Notes:
1. New York Times, November 26, 1919
2. The Rough Writer, The News of the Volunteers at Sagamore Hill, Volume 9, Issue 3
3. The opening paragraph of the act, "Purpose and Policy of the United States," stated: "It is necessary for the national defense and for the proper growth of its foreign and domestic commerce that the United States shall have a merchant marine of the best equipped and most suitable types of vessels sufficient to carry the greater portion of its commerce and serve as a naval auxiliary in time of war or national emergency, ultimately to be owned and operated privately by citizens of the United States; and it is the declared policy of the United States to do whatever may be necessary to develop and encourage the maintenance of such a merchant marine."
4. The Bridge to France, 1927, Edward N. Hurley
5. TIME, March 15, 1926
6. TIME, January 29, 1928
7. TIME, January 19, 1931
8. New York Times, September 1, 1921
9. The Audubon Ark, A History of the National Audubon Society, Frank Graham, Jr. with Carl Buchheister, published in paperback in 1992 by the University of Texas Press, Austin, TX; originally published New York: Knopf, 1990. Page 181 in the paperback edition.
10. The Roosevelt-Astor Espionage Ring, 1981; Quarterly Journal of New York State Historical Association, Volume LXII, Number 3 by Jeffery M. Dorwart
11. New York Times, May 8, 1912
12. The Roosevelt-Astor Espionage Ring, 1981; Quarterly Journal of New York State Historical Association, Volume LXII, Number 3 by Jeffery M. Dorwart
13. Ibid.
14. Astor letter, 1938; Franklin D. Roosevelt Library
15. The Belle and Kermit Roosevelt Papers, Library of Congress, Box 19
16. Ibid.
17. TIME, August 31, 1929
18. "The 1929 Stock Market Crash," Bierman, Harol, Cornel University, EH.Net Encyclopedia, March 26, 2008.

19. Ibid.
20. Ibid.
21. The Belle and Kermit Roosevelt Papers, Library of Congress, Box 115
22. Ibid.
23. Ibid., Box 117

## CHAPTER VII - ADVENTURES IN DISTANT LANDS

*March by march I puzzled through 'em,*
*turning flanks and dodging shoulders,*
*Hurried on in hope of water,*
*headed back for lack of grass;*
*Till I camped above the tree-line --*
*drifted snow and naked boulders --*
*Felt free air astir to windward --*
*knew I'd stumbled on the Pass.*

*"The Explorer," Rudyard Kipling*

The first quarter of the 20th Century was an age of
hectic discovery and manic exploration. The race for being
the first to the poles, discovery and analysis of the ancient
civilizations of the Middle-East and South America along
with the discovery of new species and many other major
challenges became competitive events for the world's
scientific community. Typical of the age (trekking to far-off
places to secure examples of rare or unknown species of
flora and fauna) was a major interest of the world's leading
collecting institutions. Many animals that today are
commonplace in zoos and museums were either only
rumored to exist or not even yet discovered. Even large
numbers of known species were not yet owned or displayed
by the major institutions. The geographic societies, zoos
and museums were anxious to acquire and display life-like
settings of the world's rare life-forms. In the 1920s Carl
Akeley of the American Museum of Natural History was
collecting for and planning the African Hall in New York as
many museums were competing for the new fossil
discoveries in the American West.

At that time, wealthy and adventurous dilettantes
served as hunter-naturalists combining sport, exploration
and game-harvesting with the noble intent of expanding
man's knowledge of the world. Earlier, famous hunters
such as Frederick Courtney Selous, George Cornwallis
Harris, George Thomson and many others had contributed

both their lives and names to the discovery of new species. The Boone and Crockett Club was originally created by Theodore Roosevelt in 1887 for the protection of America's dwindling wildlife. The organization also acquired the various best examples of America's antlered animals and began documenting the most dramatic specimens obtained by hunters. The Rowland-Ward Record Book was devised to document the largest and most magnificent of the world's animals. Kermit and his brother Theodore Jr. continued this tradition and were participants in this era of grand, adventurous exploration.

Although immersed in the shipping industry with business interests requiring Kermit to travel to the four corners of the world, his insatiable thirst for wilderness adventure could not be satisfied in the board room. Adventure and discovery in wild romantic places, along with a deep interest in literature were major forces of his personality. His curiosity for the mystery of distant lands, indigenous peoples with their unique languages, hunting adventures and particularly the undiscovered secrets of natural history were always foremost in his mind. *"Though I have done a certain amount of roughing it and hunting during my life, compared to Kermit I am a beginner,"* noted his brother, Theodore Jr., also a seasoned world traveler, hardened combat soldier and keen student of natural history. He continued:

> *"Every continent has seen the smoke of his camp-fires. His business is shipping, which takes him all over the world, and as a result he has been able in the course of his work to hunt in India, Manchuria, and various parts of the United States and Mexico."*[1]

This observation, notwithstanding his previous wilderness travels with his father to Africa and South America and his own hunting expeditions to Canada and Korea, place Kermit in a select group of 20th Century explorers and hunter-naturalists. Due to this restless nature, the conventional life of a corporate executive could no longer satisfy his wandering urge and in 1925 he once again embarked upon a long expedition to the unchartered corners of the world.

*Pursuing the Marco Polo Sheep in Turkestan*
Following TR Jr.'s defeat to Alfred E. Smith in the New
York Gubernatorial race of 1924, he and Kermit decided to
take time off for an expedition to the mountains of Central
Asia in pursuit of the elusive Ovis poli. As in the past with
their father, their plan was to combine a big game hunting
trip while collecting museum settings for science. This
strange wild mountain sheep with its age-old legends
would provide the perfect quarry while enabling the
brothers to explore a region of the world along with its flora
and fauna that until that time had only marginally been
investigated. As Kermit and TR Jr. began to explore the
high regions of Asia, Theodore Roosevelt's friend, Roy
Chapman Andrews[2] of the American Museum of Natural
History, was making remarkable discoveries of dinosaur
fossils to the northeast in Mongolia: the early origins of
man and his migration were his focus. Both Andrews and
the Roosevelts would be trekking in adjacent regions of
Asia generally unexplored.

The Ovis poli has puzzled and even created doubt in the
minds of many people since the great 14th Century world
traveler Marco Polo first mentioned their existence to the
civilized world.[3] This animal remained a myth for
hundreds of years until 1838 when British adventurer
Lieutenant John Woods explored the Pamir Mountains in
Afghanistan near the Chinese border. Woods returned and
presented to the astonished Royal Society in London a
huge set of horns, larger than any known sheep thereby
officially establishing the animal's existence. The Society
named this unique creature, Ovis poli; the Marco Polo
sheep in honor of the great explorer who first documented
existence of the animal. Down through the years, the
Marco Polo sheep has become the prized game animal for
hunters who are willing to spend the time, money and
enormous energy in snow laden mountains at elevations
reaching up to 20,000 feet. With the impressive spiraling
horns of this sheep extending horizontally from the
animals head in long graceful curves sometimes achieving
lengths greater than 60 to 70 inches, many hunters
consider this to be the ultimate trophy. However, in the
1920s, this animal was still a mysterious novelty with its

habitat even classified today as one of the most harsh, remote regions of the world.

❖

The Roosevelts focused on the Pamirs, Turkestan and the Tian Shan*[22] mountains for their pursuit of the Ovis poli which TR Jr. called the *"father and mother"* of all the wild sheep.[4] Their expectations were to also collect representatives of the region's other various fauna. The geographic diversity of high mountains, scorching desert interspersed with lowland jungle would provide a varied environment previously unstudied by science.

To finance the expedition Kermit and TR Jr. engaged the Field Museum of Natural History in Chicago and Mr. James Simpson, the wealthy head of Marshall Field & Co. The enterprise was named the James Simpson-Roosevelts-Field Museum Expedition. This venture provided the museum the opportunity to acquire animal specimens not commonly available in other institutions with the possibility of even new species. To provide professional scientific expertise on the expedition, the Roosevelt's enlisted George K. Cherrie who accompanied Kermit and his father on their South American expedition years before. Lifelong friend of the Roosevelt family, the wealthy world traveler and naturalist, Charles Sydam Cutting[5] agreed to provide photographic services for the expedition rounding out the exploration and research party to four.

For guides and camp staff, the brothers relied on the suggestions of British military officers who had experience in the mountains of Asia. Ahmad Shah, a turbaned former army sergeant-major and a tough former soldier named Feroze were employed. A syce, necessary for handling the pack animals and the four American hound dogs the brothers shipped for game tracking, was named Fezildin. Native hunters Rahima Loon and his brother Khalil were added to serve as the group's shikaries along with a cook and three coolies for odd jobs and equipment carry.

---

22 *This region is within central Asia where Great Britain and the Russian Empire conducted their strategic cat and mouse game of conquest during the 19th and early 20th centuries which the British called the Great Game. Just prior to the Great War, the British were concerned with the northern exposure to India as the Russian Empire expanded into Transcaucasia while both vied for control of Afghanistan and Persia. The only few Westerners who travelled this land were those on spying missions to gain vital intelligence for their respective countries.

The travel plan chosen for the expedition would trek an arduous route of many hundreds of miles over snow covered mountain peaks and through glacial passes, across scorching desert and via ancient caravan trails through remote villages. Their caravan's transportation relied on the local tough mountain ponies and yaks. These large rugged animals were capable of traversing the steep elevations and deep snow with little difficulty while carrying the heavy loads of both men and supplies. Beginning in the Kashmir city of Srinagar, the expedition crossed the Himalaya Mountains, passed through the Karakoram, passed onto the Takla Mahan Desert of Eastern Turkestan, thence north into the heights of the Tian Shan Mountains for the Ovis poli then on to Kargai Tash in Mongolia. Cherrie and Cutting would pursue a leisurely collecting schedule[6], stopping when necessary while Kermit and TR Jr. decided to travel light and make speed through the mountains, across Turkestan and to the Tian Shan Range while linking with the collecting team in Mongolia.

This rigorous route wore heavily on both man and beast. Temperatures at night would drop to frigid levels. Unable to stay warm at night with no camp fire due to the absence of trees for fire wood at that elevation, the only recourse was to stay dressed, huddled within sleeping bags in their tent at night. Crossing through the high mountain passes, TR Jr. noted *"but every mile stands on end."*[7] The thin mountain air at the high elevations taxed the breathing of the men and pack animals heavily laden with 150 pound loads, rendering each step an exercise in exhaustion. *"What might be an easy climb at 10,000 feet, at 17,000 sets the heart beating like a trip-hammer and the lungs gasping for air."*[8] The meager mountain fodder offered little sustenance to the laboring beasts. Many times the animals would trudge through snow belly-deep. Many frozen rivers would be forded, chilling all to the bone. At some locations the trail would lead along a narrow ledge where a slip could send animal and rider to their doom. Avalanches were frequent in the narrow mountain passes as glacial crevasses in the valleys threatened the caravan with their bottomless depths. At one location a small pony, carrying no pack, fell but could not rise. He died simply from exertion and the altitude. On another occasion during the night, one of their donkeys was killed and partially eaten by wolves within a hundred yards of their camp. A measure of the toll on pack animals in the Himalayas by previous travelers was evidenced by the numerous bones along the trail which at some locations were piled six and eight feet high.

After fording one river to avoid a shorter route across a treacherous glacier, they met two men from another caravan who attempted the dangerous glacier crossing. Also deciding on the apparently easier river ford, they had to wait four days for the water to recede. While delayed, starvation claimed the life of one man and eleven pack-animals, forcing the two survivors to eat horse-flesh.

In the 1920s, caravan travel in the Himalayas differed very little from the past ages. Travel through the precarious mountain passes was weather and seasonal dependent. Kermit's pack animal caravan experienced the same dangers that have plagued Himalayan travelers for centuries. When crossing the high Karakoram Pass their eighth animal, a pack-pony, fell off the trail. His group lost many beasts through this dangerous route; all totaled, thirteen animals were sacrificed during their twenty-five-day trek across the Himalayan range. The companion caravan of a Rajah of Baltistan and his wife joined them for a portion of the trek. The Mrs. Rajah was a veiled purdah[9] hidden within a litter carried by four servants. Kermit commented on the precarious situation of the swaying litter when skirting the narrow ledges above the numerous cliff faces where a misstep would send the mysterious aristocrat and her entourage into oblivion. Offsetting the dangers of the mountain travel, the trek also passed through picturesque villages and ancient monasteries, meeting colorful and exotic people.

The expedition marveled at the culture and customs of the Buddhist worshiping mountain people. At Nurla they witnessed a Buddhist ceremony where a priest conducted a most extraordinary service: In amazement Kermit commented,

*"He scattered incense, and genuflected mystic signs. He then took a small dagger, which he ran through a hole in his cheek, plunging it in up to the hilt, so that*

127

*the blade appeared between his teeth. Next he took two sabres, and, intoning a dirge-like chant, swung the swords about his head in the approved Cossack style. Suddenly he stripped himself to the waist, placed the point of each sword in the pit of his stomach, and, running a short distance, plunged forward to the ground, balancing himself on the swords."* Fortunately, *"Before he could repeat this performance the two assistant lamas rushed up and took the swords from him."*[10]

After descending the Karakorum onto the Depsang Plain they entered the range of the Tibetan antelope where Kermit and TR Jr. collected three of the animals for a museum setting. Up to this time, the hunting was meager although Cherrie and Cutting were successful in collecting a trove of birds and small mammals on their slower, circuitous route.

In the lowland town of Karghalik, the expedition members were feted by the Amban, the town's ranking official and his family. For the occasion, Kermit and TR Jr. donned a pair of tuxedos and top hats they packed for just such an eventuality. By civilized standards, they presented quite a bizarre appearance decked-out in opera hat and tails while riding ragged, half tamed pony's through the streets of the remote town. Even typical today in many foreign lands with obscure cultures, indigenous peoples are often very impressed with an overt show of formality and officialdom. The Roosevelts realized this with the evening dress. They even secured from Chinese officials before embarking on the trip, obsolete, ostentatious and beribboned documents written in Chinese to impress any remote peoples they may encounter. Their ceremonious dinner with the Amban and his entourage was a big success. Along with the numerous supplies packed for the trip, Kermit, always appreciative of strong spirits, contributed brandy, sloe gin and champagne to the fare as Cutting provided entertainment with song.

Throughout the trip, the expedition split and then regrouped to enable Cherrie to collect museum specimens on a more leisurely pace and for Cutting to proceed ahead to confirm all of the administrative incidentals in crossing remote lands. At Yarkand, Cherrie took a delayed passage to Maralbashi as Cutting headed to Kashgar to address travel arrangement there. The overland journey in the Takla Mahan Desert over a well-used ancient trail enabled the Roosevelts to overnight in many villages. Their sleeping accommodations varied between sleeping bags under the stars or a flea infested slumber in a serai, the central Asian version of a roadside motel. The serai were the standard hostelries for the locals which included accommodations for their livestock under the same roof. The evening meal would be from a communal pot enabling the plunging hands of all the guests to dig for their hand-dipped morsels as they squatted under a lamp. *"The evening meal over, they would sing spirited ballad songs with a swinging lilt to them or lugubrious dirges and indescribably monotonous chants."*[11]

After two-and-a-half months of hard travel since leaving Srinagar on May 19, 1925, crossing the Himalayas fording wild rivers and crossing threatening glaciers, the caravan finally arrived in the game-rich Tian Shan Mountains. Here the Roosevelt's were rewarded for their arduous trek. After some dishearteningly missed shots with TR Jr. losing a wounded roe deer, they began to harvest the desired specimens for the museum. Within a short time, Kermit shot two ibex: one measuring fifty-five*[23] and a half inches and another with forty-seven inch horns. He later shot a fine Siberian Roe Deer. Hunting in the high mountains is a very difficult proposition. Their quarry, the roe deer and particularly ibex are ideally adapted to the high elevations and precipitous cliff faces and rocky crags. The ibex is a wild mountain goat that can prance across sheer cliff faces while maintaining traction on only the tiniest of cracks and ledges. They can traverse vertical crags with fast bounds and hops while maintaining perfect balance. The males are an impressive animal sport long beards and great scimitar horns that can reach sixty-inches.

Despite being acclimated to the high country, when chasing wild game Kermit and TR Jr. were continually challenged by the thin air. The effort and danger of

---

23 *The Rowland Ward record book currently lists (in 2010) the world record of Tien Shan Ibex at 54 ½ inches taken by Kermit Roosevelt.

negotiating the incredible terrain of mountain ledges and slopes while slipping on steep slide rock was back-breaking and nerve rattling work; *"We climbed along the edges of precipices 'with a drop into nothing below us as straight as a beggar can spit'"* commented TR Jr. After spotting the often tiny specks moving on the ledges, they would mount their ponies and ride until the topography became too steep or rocky for their mounts. They would tether the horses and begin a long stalk, hoping not to be spotted by the keen eyesight of the game. Following the shot, if an animal was wounded, the hunter would necessarily begin to follow the blood trail which invariably would lead across the most difficult and dangerous route. Even when taking the animal with a clean kill, there was always the possibility it would fall down a precipitous slope either breaking a horn or ending in an inaccessible location.

As their caravan moved on into the heart of the hunting country, Kermit had the good fortune after a long stalk to shoot five Ovis Karelini, a form of wild sheep, after rapidly expending fifteen shots. Four of the animals horns ranged from forty-four to forty-six inches. However, the fifth measured a whooping sixty-one inches, the largest yet recorded at that time. On another occasion, TR Jr. took three ibex, the largest measuring fifty-two inches. Later, Kermit, following a difficult climb and taking a long 250-yard shot, took an ibex with huge fifty-nine and a half inch horns, the largest of recorded ibex heads.

Harvesting museum settings for the Field Museum being the focus of the expedition and not a sporting enterprise for trophy heads, Kermit and TR Jr. were obliged to also hunt the more common females and young of each species. This activity was approached with much less enthusiasm, so the brothers shared this hunting responsibility with their shikaries who would also independently hunt with gun in hand. When not hunting or traveling across the central Asian wastelands, Kermit, always the intellectual, would engross himself in reading. A sample of his wilderness library included: *The Egoist*, *Westward Ho*, the familiar *Pickwick Papers*, *Jorrocks Jaunts* and the *Romany Rye*. The poetry of Kipling and Edward Arlington Robinson also resided within his saddlebags.

The Roosevelt's first encounter with the near mythical ovis poli came close to being a life and death survival struggle. After climbing steep ridges for six hours in heavy weather and wounding two suitable rams, the hunters began to track the animals as they scampered away. The going was impossibly difficult as the men sometimes floundered in arm-pit deep snow. The steel gray sky began to discharge a heavy snowfall as high winds whipped the air into blizzard conditions obliterating the track. Despite the possibility of losing the wounded animals to the fastness of the mountains or the ravenous hunger of a wolf pack, the only recourse for the men was to return to camp and hope for locating the animals if the weather broke the next day. Conditions were so poor on their descent, Kermit commented: *"Working our way down to the valley we found our yaks, so frosted with snow that they looked like animated birthday-cakes."*[12]

Anticipating a near fruitless search the next morning, the brothers were relieved to learn during the night the high winds had blown much of the snowfall clear of the mountain slope revealing remnants of the animals' spore. Some of the native guides believed the slope was too steep to climb, but the Roosevelts insisted and the tracking began anew. After trekking the mountain ridges and glassing the valleys one of the sharp-eyed guides spotted seven wolves near a small ravine and knew the wounded animals must be close therein. Unfortunately, although serving as markers, the wolves destroyed the body skins rendering the animal hides useless for museum display. However, the great horns and head skins were intact and suitable for mounting on any smaller animals they later collected.

After tough days of mountain hunting, occasionally at elevations of 17,000 feet, the expedition finally collected eight ovis poli specimens suitable for the museum's collection. Travelling from Srinigar across some of the highest mountain ranges in the world while traversing the Kashmir, skirting Tibet, trekking through Turkestan and into Mongolia, the expedition covered over 2,600 miles by the time they returned. This distance was covered on foot, yak, pack pony and camel over a six-month period ending in November 1925.

Besides the ovis poli, the expedition collected over 170[13] male and female mammal specimens including ibex, deer, antelope, bear, wolf, gazelle, mountain lion and even a rhinoceros in Nepal. As the Roosevelts hunted mammals, Cherrie collected many dozens of bird skins and 70 amphibians and reptiles[14]. This trove of rare animals served to be a great addition to the Field Museum's collection.

### In pursuit of the Giant Panda

The urge to engage in adventure travel in the faraway exotic regions of the world continued to tug at the Roosevelt shirtsleeves. In 1928 Kermit and TR Jr. once again began planning and packing for an expedition into the far side of beyond. TR Jr. had just completed his campaigning for Herbert Hoover's successful ascension to the White House, and Kermit was able to break away from his executive duties enabling both to travel for an extended period. After much consideration of various remote and yet unexplored regions of the world and collecting possibilities of uninvestigated species, they decided to explore northern Burma, central China and Indo-China. Their goal was to bring back the skin of the Giant Panda along with lesser, but equally strange animals.

At that time, the Giant Panda was a mysterious and near unknown animal. The only reference to the bei-shung, or "white bear" was made by French missionary and naturalist Pere David in 1869 but he only secured furs of the creature and had not seen a live example in the wild. The first European to view a live version of the panda was in the 1913-1915 Walter Stötzner expedition. A live Giant Panda was not captured and brought to the United States until 1936 when Manhattan socialite and fashion designer Ruth Harkness turned to world exploring and fulfilled her husband's dream by bringing a live panda back from China. The animal was originally thought to be related to the raccoon family, and it was not until the 1990s when scientists, using molecular analyses changed its classification to that of a bear. Today, they are rarely observed in the wild and, due to their diminishing numbers, are on the endangered species list and are highly prized by the world's zoos.

Besides the Giant Panda, the Roosevelts desired other mammals that could offer the possibility of new species being discovered in the generally unexplored regions of Burma and China. The golden monkey, takin, McNeill's stag, burrhel, serow and ghoral were rare and unusual species that were also on their collecting list.

❖

As in past Roosevelt expeditions, Chicago's Field Museum was called upon for both technical support and sponsorship. Kermit and TR Jr. travelled to Chicago to present their plan to President Stanley Field of the Field Museum of Natural History.

At a dinner in the home of Field, the brothers met museum patron William V. Kelly who immediately agreed to finance the venture which would be called the William V. Kelley-Roosevelts Asiatic Expedition. The next step was organizing the expedition's team.

British scientist and Indo-china veteran Herbert Stevens would accompany them to China while the notable American naturalist, Harold Coolidge would lead the scientists when the expedition proceeded to Indo-China. Naturalist Russell Hendee, University of Michigan's Josslyn Van Tyne and Doctor Ralph Wheeler also joined the group. Roosevelt friend and companion on the Himalayan expedition, C. Sydam Cutting, would take still and motion pictures. Shikarries were hired in the Kashmir, and porters would be hired from the local native populations as the expedition travelled.

A major hurdle for the expedition was the myriad of languages and language dialects they would encounter as they moved through the isolated, near wilderness regions of Asia. Luckily a young Chinese-American by the name of Jack Young was recommended to the Roosevelts by the Chinese Minister. Young had worked for the Chinese Government near the regions the expedition planned to cross and he spoke many of the local dialects. After completing a crash course in skinning small mammals and birds at the museum, he joined the expedition.

Their expectations were to live off the land when able; however, packing-in food was also a necessity. Preparation of the large store of food was handled by Kermit's old Amazon companion, Anthony Fiala. The large cache of supplies included guns, tents, scientific and navigation equipment, books, gifts for the natives, bush clothing and even evening dress for when meeting local officials. The route of travel began in northern Burma on December 26, 1928 and continued north into central China crossing the Yangtze River then south to Hanoi in Indo-China. They would trek over 2,000 miles of jungle and mountain passage by horse, mule and yak.

Burma and China in the early 20th Century were very primitive with little contact with the outside world beyond the occasional European missionary. The native people barely travelled beyond their immediate villages and most were steeped in age-old superstition; living in the same manner as their forbears' hundreds of years before. Their definition of a road was usually nothing beyond a mule trail with a town consisting merely of a gathering of broken-down stone hovels. Even their guides, hired from the local population, were unsure of the trail beyond the nearest mountain or bamboo forest. Use of opium was common and a scourge to many. According to the estimate of a missionary at the time, at least eighty percent of China's population was addicted. Central government control and the rule of law beyond the few large towns were almost non-existent. Even the Buddhist monks at the occasional monastery imposed a harsh rule over the local population. The countryside was rife with warlords and bandits that terrorized the simple farmers. On many occasions the Roosevelt's expedition just missed encounters with ruthless bands of these marauders. The local village chief would frequently assign a contingent of rag-tag soldiers to accompany the caravan to the next outpost of civilization. Even the soldiers would sometimes abuse the locals. With the possibility of danger always lurking around the next turn, on some occasions, TR Jr., always the military leader, would organize the line of march like an army patrol with he or Kermit at the head of the line, one of the brothers in the center of the column and Cutting bringing up the rear. Naturally all were armed; Kermit even wore a .38 automatic Colt pistol in a shoulder holster. At one point: TR Jr. remarked:

*"As we came round a sharp bend in the trail we ran upon a Kachin with a rifle on his shoulder. Upon seeing us he jumped to one side and flung his rifle to*

*aim. For a moment it looked as if we might be in for trouble, but the Kachin, although apprehensive, was apparently on the alert for some personal enemy and a second later his face was wreathed in somewhat sheepish smiles."*[15]

❖

Similar to their routine in the Himalayas, the expedition split-up on January 5th before reaching the Chinese border. Stevens lagged behind to pursue small game at the leisurely pace necessary for the trapping and skinning of birds and small mammals as the Roosevelt's continued on to hunt big game in the north while the season lasted. As they progressed into China, Kermit became seriously ill with violent cramps, a common occurrence of the time for travelers in remote regions; the blame placed on bad water or consuming the local food. However, Kermit would continually suffer throughout his life from the ailments of his travels and lifestyle: frequent bouts of malaria, pain from previously broken bones and stressed muscles and excessive alcohol consumption. After questionable treatment by a local doctor whose medical equipment was carried in a tin box and refreshed from a day's rest, Kermit regained the strength to continue their march.

After crossing the Mekong River in China on January 11, they entered the rugged and desolate mountain gorge of the river's pass. By native superstition, the river was haunted by a monster called a Crim that ate people and cattle which the natives claimed *"some even say whole caravans."*[16] Though not molested by monsters or evil spirits as they moved on they were continually on the alert for bandit gangs. Despite having an escort of six soldiers, the caravan was forced to detour from the main trail when alerted by local villagers of a band of robbers lying in wait ahead. The region was rife with the devastation caused by the bandits.

They passed one village that was sacked and nearly destroyed three weeks earlier by the marauding bands. The bandits were cruel and ruthless with their treatment of the villagers, often severing hands and arms of their victims. The authorities in China were equally ruthless when dealing with the lawbreakers. After circling the Village of Siakwan where some bandits were holed-up, soldiers indiscriminately slaughtered all the inhabitants; men, women and children, ensuring no one would escape. On another occasion the caravan was waylaid for a day as a band of eight-hundred Tibetan bandits had routed a column of government troops ahead on the trail. Such was the type of country the expedition traversed.

When entering the high country of Yunnan, they crossed mountain ranges rising to 20,000 feet. In the high country, Kermit, with three Lolo hunters as guides, shot a male serow, a mountain antelope with horns similar to the North American mountain goat. As they continued north they entered the strange and exotic Kingdom of Muli. This isolated realm of Buddhist tribesmen greatly feared and avoided any contact with China. When a Chinese general sent a messenger to inquire of the presence of gold in the rivers, the wild mountain people of Muli cut off the ambassador's ears and left him on a barren plain to die by the side of the trail. Despite the fierceness of these people, the Roosevelts were feted by their King at a dinner where Kermit and TR Jr. reciprocated by offering him a cigar and cherry brandy along with a flashlight, travelling-chair and the gift of a .410 shotgun.

The common folk were not the only violent residents of the regions they passed through. At a mission station in Tatsienlu even the lamas displayed a degree of bloodthirstiness. When Kermit inquired if any trinkets were available for sale, a lama displayed bowls made from human skulls and trumpets fashioned from human thigh bones. A local Magistrate, just for petty offences, would execute the offender by firing squad or drowning.

Though dangerous, this region did prove promising for the expedition's hunting interests. After a long stalk in the snow, TR Jr. managed to shoot two burrhel rams with Jack Young harvesting an interesting squirrel and an assortment of birds. When passing through a heavily wooded mountain valley, local natives informed Kermit of a troupe of monkeys in the area. After splitting-up and following a long skulk through thick brush, TR Jr. spotted some movement in the branches above; a yellow shape. Firing offhand, TR Jr. hit his mark and following a heavy crash through the trees and thud he knew he had something unusual. Almost immediately after, Kermit began firing and when the smoke and dust settled, the brothers managed to harvest a collection of nine golden monkeys for the museum; providing the only complete museum group setting of this species in the world.

Within the next two days, the expedition entered a dense bamboo forest where the bamboo stalks grew six to eight feet tall. This habitat was ideal for their main quarry, the Giant Panda, and before long they began to notice signs of the animal. The fabled elusiveness of this animal was well founded. Even within its own environs the Giant Panda seemed a rarity. In search of this strange creature, the hunters struggled in very rough, dense country in temperatures that transformed the creek beds to ice. Arriving into camp after dark and empty handed, TR Jr. noted, *"Altogether it was the hardest day's hunting I had ever spent."*[17] Despite their use of dogs and supposedly experienced trackers, the next day of toil also produced failure. With the discouragement and frustration associated with the hard hunting, the native trackers resorted to the use of mysticism based upon the dubious killing of a panda ten years before. Although they doubted the effectiveness of superstition and magic, Kermit and TR Jr. humored the tracker's beliefs.

The successful hunter had been cooking pig's bones a decade earlier when the unlucky panda wandered into view, hence the belief this might work again. Now, when the cooked pig's bones failed this time, they blamed it on spirits with the assumption they hunted on a bad day: *"a day the hunting gods did not like,"*[18] according to the native trackers. Another failure resulted when the trackers erected a small temporary altar to appease the angered deities. This ended the mysticism.

The next plan was to use dogs and focus on hunting takin instead of panda. Once again, the Roosevelt's began the exhausting bushwhack through the almost impenetrably thick jungle. After six fruitless days of backbreaking work and encountering no game whatsoever, the brothers decided to move on to new country, hoping to improve their luck.

❖

As they travelled through the highlands of central China, they once again were threatened with marauding bandits. The hill towns were rife with outlaws forcing the local authorities to apply draconian measures; a local placard warned: *"All proved bandits must have their heads cut off without trial."*[19] While travelling through Yachow Jack Young saw three being executed,

> *"It is a sad commentary on conditions that at the same time three high-school boys, ranging from sixteen to nineteen, were shot because they had been making speeches against the fiscal exactions of the local soldiery, levied under the guise of anticipated taxes."*[20]

In the 1920s justice was harsh and deadly in the wilderness regions of China.

As the expedition traveled into Lololand[21] (in southwest China), spirits heightened with reports of the panda's existence nearby. The Lolo's believed the Giant Panda was a supernatural being and had come into contact with them on a number of occasions. As the panda was perceived to be a spirit, they were reluctant to kill the animal themselves but agreed to accompany the expedition as porters and guides. With ten Lolos and their dogs, Kermit and TR Jr. began the panda pursuit anew. Much to their disappointment, the dogs began to run a sounder of swine. Rather than deflate the enthusiasm of the Lolos, they decided to join the pig hunt. In rain and sleet, over hill and dale they forged on even to clambering down the drop of a forty-foot waterfall while disregarding sprains and bruises and a potential broken neck. All was for naught as the dogs lost the track. Another failed day as they returned to camp.

The next few days were an unsuccessful slog through desolate jungle covered mountains as rain and snow pelted the expedition. Passing through various villages the hunters changed Lolo guides and doubted the questionable recommendations of village elders in regard to the possibility of encountering the giant panda.

On the 13th of April, Kermit and TR Jr., along with four Lolo guides encountered tree scrapes and the recent tracks of a large panda in the snow. After dismounting their ponies they began tracking the animal on foot through a bamboo forest:

*"The fallen logs were slippery with snow and ice.
The bamboo jungle proved a particularly unpleasant
form of obstacle course, where many of the feathery
tops were weighted down by snow and frozen fast in
the ground."*[22]

Tracking the animal for two and a half hours and
soaked through to the skin and shivering, the hunters
came upon a giant spruce tree with a hollowed bole.
Emerging from the hole was the prize the Roosevelt's had
planned and hoped for after spending many hard days,
travelling around the world and traversing many miles of
uncharted wilderness. For a period of time, they began to
question if the large black and white apparition before
them actually existed. *"And now he appeared much larger
than life with his white head with black spectacles, his
black collar and white saddle."*[23] Both brothers fired
simultaneously as the animal, groggy from sleep and
unaware of the imminent danger, began to skulk away.
Although wounded, the panda bounded away but only
covered seventy-five yards before falling to their bullets.

Celebrations reigned high that night after the arduous
task of hauling the heavy bulk of their trophy back to the
village. A slaughtered sheep was ordered for everyone and
Kermit and Ted mixed a hot toddy from their flask of
brandy for a toast as the natives downed prodigious
quantities of corn wine. Concern for the spirit gods
precluded the shikaries from touching any of the skinned
panda carcasses. So great was the religious worry that a
priest was summoned to cleanse the house and
surrounding area where the panda lay.

Despite having taken a great and extremely rare trophy,
the Roosevelts were up the next morning anxious to
continue on the hunt with the takin[24] as their quarry. After
fruitless days in search of this elusive animal, they
reluctantly moved on leaving the remote and hostile
Lololand as perhaps the first white men to ever venture
into their realm.

❖

Upon completing their trip at the railhead at Yunnanfu
in southern China, Kermit began receiving urgent
telegrams to return to the United States immediately. His
wife Belle was ill and business issues required his

immediate attention. On May 8, he started for Haiphong in French Indochina (Annam). He travelled through Kwang Ngai and Hue before reaching Saigon where he left on May 17th as the remainder of the expedition began to explore what is now called Viet Nam. Prior to Kermit's unexpected return to the States, the Roosevelts planned to rejoin the Annam portion of the expediton on the Mekong River.

Herbert Stevens separated from the Roosevelts in Likiang and continued alone collecting through Yunnan and Szechwan. His collection numbered around five-hundred specimens. Harold Coolidge, Russell Hendee, Josselyn Van Tyne and Ralph E. Wheeler continued on a separate expedition in Annam and Laos. On the 14th of May, Hendee started down the Mekong and shortly after developed a serious fever and on June 6 died in a hospital in Vientiane.

The expeditions of Kermit and TR Jr. into the wild and remote regions of the Himalayas, Burma and central China along with the scientific team in Annam were remarkable for their acquisition of strange and little-known animals which added to the collections of major museums and man's knowledge of the zoological world. But also for their logistics and traditional method of travel in a manner that in a short period of time would become quaintly obsolete as the 20th century progressed with air travel and advances in radio communications. During their almost five-months of travel on the 1928-29 expedition, the Roosevelts covered two thousand miles of travel by horseback, foot and boat without the aid of detailed maps, wireless radio or satellite navigation. They traversed high mountain ranges and exposed themselves to possible bandit attack on many occasions. Within a short period following their trip, some of these remote sections of Burma, China and Annam would be contested ground between the British and American forces with the Japanese in the Second World War.

*Hunting the tawny feline in mountain snows and jungle heat*

While on one of his business trips to Japan, Kermit decided to spend a three-week sojourn in the mountains of North Korea. At that time, the Korean peninsula was a primitive and isolated region, ruled by the Japanese

Empire. In December 1922 he decided to hunt one of the largest, most elusive and rare of the big cat species, the Siberian or Manchurian Tiger.25 The Korean Tiger Kermit pursued is larger than his lowland cousin and wears a heavier coat of fur to enable survival in harsh mountain terrain. At that time, they were in profusion in Korea and greatly feared as having a reputation for frequently devouring the local peasantry. However, as all wild cats are solitary and elusive, the Korean Tiger's mountain habitat made it especially difficult to locate and hunt. Despite tramping numerous miles on foot and mountain-pony and scaling snow covered peaks ranging up to six-thousand feet, the only game his party secured was wild boar. During the adventure, Kermit and his party suffered from the harsh conditions. On one occasion he commented:

*"We climbed up six thousand feet, part all but perpendicular, over rocks and solid sheets of ice. When we reached the top we were puffing and panting at furnace heat, but two minutes facing the icy wind that whipped over the ridge set us shivering, and we plunged down through the deep snow that on the other side had taken the place of ice."*26

Although failing in the opportunity to collect a fine specimen, he experienced an age old primitive way of life in a land that would soon become one of the most isolated and troublesome regions in the world. In a few short years following the Korean War, this land would suffer not only the demise of the tiger but would also be sealed to the outside world.

In 1923 Kermit again decided to try his luck on a tiger hunt and this time with his wife Belle in the Mysore State of India. India at that time was still in colonial thrall to the British Empire and managed under the British Raj in the spirit of Rudyard Kipling. Traditional hunting in the princely states was still legal and in vogue; the age-old exotic pukka lifestyle still evident. Today in India, all animal species are held in high religious reverence and sport hunting is outlawed throughout the country. Game animals abounded then and the Indian Tiger was still fairly common.  Kermit and Belle were the guests of a well-heeled American industrialist friend of his and were shown every courtesy by the local officials during their stay.  Days would be spent roaming the lush and exotic forests on the Mysore plateau as evenings were spent in congenial banter following a sumptuous Indian dinner.

The Roosevelts daily technique was to still hunt and stalk which required a quiet, stealth movement through the jungle in the hope of stumbling upon a cat or they would alternately conduct a drive by the local peasants as the hunters remained stationary.  To mount a drive, the plan was to enlist a numerous contingent of natives formed into a line and move forward while shouting, banging drums, pans and any loud utensil as the hunters were strategically placed in trees or machans on elevated platforms ahead of the line of march.  The shikarries (experienced Indian hunting guides) were placed on the flanks of the line preventing the tiger from breaking out and scrambling beyond the line of natives.  This method would drive all game toward the posted shooters including any tiger wandering about in the neighborhood.  The stalking method, conducted on the ground was perhaps the most difficult and dangerous for the hunters although the elevated position of the machan provided greater visibility and a greater degree of safety for the shooter.  Concern for the exposure of the native beaters on the ground naturally was of scant consideration.

Although Kermit believed that cats never looked up, on one occasion a tiger stood under Belle's tree and looked straight up at her at an angle that precluded her taking an effective shot.  While perched in their elevated stands, Kermit and Belle marveled at the diversity and antics of the wildlife.  Hawks, and owls and jungle fowl and peacocks preceded the beaters:  *"These last were a most beautiful sight as they flew past, their tails spread, their gorgeous plumage blazing in the sun."*[27]

After many fruitless drives, Kermit finally wounded a large tigress that required him to track a mile and a half before the natives came upon her body.  As is typical when hunting with indigenous people everywhere, the tiger kill caused a commotion among the natives.  *"Our village friends were wildly excited.  They lashed the tigress to a pole and formed a triumphal procession shouting and singing and beating their drums.*"[28] Care was taken to ensure the locals would not steal the whiskers and claws for use in native medicines. Besides tiger, the hunters successfully pursued guar, black buck and sambur. During their hunt, Belle was able to bag a leopard. She even shot a fifteen-foot long python that when skinned; they discovered the snake had engorged a spotted deer doe.

In November 1925 upon returning from the previously described high mountains for ovis poli and securing a wildlife collection for the Field Museum, Kermit and Tr. Jr. accompanied by their wives decided to hunt in Nepal. During their years of marriage to the two Roosevelts, both women had become avid adventurers and fairly skilled shooters who also shared a love for wild places. After many shooting and sightseeing trips throughout India, at the invitation of the Maharaja, Belle and Eleanor met the brothers in Kashmir and travelled to one of the Terai valleys of Nepal for a tiger hunt. Living accommodations were similar to that of an African safari: sleeping and dining tents clustered around a large log fire for mitigation of the evening chill. Although encircled by huge snow covered mountain ranges, the valleys were enshrouded in high, dense jungle that precluded any chance of hunting on foot.

Unlike the Indian method of hunting tiger from elevated stands as long lines of beaters would drive game to the stationary shooters, in Nepal Elephant transport was the only possibility for forging through the near impenetrable tangle of growth. Live bait would be staked at numerous locations throughout the surrounding jungle at night and checked in the early morning for a recent kill. Much of the excitement of hunting from the back of an elephant was simply the ride itself:

> *"The long line of elephants in solemn procession
> were a source of never-failing joy. There was always
> their preposterous conformation to ponder over; the
> enormous flapping ears and the ridiculous minute
> inquiring eyes; the strange toothless leer of the
> tuskless ones; the great loose knees which turned
> outward with a baggy shuffle and the delightful
> incredible toe-nails. The whole massive an otherwise
> dignified creature."*[29]

143

When a recent kill was located, the hunters would change their mounts from being perched on a pachyderm seated on a pad for travel to another equipped with a howdah, a wicker basket for hunting which provided a higher measure of safety for the hunter should a tiger attempt to charge and jump the back of the beast. The transfer to the howdah was an adventure in itself. According to Belle,

> *"Once arrived at the kill we descended from the pads and mounted our howdahs, even with our elephant kneeling. The best method of egress was a flying leap through the air from pad to howdah elephant."*

Although even-tempered and used to the hunting routine, an elephant would occasionally spook and charge off with mahout (the native elephant driver) and hunter hanging on as the beast rampaged through the undergrowth. On one occasion Eleanor's elephant was charged on all sides by an angered tigress with four cubs. Her mount dashed off into the jungle with the startled riders clutching desperately on their precarious perch; four elephants hastily pursued and secured the frightened beast.

During their week-long tiger hunt in Nepal, the Roosevelts bag was eleven tigers with Belle also taking a rhinoceros. Although the existence of both of these animals are now very endangered and even then were known to be diminishing, the Roosevelts believed, as TR did two decades before, that as they were collecting for a museum, the killing was for the advancement of science. The morality of their belief based upon today's ethics must be decided by the reader.

During Christmas week Kermit and Ted decided on collecting fauna in what Kermit termed as "Mowgli Land." They were joined by a Goanese collector for the Bombay Natural History Society. The experienced Baptista had collected mammals and birds through much of India, Assam and Nepal. On this trip, Kermit shot another tiger measuring nine-feet, eight inches. During their short stay, Kermit managed to collect both a black buck and two chinkara for the museum. Chinkara is a small and graceful Indian gazelle.

One of the most exciting segments of their Asian journey was when Kermit and Ted decided to try their hand and horsemanship with the traditional British-India sport of pig sticking. Both experienced horseman, Kermit and Ted well realized the great danger to both rider and horse in attempting to skewer a large wild boar with a seven-foot long spear while riding hell for leather on a fleet horse. Over hill and dale, through brush and jungle the brothers rode with their British Army companions. On one headlong chase *"Ted's horse came down twice; once it threw him into the middle of a thorn-bush, and he came up looking like a prize-fighter at the end of a stiff battle.*[30] Whilst on the chase, one of the event's organizers, a Captain Head, released his spear into a boar on the run. As the beast tore loose from the weapon, it glanced up pinning Head's leg to the horse and toppling both resulting in serious injury to rider and death to his mount. Although neither Kermit or Ted succeeded in skewering a pig, both *"... had some grand gallops and enjoyed our time to the full."*[31]

As the son of an ex-president, embarking on numerous and varied expeditions and hunting trips, Kermit along with his various companions were treated as VIP's in every foreign land he visited. Even when traveling to remote and uncharted regions the local officials, whether Indian Maharajas, British Army Officers, diplomats on station or local tribal chiefs; all would provide the best in credentials, advice and accommodations. His main problems were always those which any who decides to engage in rough, dangerous travel confront: inconvenience, probable hardship, hostile locals, harsh environment and aggressive animals. However, his prime years when in the bush inured him to what most travelers would consider unacceptable misadventure. As Kermit related in the opening of his fine little book "The Long Trail":

*"...it is when men are off in the wilds that they show themselves as they really are. As in the case with the majority of proverbs there is much truth in it, for without the minor comforts of life to smooth things down, and with even the elemental necessities more or less problematical, the inner man has an unusual*

*opportunity of showing himself – and he is not always attractive."*

Unfortunately, the weight of this axiom, which Kermit so well understood defined his "inner man" later in life, and when not "off in the wilds" he became the very characterization of the man he defined as "not always attractive."

Notes:
1. East of the Sun and West of the Moon, 1926, pg. 1; Theodore Roosevelt and Kermit Roosevelt
2. Kermit became good friends with both Andrews and his wife Yvette and in 1924 became godfather to her son, Kevin Maxwell Andrews. Belle and Kermit Roosevelt Papers, Library of Congress
3. "There are great numbers of all kinds of wild beasts; among others, wild sheep of great size, whose horns are good six palms in length. From these horns the shepherds make great bowls to eat from, and they use the horns also to enclose folds for their cattle at night." The Travels of Marco Polo
4. East of the Sun and West of the Moon, 1926, pg. 3; Theodore Roosevelt and Kermit Roosevelt
5. In the 1930s, C. Sydam Cutting was the second westerner to reach the Forbidden City of Lhasa in Tibet, which was long off-limits to outsiders. While in Tibet he developed a friendship with the 13th Dalai Lama and acquired a pair of Lhasa Apso dogs. He is credited with introducing the Lhasa Apso, a Tibetan breed of dog to the United States. In later years he built the Hamilton Kennels in New Jersey and propagated those which he acquired in Tibet. The American Kennel Club recorded its first Lhasa Apso, "Empress of Kokonor" in 1935
6. Ibid. pg. 28; Cherry already began his collecting responsibilities for the Field Museum during their sea passage through the Red Sea where he shot four different species of hawk from the decks of their ship
7. East of the Sun and West of the Moon, 1926, pg. 8; Theodore Roosevelt and Kermit Roosevelt
8. Ibid. pg. 56
9. The Hindu or Muslim system of sexual segregation by using a screen or curtain to keep women in seclusion
10. East of the Sun and West of the Moon, 1926, pg's. 40 and 41; Theodore Roosevelt and Kermit Roosevelt
11. Ibid., pg. 88
12. Ibid., pg. 232
13. Courtesy of the Chicago Field Museum of Natural History
14. AMPHIBIANS AND REPTILES of the JAMES SIMPSON-ROOSEVELT ASIATIC EXPEDITION by Karl P. Schmitd, 1926, pg. 167, Field Museum of Natural History

15. Trailing the Giant Panda, 1929, pg. 30; Theodore Roosevelt and Kermit Roosevelt. The Kachin were a primitive, warlike indigenous people living in northern Burma
16. Ibid., pg. 56
17. Ibid., pg. 178
18. Ibid., pg. 180
19. Ibid., pg. 188
20. Ibid., pg. 189
21. Expedition News, June 2003 – Volume Ten, Number Six. Lololand is the home of the Lolo tribe. "Lolo' was a pejorative Han Chinese term meaning 'barbarian' because of their primitive lifestyle and social hierarchy. The Lolos lived in the vast unmapped territory in southwestern China known as Lololand. Today the Lolos call themselves Nuosu and are under the blanket term of Yi with six other ethnic minority groups in the region. Aside from the Lolos reputation as fierce, barbaric and capable warriors, the Lolos had a caste system in place that revolved around the practice of slavery." Kermit and TR Jr. described the Lolos as being similar to American Indians: "Wild-looking fellows with their black turbans and great capes. One mountaineer had his hair cut in a scalp-lock like an American Indian."
22. Trailing the Giant Panda, 1929, pg. 223; Theodore Roosevelt and Kermit Roosevelt.
23. Ibid., pg. 225
24. Takin: a rare horned mammal in the family Bovidae. The Takin, weighing up to 700 pounds wears a heavy coat of fur and is on the endangered species list. The Takin is thought to be the origin of the mythological "golden fleece."
25. The Korean Tiger is now extinct on the peninsula having disappeared in the first half of the 20th Century. However, biologists believe the species may still survive in small numbers across the border in China.
26. Cleared for Strange Ports, 1927, page 56; Kermit Roosevelt and family members.
27. Ibid., pg. 158 Kermit's observation.
28. Ibid., pg. 178
29. Ibid., pg. 229. "FROM THE LAND WHERE THE ELEPHANTS ARE" by Belle Willard Roosevelt.

30. Ibid., pg. 215
31. Ibid., pg. 216

# Chapter VIII- Returning to Combat; World War II

*Back to the Army again, sergeant,*
*Back to the Army again.*
*'Ow did I learn to do right-about-turn?*
*I'm back to the Army again!*

*"Back to the Army Again" Rudyard Kipling*

The decade of the 1930s was an extremely unstable period for America and the industrialized nations across Europe. With much of the Western World mired in economic depression and job loss, many people began to question the efficacy of the capitalist system and democratic principles were increasingly being blamed for the troubles – people were looking for leadership that didn't seem to exist. Not surprisingly, faltering economies based upon free market exchange began to turn a growing number of people inward or towards radical forms of government. To some, communism appeared to offer solutions, with fascism rising as a counterbalance. Even nature seemed to work against the interests of Americans as much of the Midwest farming regions turned into massive dustbowls and coupled with manufacturing loss in the east forced mass migrations of people to relocate while abandoning family homesteads and the familiarity and security of their birthplaces.

As many nations were in a continual state of economic and social decline, one nation in Europe was energized by a charismatic leader who headed a political party that offered hope and salvation. The rise of the National Socialist or Nazi Party and its leader, Adolph Hitler mesmerized the German population and began a massive industrial and military buildup, all in contradiction with previously mandated strictures imposed by the victors of the Great War. Following the devastation of Europe at the end of the First World War, the victorious allied nations with the firm expectation of ensuring that Germany would never rise militarily again to threaten the world order, forced a set of rigid requirements on Germany at the Treaty of Versailles. A mandated loss of industry and industrial territory, payment of reparations, a severe reduction in military capability and reduced borders within a demilitarized zone along with a loss of overseas colonies all were designed to render Germany a broken and benign power.

The instability of the Depression and the severe economic condition of Germany in the early 1930s enabled Hitler to gain political traction with both the masses and the industrial and political leaders in the country. The fear of communism, the scapegoating of Germany's Jewish population and the German citizen's hope for a better life provided Hitler and his Nazis the opportunity to gain high political office and create a total dictatorship. During the early to mid 1930s as Hitler consolidated his strangle-hold on the government, he began to rebuild Germany's industrial infrastructure and rearm her military, all in violation of the treaty commitments that were codified two decades earlier. An economically troubled and war-weary Europe which suffered the loss of four and a half million of its population in the Great War benignly looked on and was simply unable to respond to the growing threat. The great powers of Europe became helpless as the German Reich invaded Austria, forced the cession of the Sudetenland and finally, the occupation of the rest of Czechoslovakia. The change in Europe's pusillanimous, idle posture began on September 1, 1939 when Germany's war machine invaded Poland. On September 3, Britain and France declared war on Germany and the Second World War began.

The United States, still struggling with the debilitating effects of the Depression, looked on with disinterest. President Franklin D. Roosevelt, realizing the precarious position of Britain, began to recognize the potential threat to the free world if Nazi aggression, allied with Italy and Russia, was permitted to spread across Europe and defeat the U.S.'s former allies. However, the American people, always apprehensive of Europe's ageless, internecine warfare and still mindful of the slaughter of the recent "war to end all wars" were adamantly opposed to any U. S. involvement. Despite the opposition from those overwhelmingly supportive of neutrality, FDR worked behind the scenes to assist his new friend, Winston Churchill, and his beleaguered island nation. The United States would not formally enter the war until the bombing of Pearl Harbor by the Japanese on December 7, 1941.

Kermit, ever the warrior, hastened once again to enter the fray as the only Oyster Bay Roosevelt at that time sympathetic with FDR's concerns. Despite his advancing age, growing marital problems and alcohol abuse, he was determined to join a combat unit and fight Germans as the United States stood idly by. In September 1939 Kermit met with his friend, Winston Churchill who was then First Lord of the Admiralty and requested a commission in a machinegun corp: *"being willing, if necessary to give up his United States nationality in order to be able to fight against Germany."*[1] Churchill thought that this offer of service by a prominent American was one which should be accepted, and he understood from the Secretary of State for War, that the necessary arrangements had been made. The deal, approved by the King, was to commission Kermit as a Second Lieutenant in the Army with immediate promotion to the rank of acting Major.[2] In December Kermit was assigned to the Machine Gun Training Center with the Middlesex regiment at Mill Hill.

❖

In August 1939 on the cusp of the German invasion into Poland, Germany and Russia signed a non-aggression pact and secretly developed plans to carve-up eastern Europe. Russia, in her alliance with Germany, albeit distrustful of her intentions, began to strengthen her borders but the strategic location of Finland in the northeast lay only twenty miles from the outskirts of the City of Leningrad. To secure her northern flank, Russia demanded concessions which the Finnish Government rejected. On November 30, the Russians attacked along the Finnish frontier and simultaneously bombed Helsinki, the capital of Finland. For many weeks the Finns pummeled the Russian Army, inflicting terrible carnage on the overconfident Russian troops who were unprepared for the intense cold and snow of this Winter War. However, despite heavy Russian losses the Finns were greatly outnumbered and after numerous engagements began to be overcome with fatigue and run short on ammunition.

The world stood by in horror during this violent invasion by a huge, belligerent nation of a small and valiant country, even the isolationist American people were shocked by the violence. As the tragedy was unfolding, the British were working behind the scenes to aid the Finnish forces. Prime Minister Neville Chamberlin wrote to French Premier M. Daladier pressing his government to send help to the Finns as the British High Command began to plan for an international force of volunteers to aid the Finnish resistance. As of February, the Finnish Air force had received 52 of some 400 aircraft promised by the British and more were arriving at a rate of five to eight a day.[3] Anti-aircraft guns and munitions were also being supplied. Kermit suggested to the British that they invoke the support of FDR. At a meeting of the War Cabinet the British High Command noted: *"As, however, there is a good deal of unfriendliness between the Democratic and Republican sections of the Roosevelt family, this was thought to be not adviseable."*[4]

The British, concerned with maintaining the appearance of neutrality in the conflict established a shadowy, unofficial organization named the Finnish Aid Bureau under the direction of an equally mysterious individual named Harold Gibson. The Bureau was a recruitment and management agency for an international force of volunteers that would assist the Finnish resistance. The concept of the international force was a throwback to the multi-national group of volunteers who fought in the Spanish Civil War in 1938. To ensure anonymity, the British Government opposed any active military personnel serving in the volunteer force. Eager to see action, Kermit, with the aid of Churchill lobbied for command of a combat unit and the Finnish volunteer force was decided upon. The British High Command initially balked at assigning Kermit to lead the force. Such an appointment might be regarded in the United States as an attempt by the British to involve that country in the war. Despite the haggling over political concerns, Kermit was finally cleared to command the unit. However, to maintain the appearance of a civilian volunteer force, Kermit had to resign his newly appointed army commission with the Middlesex Regiment. The idea of a new adventure that could renew his self-respect and redeem him in the eyes of his family was a great boost to Kermit's morale – in his eyes the operation would be a *"crusade."* He later commented for the London Times₅: *"I felt that in fighting for the Finns I should be ranging myself against the O.G.P.U. (Russian secret service, forerunner of the KGB) and the Gestopo and all the forces which are troubling the world today."* On February 4, 1940, Kermit made a lengthy radio broadcast against Germany to the British people on the B.B.C. stating the necessity to mount a *"...modern Crusade to save Finland."*

The plan was to ship fifty volunteers a week for a total unit size of approximately five-hundred fighters along with field guns and 30,000 rounds of ammunition. However, fate intervened and Kermit's pursuit of redemption and glory in battle evaporated. Before departing with the first contingent of volunteers, Kermit's ill health gained control, and he was forced to enter the hospital rather than begin execution of the ill fated operation. During the early months of 1940, Kermit lived in a state of constant, extreme pain. On February 2 he left the hospital in London to spend a one week leave with Belle at the Ritz. She arrived in England and attempted to nurse him to health in the London hotel where he received a constant round of doctors and dentists along with occasional nurse care. Belle was frantic at his weakened condition and vainly attempted to nurse him and constrain him from his obsession with pursuing a combat role in the war.

On some occasions he was unable to leave his bed. In her diary*[24] she recorded:

> *"Up all night – really frightened – doctor came about eleven – took charge but left me alone with very sick man from 11:30 to 3 o'clock – no medicine – could not keep father in bed – with difficulty and anguish kept him from going out – lovely day nurse finally arrived with doctor when I had about exhausted all strength and arguments."*

---

24 *Following this period Belle sent their son, Kermit Jr. a copy of her diary in letter form while in England with Kermit from February 1, 1940 to April 30, 1940. The diary (with others of the period) now resides in the Library of Congress in Washington DC in the Belle and Kermit Roosevelt Collection.

Then *"...good case of flu with probable pneumonia."* To add to Kermit's ongoing misery he was suffering from bad teeth. On March 12: *"Drained abscess continually but couldn't remove tooth. Pieces of bone coming off. Kermit lived in much pain. Poison in blood."* On March 19: *"Kermit had dysentery."* March 29: *"Doctor found a spreptecarcus* (sic) *in K's. intestines."*

Despite his numerous and dreadful ailments, Kermit still had enormous vitality to endure pain and spring back. On March 7, after resigning his commission with the British, he was sworn into the Finnish Army. However, at fifty-one he was clearly beyond any condition for war making let alone overall command of the volunteer force. Having overruled Kermit's stubbornness towards military service, the Finnish volunteer operation continued with a new commander and over the next few months became an embarrassment to the British Government as none of the volunteers saw action. On March 13, 1940, the exhausted Finns closed a peace agreement with the Soviets and capitulated to Russia ending hostilities. The hundreds of volunteer fighters that shipped to Finland without Kermit never fired a shot. Some returned to England, some remained, and the whereabouts of others were never recorded as the entire shadowy campaign became a failed footnote to the dramatic conflict that followed across Europe.

Following a short recuperative stay in a London hospital, Kermit once again stubbornly set his sights on a combat role and began to angle for command of a fighting unit; he just would not recognize that his days of martial glory had passed. He obsessed with the desire to enter the war in a combat role and used every contact he knew in England, from royalty to the Prime Minister. The Roosevelts engaged in a hectic round of social activity: Belle dining with royalty including Winston Churchill while Kermit played golf, visited London clubs, and shot pheasant as he campaigned with military officers for a command. In April he reapplied to the British Army, and on the 22nd, he met with Lt. Colonel C. McVean Gubbins of the Royal Artillery. Gubbins was a career military officer, a war hero in World War I, an author, linguist and military strategist. He commanded a group of special assault troops that later became the famed British Commandos.

Kermit immediately developed a liking and trust in him. In his new assignment, Belle recorded in her diary, Kermit would,

> *"Laison between Norwegians and* (the) *War Office – very important setup – taking wireless equipment and wireless men – two lots going, as Gubbins indicated."*

The mission was classified Top Secret.

In the spring of 1940 the German High Command became concerned that the Norwegian port of Narvik, critical for the shipment of iron ore from Sweden was in jeopardy. Additionally, Germany, gaining command of the sea bordering Norway, would undermine the Allied blockade of Germany. Coincidently, both Germany and the British arrived at the same strategic conclusion at the same time as German troops landed on Norwegian soil. The British began a coastal mine-laying operation. A series of naval engagements ensued with German landing operations at Narvik following a British evacuation under heavy air attack. The campaign occurred at the beginning of April and ended on June, 10 with Germany prevailing. On April 25th Kermit, in anticipation of serving in the extreme conditions of cold and snow in Norway left for Scotland to work with polar experts Andrew Crofts and Quintin Riley. He eventually reached Narvik and distinguished himself assisting in the evacuation under heavy German bombing and strafing runs.

By the end of June Kermit was once again back in England and high and dry in his pursuit of combat, writing to Belle: *"This looking for something to do is hard work, always being asked for advice and then doing nothing to do oneself."*[6] His luck and influence with the British War Office once again landed him a trip to the Middle East with the Middlesex Regiment. However, the assignment was more of a tedious exercise in boredom than an opportunity to gain valor while engaging the enemy. Writing[7] to his friend and former commando from Norway, polar explorer and military officer, Lt. Cdr. Quintin Theodore Petroc Molesworth Riley:

*"That's a long trip out* (to Egypt) *by way of the Cape, six to seven weeks with one port of call. It was interesting in the desert, but the Italians just didn't have any fight in them. I thought surely we'd hear from them around Massawa where they had destroyers, submarines and airplanes, but although we had forty four hundred troops packed like sardines aboard our ship, we never saw an Italian.*

*"On patrol it was the same way; you could never get in more than a couple of bursts before they legged it."*

The idleness and lack of action began to wear on Kermit and he turned to drink to pass the time. Adding to his deteriorating situation, dysentery began to trouble him: *"I had bad luck in having two attacks of dysentery, one quite severe – the head surgeon died in the bunk next mine; but I'm all right now.* The combination of his physical ailments and excessive drinking resulted in his being recalled to England and mustered out of the military.

Notes-

1  Declassified Top Secret record of the British National Archive; Conclusions of a Meeting of the War Cabinet held at 10 Downing Street, held on Tuesday, September 19, 1939.
2  Ibid., Saturday, September 23, 1939.
3  Ibid., February 9, 1940.
4  Ibid., date unknown by author and not recorded in British Archives.
5  The Times, March 4, 1940; "British Volunteers for Finland – Mr. K. Roosevelt in Command.
6  Letter, Kermit to Belle dated 28 June, 1940; Belle and Kermit Roosevelt Collection, Library of Congress
7  Letter dated 23 February, 1941; Kermit Roosevelt to Lt. Cdr. Quintin Theodore Petroc Molesworth Riley in the Liddell Hart Center for Military Archives, King's College, London

# CHAPTER IX- DEƒCENT INTO OBLIVION

*WHENEVER Richard Cory went down town'*
*We people on the pavement looked at him:*
*He was a gentleman from sole to crown,*
*Clean favored, and imperially slim.*

*So on we worked, and waited for the light,*
*And went without the meat, and cursed the bread;*
*And Richard Cory, one calm summer night,*
*Went home and put a bullet through his head.*

*From "Richard Cory" by Edwin Arlington Robinson*

Kermit's upbringing instilled in him a fascination with literature and languages, an overwhelming urge to pursue adventure in uncharted foreign lands and perhaps above all, the need to engage in war. Unlike his father, who needed to prove his manliness and patriotism to absolve the family name of what TR considered the disgrace of his father's avoidance of combat in the Civil War, Kermit's obsession with continuing in military service was more complex.

War meant adventure, an absolute patriotic duty but also the vehicle to maintain his self respect. Knowing that his lifelong predilection towards substance abuse had broken his mother's heart and imposed untoward hardship on his family, he believed useful military service could be a redeeming endeavor. However, as he approached middle age, the debilitating attacks of malaria and the numerous bruises and scrapes from his careless life coupled with the years of physical abuse sustained from alcohol and drugs diminished his once robust physical constitution to that of a walking skeleton. His once wiry and tough frame now was being reduced at middle age to a bloated hulk constrained by weak and spindly arms and legs. Gone was the stamina in frame and strength of character. This failure coupled with his substance abuse began a cycle of descent that destroyed his self-image and self-respect.

In the fall of 1939, hoping to regain his shattered sense of self, although physically unfit, Kermit once again enlisted in the British Army as he had during the Great War.  Belle gained a degree of relief and hope by believing Kermit's entry in the war and separation from his old haunts and wayward lifestyle would enable him to recover.

At the end of 1940, Kermit was a virtual physical and mental wreck since his return to England from military service in the Middle East with the British Army.  Besides alcoholism, he developed an addiction to paraldehyde, a drug used by those suffering from severe, acute alcoholic intoxication.  An enlarged liver, dental problems and recurrent bouts of malaria and various other diseases added to his anxiety and suffering.  Kermit continually struggled with the realization of his total breakdown and incapacity.  His physical and mental deterioration was exacerbated by his inability to pursue his lifelong desire to engage in adventure and for a Roosevelt, serving in war with valor was the ultimate.  But yet, as many who are afflicted with substance abuse, he was unable to escape its dreadful grasp and continued with his destructive lifestyle.  His natural tendency for periodic bouts of melancholia was heightened by drugs and alcohol and contributed to his feelings of failure in the war.

As the specter of America's entry into the war loomed large, in June 1940 frustrated with America marking time as Nazism marched across Europe and perhaps to further ingratiate himself with his influential cousin Franklin, he broke a long-standing tradition of the Oyster Bay Roosevelts and wrote to FDR from England and asked his assistance to change his party affiliation from Republican to Democrat.  He argued against the *"Republican isolationist party"* in favor of joining the *"aggressive Democrats."*  However, this wasn't the first time Kermit had imposed upon his cousin for a favor.  While with the International Merchant Marine Company in 1933 as his business interests faltered, he asked FDR to have the Congress influence British shipping companies to repay $11,000,000 he claimed was owed the company writing: *"...we possess a very real nuisance value which can be exerted against the British shipping interests...."*[1]

Unlike the rest of his siblings, Kermit and Belle were the only family members to maintain a friendly relationship with FDR and Eleanor. In fact, Belle maintained a very close and tender relationship with both FDR and Eleanor throughout their lives. She would visit the White House many times, bestowing little gifts that buoyed the enormously challenged wartime President: bottles of Scotch and Rye from her father's stock, a cocktail shaker for Christmas and small knickknacks for his study. Basically, Kermit was apolitical and unlike his brother Ted Jr. never displayed any interest in carrying on the family legacy of politics. During an interview with historian, Joseph P. Lash, Kermit Jr. commented: "*My father was the only one of TR's sons who never expressed himself publically on any political issue.*"₂ The rift between the Oyster Bay Republicans and the Hyde Park Roosevelt Democrats with the exception of Kermit and Belle became very venomous through the years dating back to the 1920s as TR Jr. pursued and failed in politics as his cousin FDR gained success. The ongoing battle became hateful during the 1930s when TR Jr. and Alice, both conservative Republicans, publically accused the liberal FDR of attempting to turn the country toward Socialism with his New Deal policies. Both began campaigning across the country against the President, his administration and his growing resistance toward the increasingly aggressive Nazi regime. TR Jr. even became prominent in the America First movement in stern opposition to any U. S. involvement in the growing European War. Sharp-witted Alice maintained a spiteful, critical attitude toward FDR (whom years before she derisively called a feather duster) and Eleanor for the rest of her long life. Following the war, brother Archie became an extreme conservative speaking out publically against the liberal policies near and dear to his Hudson River cousins, even joining the John Birch Society. Kermit and Belle's friendship with the White House even began to cause a degree of friction with TR Jr. Although resisting FDR in every way possible, the entire Oyster Bay Roosevelt clan, including the aged Edith, immediately did an about-face in support of the war effort following the attack on Pearl Harbor when many of the family, as they did in the Great War, began pulling strings and volunteering to enter the fray in uniform.

As the war progressed, with American involvement in 1941, TR Jr. would serve with distinction as a field-grade officer under Patton. Archie would also gain military honors as an Army officer in the Pacific. In comparison to the former martial competition with his brothers in the Great War, Kermit's feelings of inadequacy became overwhelming and uncontrollable and simply added to the solace he gained in a bottle of alcohol.

By the end of 1940, Captain Kermit Roosevelt had returned to England and in May 1941 he was discharged from the British Army for health reasons. Not willing to be cashiered out of both the military and the war, in desperation he personally appealed to his friend, Prime Minister Winston Churchill; his efforts were in vain. After reviewing Kermit's condition, Churchill agreed with the army's medical report, and Kermit was forced to withdraw from the military and return to the United States where he entered a hospital for treatment of his numerous ailments.

Earlier in the 1930s, as Kermit's depression induced descent into alcoholism and drug addiction continued to grow, his roving eye for the opposite sex settled on a mysterious woman named Herta Peters*[25], and they began a not so concealed relationship. Upon returning from Europe, he rekindled his illicit relationship with Peters adding to his mounting problems. Although Kermit had flings with many shady women in the past, Peters became a continuous companion if not obsession. His ongoing philandering with Peters rocked his marriage with Belle. Although very distraught and aware of his affair, Belle continued to maintain appearances and discretely ignored her husband's infidelity, feeling impassionedly that their many years together were worth saving. Belle even went so far as to maintain a communication3 with Peters:

> *"At first Belle denied what was happening. Then she became obsessed with preserving appearances. Finding out who Peters was, Belle invited her to their apartment and introduced her as 'a family friend.'"*

---

25 *In the excellent study of the Roosevelt children, "The Lion's Pride" by Edward J. Renehan Jr., he records Kermit's mistress as named Carla Peters. However, "The Louis Nichols Official and Confidential File and the Clyde Tolson Personal File" within the Confidential Files of the Federal Bureau of Investigation cite her name as Herta Peters.

*Kermit with wife Belle. In early middle age Kermit is clearly showing signs of bloat and fleshy face; indications of his hard living. Note what appears to be a missing thumb on his left hand.*

Kermit characteristically adopted a nonchalant attitude and continued with the illicit affair and began even rooming on and off with Peters. During these difficult times, Belle continued living in denial while maintaining the hope that Kermit's infidelity was only a temporary affair, even writing to FDR's private secretary, Marguerite "Missy" LeHand in March 1941 that she had received *"lovely batches of letters from Kermit this last week."*₄ This was one of the many desperate letters she wrote to FDR informing him of Kermit's deteriorating condition and requests for help.

Despite his busy schedule and overwhelming focus on war preparation, FDR was determined to use his influence to aid his faltering cousin. He searched for a safe occupation for Kermit in a remote region removed from the negative influences of his party life and end his potential for creating a family scandal in public.

Belle and FDR were not alone in searching for a solution to the unraveling of Kermit's life; his old friend, Vincent Astor, also became involved. In early July 1941, at the behest of FDR, his friend and senior aide, General Edwin M. Watson directed Assistant Chief of Staff, General Sherman Miles to find an isolated and benign job for Kermit, with the goal of stationing Kermit out of sight and out of mind where he could engage in no mischief. Frustrated with attempting to corral and dry-out Kermit, Miles informed Watson:

> *"Commander Astor concurs with me in believing that there is nothing more to be done in this case short of using actual force, and that there is no hope of getting him fit to travel as long as his woman retains her hold on him."*₅

Watson's orders to Miles were:

> *"Have Kermit Roosevelt come to Washington Friday, work him at G-2 reading maps and studying country, have Walter Reed do dentistry and have a squad put him on a boat."*

This last order implied the use of force if necessary. Miles responded with a suitably exiled location: *"He will be doing work for our government especially in the veld region of South Africa with the consent of local authorities."* When this bogus assignment apparently fell through, FDR wrote in desperation to F. Trubee Davison, former President of the American Museum of Natural History, requesting a favor. He asked Davison if while in South Africa Kermit could *"...assist your work and indicate to him a mission or line of investigation you would like him to cover."*[6]

Kermit didn't make it to Africa and wasn't even aware of his cousin's scheming but was forced to undergo a thorough physical examination the following month. While in the hospital, his excuse to the examining neuropsychiatrist for his drug addiction was that he used drugs frequently for the withdrawal of alcohol. Results of the physical recorded that *"his movements were uncoordinated and he spoke in a confused manner, saying that he had been drinking excessively because of a return of an old dysentery."*

In July 1941 Kermit went missing and FDR and Astor, at the frantic concerns of Belle, enlisted the services of the FBI through Director J. Edgar Hoover to assign federal agents to locate Kermit. The agents found Kermit in New York, apparently living with Peters. Trouble over Kermit's lifestyle was not the only concern. During war time, the companion of the President's philandering cousin, also a nationally known figure raised questions about Peter's background and the potential for her being an enemy agent. The FBI continued to maintain an on-again, off-again surveillance of both Kermit and Peters throughout the month of July and maintained an open file on his whereabouts through September. Watson became frustrated with acting as a coordinator between the White House and the FBI although his intercession was necessary to avoid having FDR continually involved with Kermit's escapades. He also resented using government resources for what he believed was nurse-maiding Kermit, noting *"I know he's worthless – the fellow, and it makes me sick at the stomach"* notifying his boss, FDR, *"Vincent says things are going about as bad as possible with Kermit."*[7]

The simple fact is that aside from familial loyalty, Kermit's aberrant behavior could have been a great embarrassment to the administration by feeding FDR's many detractors with juicy gossip. And during war time, Kermit, who was a close relative and confidant to the President as well as a nationally known figure and former military officer, could pose a threat to national security, a far descent from his failed patriotic intentions.

As the months wore on Kermit would disappear for periods of time as Belle, Astor and a friend, Major Head would go on a frantic search for him. On one occasion Miles had a Colonel Winslow follow him. Following Kermit's intermittent disappearances and resurfacings, he ended up in a hospital at the Air Force Replacement Training Center in Santa Ana, California, after absconding to the west coast with Peters. A letter sent to the President on April 9, 1942, from military physician, Russell V. Lee, stated:

> *"I am writing you at the request of Mr. Kermit Roosevelt, who desires that you be given an estimate of his physical condition at the present time with view of him qualifying for a commission in the Army. I find his condition now very much better that I have ever found it, and I believe that he is now able to pass the army physical examination, I truly believe that our principal problem is now solved and will not recur again."*

This optimism was ill-placed despite Kermit's desire to convince his cousin of improvement and ability to serve in uniform.

The evasive nature of Kermit's wanderings stymied the bureaucratic efforts of the government to keep track of his whereabouts and on April 30, a Lt. Col. M. D. Taylor wrote to Lee, questioning Kermit's location. He once again had a backslide and in late April his brother Archie signed him into the Hartford Retreat in Connecticut for one year, a sanitarium where he could not leave on his own volition. He was even denied the use of a telephone. Archie wrote to FDR *"K. is in the Hartford Retreat under voluntary commitment, with a court order in case he tries to get out within four months."* After a four-month detoxification in Connecticut, Kermit's condition appeared to bounce back to normalcy to a degree where he was released and his cousin arranged for a commission in the army. He was ordered to active duty as a Major, effective July 15, 1942, and assigned to Fort Richardson, Alaska; out of sight and hopefully, out of mind. Although Alaska was attacked by Japanese planes at Dutch Harbor that same month, Alaska was still a faraway backwater for any military assignment.

The expectation by the White House was that his duty as a garrison soldier outside of Anchorage would enable him to maintain his sobriety and ensure the end of his scandalous threat to the family and the President. Upon reporting for duty on July 29, Major Kermit Roosevelt was assigned as Assistant Chief of Staff in Operations. His driving urge to engage with a combat unit was stifled by his desk job, so he unofficially hitched rides on reconnaissance flights and maintained a friendship and fleeting involvement with Major Marvin "Muktuk" Marston, who was organizing a tundra army of Eskimos to guard the eastern coast of Alaska. However, desire a fighting role as he may, he was denied any official combat duty.

On December 2 he was reassigned to staff work in the G-2 intelligence section at Fort Richardson. Later stated: *"His duties included procuring, compiling and recording information for the 'Alaska Digest'. Such duties necessitated pursuit of information work."* The Alaska Digest was *"a compendium on the economic, geographic and political aspects of Alaska"*.[8] According to testimony given on June 9 during the investigation following Kermit's death, from January 25, 1943 to February 20, 1943 he was in the base hospital receiving treatment for hemorrhage. His diagnosis was *"secondary anemia moderately severe due to intestinal bleeding of unknown cause."*[9] Following six blood transfusions for massive blood loss, he was transferred to Barnes General Hospital in Vancouver, Washington, where he underwent extensive testing and had some dental work attended. He complained his current illness began on January 19 when he first noticed dark reddish stools and increasing weakness and dizziness. Later he was too weak to rise from his bed. While at Barnes, he gave a past medical history of bacillary dysentery in 1912 and 1922, Asiatic cholera in 1931, amebic dysentery in 1939, 1940 and 1941 while serving in the British Army and malaria on several occasions.

Despite Kermit's distant isolation, concern was still evinced from the White House. On March 18 FDR sent a memorandum to Watson stating he *"thinks it would be a fatal mistake to assign K. to the United States and I am inclined to recommend Hawaii."*[10] Kermit's frame of mind at this time was clearly troubled.

167

While at Barnes, Kermit was informed that he was virtually under arrest. He called the White House and requested a Court Martial to clarify his position. Fearing a public scandal, General Watson then placed a call to the hospital administration permitting his release. On April 17 he was declared "clinically cured" and "general condition good" by the Barnes medical staff and on April 20 he received orders from the War Department returning him to full duty. However, confusion clearly abounded in regard to Kermit's condition and suitability for service. No mention is made in any of his medical records at Barnes for this period of any abnormal mental state or any alcoholism or any requirement for detoxification. In fact, he was released for return to his former duty station. However, the record indicates that by this time he was persona non grata at Fort Richardson. On April 24 the War Department in Washington received a radio message from Headquarters, Fort Richardson stating: *"...he is considered physically unfit to be again subjected to Asaskan* (sic) *Service and it is requested that he not be reassigned to duty (Sgd. Whittaker DECOM ADC) in this command."*[11]

Records indicate he returned to Alaska on April 23. However, on April 29 an incoming message from Fort Richardson to the War Department stated Kermit was awaiting transportation back to Alaska. A May 11 message from Fort Richardson informed that Kermit was still in Seattle and once again requested that he not be *"summoned to service in Alaska."* No reason was given for these rejections by the Alaska command of Kermit continuing duty in Alaska. This request was overruled by the Secretary of War and on May 18 he arrived at Fort Richardson. On the 20th of May he was back at the post hospital complaining of *"having a hard shaking chill"* which was attributed to his history of malarial infection. A June 2 letter from Camp Roberts in California to Barnes requests *"...present status of officer"* and claims, *"To date Major Roosevelt has not reported at this station."* A response from Barnes: *"Letter orders dated April 3, 1943 were received at this General Hospital from the Adjutant General, directing Major Kermit Roosevelt, 0-188985, Infantry, to report to another station."* Interestingly, this transmittal was sent on June 10, six days following his death!  Ongoing confusion clearly abounds within the military as to his whereabouts during this period and astonishing misinformation about his condition.

The official inquiry claims that in the early morning hours of June 4, 1943, Kermit arrived back at his billet in a drunken state and killed himself.  However, much confusion, inconsistency and omission exist in the official record about the manner and time of his death.  The technical details of his supposed suicide also raises questions along with the conduct and thoroughness of the general investigation.

Notes:

1. From copy in Kermit Roosevelt military file, National Archives.
2. Joseph P. Lash interview, 1/18/67. Ibid.
3. The Roosevelts, an American Saga, by Peter Collier with David
   Horowitz pg. 382
4. Letter dated March 14, 1941; Belle to FDR; FDR Library.
5. Memo dated July 29, 1941; General Sherman Miles to General Edwin M. Watson. Ibid.
6. Letter dated July 21, 1941; General Edwin M. Watson to F. Trubee Davison. Ibid.
7. Memo dated August 27, 1941; General Edwin M. Watson to FDR. Ibid.
8. Testimony of Lt. Col. Walter F. Choinski, taken at Fort Richardson
   Alaska, June 9, 1943; letter residing in Kermit's military file at the National Archives.
9. Kermit Roosevelt military file at the National Archives.
10. Incoming message; War Department Classified Message Center; Ibid.
11. Ibid.

# CHAPTER X - A SPECULATION ON HUMAN TRAGEDY

*O God, my God, where'er Thou art,*
*Keep my beloved in Thy Heart*
*Fold in thy Heart that head so bright*
*Heal him with Thy most gentle light*
*And since Thou mad'st forgetfulness*
*Forget what'er Thou find'st amiss*
*And since Thou mad'st remembering*
*Remember every lovely thing,*
*And then my God look down and see,*
*And pityingly remember me.*

Kermit's epitaph; June 4, 1943
Fort Richardson, Alaska
By his mother, Edith Roosevelt

The loss of her second son, Kermit, was a severe blow to the frail Edith in her eighty-second year. Although the family sheltered her in every way possible, she was always aware of his frailties and potential for self destruction since he was a youngster. Edith went to her grave five years after Kermit, never knowing the true story of his death, having been led to believe a failed heart as the cause. In fact, the government and the family concealed the official nature of his death from the public for decades.

The pattern of his slow, self-destructive decline was not new to the Roosevelt family, nor would Kermit be the last. Earlier members of the Roosevelt clan also lived a life of calamitous conduct. The potential for him growing into manhood and developing a disturbing, troubled life was recognized early on by both Theodore and Edith and weighted heavily on them. As a youngster Kermit was a brooding and frequently melancholy boy. His was an introspective, solitary soul who was the opposite of the large gaggle of noisy children in the Roosevelt household. While playing in the roughhouse environment of the family, his siblings would pursue every challenge and attack every game with gleeful energy with Kermit also participating but

171

in an ambivalent and laidback manner. As his mother's favorite, he would be considered somewhat of a "mama's boy" today, making him more of an outcast among the other children.

When his father was in the White House and Kermit was a young student at Groton, he developed an interest in an obscure, down and out poet named Edwin Arlington Robinson. The poem by Robinson that initially captured Kermit's interest was a maudlin piece named "The Children of the Night" with opening lines that begin:

> For those that never know the light,
> The darkness is a sullen thing;
> And they, the Children of the Night,
> Seem lost in Fortune's winnowing.
> But some are strong and some are weak, --
> And there's the story. House and home
> Are shut from countless hearts that seek
> World-refuge that will never come.

Aside from the poem appealing to Kermit's dark, brooding nature, perhaps he sensed a kindred spirit in Robinson. For a portion of his life, Robinson was a failure who sank into poverty and alcoholism and at one time was reported to be suicidal. When Kermit showed the poem to the President and pestered him to assist Robinson, his father was so impressed with Robinson's work that he arranged a sinecure for the unemployed poet at the U.S. Customs House in New York City. With Roosevelt's support, his career was energized, and he eventually received three Pulitzer Awards and published twenty-eight books of poetry during the remainder of his life.

As Kermit was growing up, deep disturbing emotional problems loomed within the Roosevelt family. In 1896, cousin James West Roosevelt, a physician, was suffering from alcohol and drug addiction and died at the young age of 38. However, the death of Theodore's younger brother and Eleanor Roosevelt's father, Elliot, in 1894 brought the horrors of substance abuse much closer to home. Eerily similar to his nephew Kermit, Elliot was a precocious, bright youngster; the leader of the pack of his young siblings who loved books and had an interest in nature. Early on he was considered to become the most successful of the Roosevelt children. He excelled in athletics and when older enjoyed playing polo, riding to the hounds and the adventure of traveling to far off lands for big game hunting. He was gregarious and socially popular, although lurking below the surface were feelings of anxiety, self doubt and melancholy that as a youngster would manifest in a series of peculiar physical illnesses. He would eventually become obsessed by the perceived competition with his brother, Theodore - as his brother's star was on the assent, Elliot's was in decline. As his brother attended Harvard College, began to excel in politics and even became a published author, Elliot was incapable of even entering college. His life seemed to have set a similar pattern for the way Kermit's would evolve and then decline.

Like Kermit, he developed a taste for alcohol at a young age. In August, 1880 while still young men, Elliot and Theodore traveled to the west on a hunting trip as Elliot began displaying his growing taste for alcohol. In a letter to his sister, Corrine, Theodore humorously commented:

*"As soon as we got here he took some ale to get the dust out of his throat; then a milk punch because he was thirsty; a mint julep because it was hot; a brandy smash to 'keep the cold out of his stomach'; and then sherry and bitters to give him an appetite. He took a very simple dinner – soup, fish, salmi de grouse, sweetbread, mutton, venison, corn, macaroni, various vegetables and some puddings and pies, together with beer, later claret and in the evening handygaff."*[1]

Although familiar and concerned with Elliot's physical and emotional problems, the family did not yet realize his insidiously growing dependence on drink. However, within a few short years this would change. Just prior to his early death at age 34, Theodore commented that Elliot *"...had been drinking whole bottles of anisette and green mint, besides whole bottles of raw brandy and champagne, sometimes half a dozen a morning."*[2]

Elliot's decline would be astonishingly fast. As he matured he became a bon vivant and world traveler, always gracious to anyone who would share a drink and carouse with him. Hunting tigers in India or hobnobbing with British Army officers and royalty in England seemed to represent his prime interests and consumed much of his life. Assuming responsibility with the challenge of settling down with his wife and growing family, securing a job and conforming to a degree of respectability were beyond his reach. His deep seated feelings of doubt and general uselessness were satiated by drink which only compounded his emotional decline. Threatening suicide, he spent time in and out of sanatoriums. Adding to this he began cavorting with various women and would disappear for periods of time, abandoning his wife and children. Bouts of drunken stupor interspersed with periods of delusion occupied the shadowy life he shared with his last mistress, a woman named Katy Mann. Elliot's philandering escapades with Mann became a major crisis for the family when she claimed to have borne his illegitimate child and demanded a ransom to keep the disgrace concealed.

Compounding his misery and feelings of guilt, at the end of 1892, his wife Anna died of diphtheria and son, Elliot Jr. died of scarlet fever a few months later. Little ten-year old Eleanor who idolized her father was perhaps the most heartbreaking victim of Elliot's decline. She was shuttled between family members, sustaining a lifelong emotional wound resulting from her father's continued absences and his destructive behavior. Unwilling to rehabilitate himself and spiraling down into a drunken madness, he died in a derelict state on August 14, 1894, following a seizure.

Even Kermit's father displayed signs of a depressive disorder, albeit without any resort to alcohol or drug usage. Contrary to his brother Elliot, Theodore attacked his demons by incessant action. Certainly, the loss of his mother and wife, both on the same day, must have evoked an enormous reaction which no doubt affected him for the remainder of his life. Following the death of his beloved Alice Lee, he shunned his newborn daughter Alice and relegated her care to his sister Bamie. Following the tragic loss, he recorded that the light has gone from his life and he withdrew to the western Badlands to sooth his shattered emotions; never again mentioning Alice Lee's name. However, aside from his boisterous demeanor,

Theodore Roosevelt did show signs also of having a predisposition for melancholia for much of his life.

Some theorize that Theodore's manic personality was a subconscious response to keeping his natural anxiety at bay. Hence, his famous comment: *"Black care rarely sits behind a rider whose pace is fast enough."* Perhaps conquering the struggles of his own overwhelming emotions by shear willpower and activity while witnessing how idleness combined with substance abuse affected his brother reinforced Theodore's lifelong penchant for being a teetotaler. This strong disdain for any usage of alcohol even incited him to sue in court and win the case with a newspaper editor who slandered him in print as being an alcoholic.

Kermit's lifelong problems within the next generation of Roosevelts seemed to have followed his Uncle Elliot's in close order. Kermit was a world traveler who enjoyed many of the same activities as Elliot: hunting, the unusual and unique features each discovered in people and places around the world and both had an eye for the ladies. Elliot was an outward and gregarious personality, addicted to social carousing so was Kermit, but both harbored an inner emptiness that continually depressed their personalities. Each for a period of time seemed to find solace in alcohol and drugs and both sacrificed their families to their uncontrollable lifestyle. In the end, both ended their own lives at a relatively young age; Elliot by alcohol poisoning and Kermit by gunshot.

However, Kermit's succumbing to the demons that led to his death did not end the emotional problems within the Roosevelt lineage. Kermit's youngest child, Dirck, born in 1925 began to show signs of emotional distress at an early age, similar to Kermit's Uncle Elliot. Dirck displayed signs of trouble when unable to cope with his entry to Groton, writing home after just arriving, *"Groton disappoints me greatly."*3 Unable to get on with the other students and address his studies, he withdrew from the normal socializing at the school and began to display a bizarre conduct. In one well publicized event in 1938 which the New York Times characterized as "Dirck Roosevelt Goes Adventuring," he and another student ran away from school, initiating an eight-state, law-enforcement hunt that ended a few days later in Baltimore. While on the lam, the police located a note left by 13-year old Dirck stating *"If a man feels it necessary to take his own life, should he be condemned?"*[4] During this period, his father's life was totally distracted with his own problems of drinking sprees and on again, off again departures with his mistress.

In 1943 Dirck was inducted into the service where he spent much time in military hospitals with severe emotional problems. Following the war, he attended Oxford University and then knocked around Europe, continuing to exhibit eccentric mannerisms. When in Spain he was arrested for a homosexual pass at a man that earned him expulsion from that country. After returning to the United States and leading a confused and pointless life, Dirck eventually committed suicide at his mother's house in 1953.

Admittedly, it is somewhat presumptuous for an author to attempt the dissection of someone's character and inner motivations. Our life's conduct is influenced by many factors: heredity, environment, education, upbringing, etc. and besides, attitudes and standards of morality change over time making the speculation of a complex person, living in a different era exceedingly imperfect. For example, even into the 1950s, topics such as divorce and illegitimacy were considered taboo and not openly discussed in polite society. If an acquaintance or member of the extended family was divorced from their spouse or bore an illegitimate child, they were at once the source of hushed rumor and innuendo, hence, Elliot's imposition of disgrace on the Roosevelt family. In the twenty-first century, divorce is so commonplace, along with common law relationships that casual living arrangements in the United States between non-wed couples threaten to exceed those who are lawfully married and more and more births are occurring out of wedlock – all taken in stride by modern society. In today's culture, excessive drinking is looked upon by many as a disease, not necessarily a character flaw. Use of tobacco today is shunned whereas in previous generations, smoking and drinking were socially acceptable and even considered to be fashionable. Conversely, non-smoking teetotalers like Theodore Roosevelt were rare during Kermit's upbringing. So, social mores are an ever changing set of concepts that are culturally dependent upon time and place with personal motivations frequently being an imponderable. However, the challenge of looking back upon a person's history and speculating on motivation must be pursued in order to consider the possibilities of why and how events unfolded and naturally to satisfy the devoted investigator's curiosity.

So what, if anything, can be concluded from Kermit's story of lifelong depression and alcohol abuse ending in a wayward life style and ultimate suicide? Was it based on an inherited character trait within his family line, an aberrant segment of DNA or just the palliative effect of alcohol and drugs soothing a fragile and sensitive personality? Or was it the inverse where a depressive nature becomes dependent on the alcohol and drugs? When a depressive nature is coupled with substance abuse, determining the degree to which one may initiate the other is a difficult, hazardous and perhaps impossible task to define with any expectation of accuracy.

Although much is yet to be learned, many researchers seem to generally agree on the causes of substance abuse. Some, such as the U.S. Department of Health and Human Services, claim the risk for developing alcoholism does run in families and that genetics within a family line partially explain the malady with lifestyle also being a factor. Others theorize that stress can play a role in excessive drinking, others speak of social influences. In Russia where alcoholism has always been extraordinarily high, the problem is attributed to both historical and cultural causes. Statistically, alcoholics have the highest rate of suicide.

Perhaps Kermit's combination of dreaminess and intellectual isolation as a youngster with his disregard for physical safety were contributing factors. His life-long depressive tendencies may have been satiated with alcohol ultimately leading to dependency. Over time, this may have begun a self-destructive physical and psychological cycle that on the one hand, where alcohol consumption quelled his misery and on the other undermined his stamina and physical capabilities leading to helplessness. Clearly he had a famous reputation to uphold as expressed by his lifelong competition with his brothers in their war time exploits and the near mythic stature of his father to emulate, hence his acts of derring-do.

In later life, the more he attempted to redeem himself in battle, the greater the realization of his physical inability that would lead to increased alcohol consumption and then again feed the cycle of physical degradation. Unlike his family and friends, the supportive relationship with Peters was one of unquestioning, non-judgmental acceptance and may have provided a modicum of relief as feelings of uselessness took hold as the family's living standard diminished. As previously stated, his spiral of decline closely patterned that of his uncle Elliot. The severe psychological trap of loneliness, shame, guilt, hopelessness and helplessness may have convinced him that death was the only way out.

*Another perspective*[26]-

A detailed analysis of all of the government documents pertaining to Kermit's last duty assignment in Alaska and the circumstances of his death defined therein raise many unsettling questions. There are inconsistencies in the testimony and omissions in the investigation. The final official circumstances and manner of his death sound somewhat improbable and raises questions of suspicion; did he commit suicide or was he the victim of some sinister plot? The following are troubling points to consider.

Autopsy:

The results of the official autopsy report, conducted by the post surgeon at Fort Richardson's 183rd Station Hospital in Alaska were completed on June 4, 1943, 3.00 PM; the afternoon following his demise. The Clinical Diagnosis stated:

> *"Wound, gunshot, head, perforating, caliber unknown, entrance through soft palate, exit through the parietal bone, course through the posterior pharynx upward through the condylar portion of*

---

26 *The following narrative is based upon 633 pages of documents contained in Kermit Roosevelt's military file acquired by the author from the National Archives. The file was closed to the public and only declassified in 1959, sixteen years following his death and even in 2010 was very difficult to obtain. Despite repeated requests to the National Archives by the author the government still resisted disclosure and only responded after the author enlisted the help of Congressman John Hall.

*occipital bone, perforating the medulla and occipital lobe of brain on left.*

The report continued: *Wound, perforating, through condylar portion of occipital bone and in posterior region of parietal bone near mid-line.* The findings stated the time of death at 11:30 AM and noted:

*There is a ragged perforating wound in mid-line of soft palate extending through the upper posterior pharynx which easily admits a surgical instrument 1 ½ centimeters in diameter. Just in the mid-line in the posterior parietal region there is a ragged wound 2 centimeters in diameter.*

The report also states: *"The right thumb has been amputated at the 1st interphalangeal joint"*. A thumb was amputated from Kermit's hand in the 1920s resulting from radium poisoning acquired when he was treated for an earlier infection.

However, an earlier clinical abstract from the Fort Richardson post hospital stated the left thumb was amputated (read amputation issue under item 3 of Provost

*A .45 caliber army service pistol of the type used in Kermit's death.*

Marshall report following). The report claims Kermit was inebriated at the time of his death stating *"Blood alcohol studies on postmortem blood revealed 2.5 mgm. per cc. alcohol."*

The stated size of the wound channel *"that easily admits a surgical instrument 1 ½ centimeters in diameter"* and a *"ragged wound 2 centimeters in diameter"* raises a question. The official investigation report lists a .45 caliber service pistol as the suicide weapon. The military .45 used 230 grain ball ammunition with a diameter of .452 inches. A 2 centimeter hole is .8 inches in diameter, 56 percent larger. Even a 1 ½ centimeter hole is .6 of an inch. The standard .45 full metal jacketed round will acquire very little expansion upon impact, even when hitting a surface much more dense than soft tissue and thin bone.

However, if a non-military soft point bullet was used it would expand considerably more than .452 with the little resistance presented by the soft tissue in Kermit's head.

The size of the wound in regard to the stated suicide weapon is questionable unless civilian ammunition was used, a type which is outlawed for military use and one which is unlikely that Kermit had access. So why such an extensive wound channel? Additionally, no mention is made of any gun residue which should have been in profusion within Kermit's mouth and within the wound channel, and why and how was the autopsy report completed a mere three and a half hours following his stated death?

*Death Certificate:*
The Territory of Alaska Death Certificate lists the name entry for the deceased's father and mother as *"Unknown"* despite the form requiring *"Every item, carefully supplied."* Clearly, as Kermit was the ex-President's son, the sitting President's cousin and a national figure in his own right, why was his parentage listed as "unknown?"

*Synopsis Report of the Official Investigation:*
On June 4 an official investigation of the cause(s) of Kermit's death began and included the testimony taken from witnesses by Claims Officer Colonel Morris R. Moore who was ordered to head the investigation through the Inspector General's Office.

Curiously, the investigation report places the time of death at approximately 8 AM, which is in conflict with the autopsy report statement of 11:30 AM. The findings of the investigation were as follows:

*"Although intoxication was a contributing cause it was not the proximate cause. At the time of and just prior to his death the deceased was suffering from an abnormal mental condition which was caused by worry over ill health and the frustration of his desire for active field duties, which rendered him not susceptible to ordinary human motives or appreciations of right or wrong and incapable of the normal control of his actions, and is considered to be as a result of military service."*

According to the synopsis of testimony prepared by Moore, at 12:40 PM on June 4, the body of Kermit was found on his bed;

*"All evidence indicated that he had shot himself with a .45 caliber automatic pistol which was clasped in his hands at the time the body was found. There were no indications of foul play or that there had been a struggle in the room or that robbery was a motive as no valuables had been taken."*

The testimony synopsis went on to state:

*"Due to worry over his physical condition and the fact that he was to be deprived of the opportunity to perform active field duties, the deceased at the time of and immediately prior to his death became mentally unbalanced to such an extent as to not realize the direct physical or moral consequence of his acts or having such realization was unable to refrain there from because of the derangement of the reasoning or volitionary faculties.*

*There were no facts available to the investigating officer from which to determine if the unsound mental condition existed prior to his entry into the service."*

Nothing in Kermit's medical reports for the year leading up to his death indicate any mental problems. Despite his multiple hospital stays, no psychological examination was administered. Additionally, the findings of the official investigation including the motive for his death were written by a claims officer, not a medical doctor. During the investigation, a number of sworn witnesses testified to his mental stability as being normal in conflict with the official version with two exceptions (see Witness Testimony).

*The Medical Report*

Although the report was signed on June 5, only one day following the death and one day after the autopsy, the report states the caliber of the weapon was unknown despite the large size hole and the immediate opinion of the officers (including doctors) who found the body and who investigated the death scene  immediately after the discovery; all who claimed the caliber was .45.

The autopsy report claims the death occurred at 11:30 AM. Testimony of the investigating officers (including the official report) claim the death was at 8:00 AM- a three and a half hour discrepancy. One investigating officer, 1st Lt. Gordon D. Skeoch, a doctor who was Chief of Out Patients at the post hospital investigated the body shortly after 1:00 PM and stated: *"The body was cold with considerable rigor mortis giving evidence of having been dead several hours."* Rigor mortis characteristically begins about three hours following death. If the body was investigated by a doctor a mere hour and a half following the autopsy report of death at 11:30, why was the body cold with rigor mortis and why did others claim (including the official report) the death was at 8:00 AM in conflict with the autopsy report?

On June 9, five days following the death, a Captain R. S. Aronson, Chief of Laboratory Services at Barnes General Hospital in Vancouver notified Fort Richardson with a request for data: *"If an autopsy was done, we shall be, of course, greatly interested in receiving autopsy material for histologic examination in accordance with existing regulations."* When not receiving the report by November 13, five months later, Aronson sent another letter to the 183rd Station Hospital in Fort Richardson requesting: *"... two copies of a statement indicating the decision of the investigating officer as to the gunshot wound being accidental, suicidal or homicidal."*

It appears that there was a considerable delay in following established protocol in defining the details of Kermit's death to the authorized officials in Vancouver. Why a delay?

*Provost Marshal report:*
On June 4 the Fort Richardson Provost Marshal, Major Edmund Meagher produced a two-page report on the initial findings. In the report he states the death was by a .45 caliber bullet that was found:

*"in the pillow under his (Kermit's) head. A single ejected shell was found under the bureau about eight feet away. A Caliber 45, Model 1911 Colt service pistol, No. 95112 was found on his chest, muzzle pointing toward his chin. His right thumb was placed near the trigger. The fingers of the right hand were over the rear of the butt. The left hand was clasped over the barrel. The left thumb, which was near the ejection slot was stained with what is believed to be gunpowder."*

This report raises questions and considerable doubt on the feasibility of his statements. The assertion that his body was discovered with the pistol in his hands and the manner in which the report claims that the body grasped it is totally improbable and raises questions as to who actually fired the piece:

**#1** - A .45 caliber 1911 pistol is a very powerful handgun with a considerable recoil.

The gun generates 7.9 foot pounds of energy with a recoil velocity of 15 feet per second. A 30-30 hunting rifle is only slightly above in energy with 10.6 foot pounds and 9.5 feet per second in recoil velocity. The .45 has a recoil operated slide such that when fired, the slide will instantly slam rearward, ejecting the spent shell and then strip a fresh round of ammunition from the magazine into the chamber on its forward, spring actuated motion. This action releases much energy, such that many people find the pistol difficult to use. One reason the American military discontinued its use as the standard service sidearm in the 1980s, selecting the 9 millimeter instead is due to the recoil being less violent, hence more accurate bullet placement.

If Kermit used this weapon for suicide, would he still be clutching the weapon in the manner stated? Or more probably would the recoil energy have displaced the piece and been thrown out of his hands?

The author believes that considering the foregoing, he would no longer be grasping the gun post mortem in the manner (officially stated) as when he initially fired the weapon.

Furthermore, the report states the left thumb was located near the ejection slot with a possible gunpowder stain. If clutching the gun as described, his thumb probably would not be near the ejection slot. A test of the same type of pistol by the author indicated the ejection slot on the .45 does not emit any gunpowder residue.

**#2** - The various reports of the inquiry (as stated earlier) conflict as to which hand was missing his thumb. Available photographs of Kermit show his left hand containing a full thumb. In fact one photo where he is sitting down indicates a perhaps vainful attempt to consciously conceal his right hand below a table he is sitting near in the picture . The service .45 contains, as a safety feature, a grip safety along the back of the pistol's handle that requires the shooter to squeeze the gun's grip as he pulls the trigger. With a part (or all) of his thumb missing, this could/would indeed make firing the gun in the stated manner difficult but perhaps not impossible.

**#3** - The report claims the spent bullet was found in the pillow below his head. In testimony by another officer at the scene, the bullet was found on the pillow. In either case, finding the bullet so close to the body is improbable.

The .45 caliber, military ball ammunition will penetrate between 27 and 29 inches of ballistic gelatin. This bullet, supposedly penetrating only a few inches of soft tissue and a human skull (with an average thickness of only a quarter inch) would probably penetrate the two pillows, the bed, and possibly the wall behind the bed and perhaps other surfaces beyond the wall before expending all of its energy. Hence, the travel distance would be considerably longer than a few inches.

**#4** - The left thumb was stained with what appeared to be gunpowder according to the report. There is no mention if the residue was analyzed to determine just what it was. Perhaps dirt from Kermit's rambling around drunk the night before, if he was in fact drunk? For the gun to be fired as stated with the bullet's trajectory angling up into his pallet and skull, he probably would have to be holding the gun upside down and angled into his mouth.

Interestingly, nothing is mentioned in either the autopsy report or the investigation of any powder burns or residue on the inside of Kermit's mouth where it surely would be deposited in profusion if the gun muzzle was close by when fired. Considering the recoil of the .45, if the muzzle was in his mouth, the gun would no doubt have dislocated his front teeth. Even if close to his mouth, the muzzle blast would have a high probability of displacing his teeth. No mention is made in the autopsy of any dislocated teeth.

**#5** - In his report the Provost Marshall mentions that on a visit to Kermit's room the night of June 3 at 7:10 PM a Lt. Collins said he *"observed a bloody footprint in the middle of the floor and a spot on the pillow. It is assumed that the Major had suffered a hemorrhage."*

During sworn testimony Collins did not mention this nor did the Provost Marshall mention this in his testimony or state if the footprint remained the next day following discovery of the body.

No mention is made of any effort to analyze the footprint, if it existed, to see if it conforms to Kermit's shoe size or any analysis of the blood.

**#6** - The report states Kermit visited a civilian friend, Mr. Zack Loussac, off base the night before his death and that Loussac called a cab for an intoxicated Kermit and sent him home sometime after midnight. Loussac mentions nothing of this in his sworn testimony. Nor is he questioned about this.

*Official Investigation:*
The formal investigation of the suicide lasted four days and included the testimony of fifteen military personnel and two civilians. Seven "exhibits" were included: two letters, one transmitting the report, the other the report of death; the witness testimony; synopsis of testimony; a

medical form; autopsy report; duty status certificate and assignment certificate.

*Witness Testimony:*[27]*

Similar to the other aspects of the investigation, the paneling of witnesses was conducted in a slipshod manner. Important questions were not asked and conflicts in testimony surfaced which were not challenged. For example: Contrary to the report implying Kermit's mind was imbalanced, much testimony found no indication that he was not in full control of his actions. Additionally, testimony relating to his supposedly drunk condition on the morning of his death conflicts.

### Z. J. Loussac (civilian friend)-

Q. *"State what acquaintance you have had with him?"*

A. *"I first met Major Kermit Roosevelt about seven years ago when he was hunting in Alaska, and renewed our acquaintance about a year ago when he was sent here with the Armed forces. During the last year I have seen him on many occasions at my apartment as well as at the different homes in Anchorage. Upon his return from the Barnes Hospital he came up to my apartment. He was apparently in good spirits and fully recovered from his recent Illness. He seemed to be quite happy over a new assignment he expected."*

Q. *"What would you say as to his mental condition and do you know whether he used intoxicating liquor or narcotic drugs and if so, to what extent?"*

A. *"I know he did not use drugs. Before Major Roosevelt went to the hospital I saw him refuse to drink on many occasions either before or after dinner. After he came back and just recently, although he appeared to be perfectly sound mentally he was apparently brooding and I think he was drinking somewhat. I asked him why he was drinking and he said he thought it would help him to sleep."*

---

27 *Witness Testimony per the Report of Investigation of the Death of Major Kermit Roosevelt o-188985, dated June 4, 1943. Conducted by Lt. Col. Morris R. Moore, Inf., Claims Officer, Alaska Defense Command. File resides in the National Archives.

Q. *"Did you notice a bruise or dark spot on his cheek and if so state if you know what caused it?"*

A. *"Yes I noticed that on Wednesday and asked him what caused it and he said he stumbled against the closet."*

**Author Analysis**

This line of questioning does not jibe with the following testimony of the cabdriver, John Johnson, who supposedly shuttled Kermit from Loussac's residence on the morning of his death. Also, no mention of the bruised cheek is followed-up anywhere in the report. No mention is made in the inquiry (or in any record) of just what new assignment was expected by Kermit nor any indication of Kermit's possible mental illness by Loussac.

### John Johnson (driver for Special Cab in Anchorage)

Q. *"Did you bring an officer from Anchorage to Ft. Richardson, Alaska, the morning of Friday, June 4, 1943?"*

A. *"Yes. Mr. Loussac called and told me that he had a Major he wanted taken to Camp but he didn't tell me his name."*

Q. *"Just where did you pick this Major up?"*

A. *"In the Loussac apartments, on the second floor, in a closet. He had one shoe and his coat off."*

Q. *"What was the officer's condition when you picked him up?"*

A. *"He was so drunk he could hardly walk. Mr. Loussac and I had to help him from the $2^{nd}$ floor of the Loussac Building to the cab."*

Q. *"Was the Major able to talk?"*

A. *"Yes. The only thing he said to me was to ask how much he owed me."*

Q. *Did he appear to be just intoxicated, out of his mind, or just how did he act?"*

A. *"He acted serious but evidently knew what he was doing. But he was too drunk to walk."*

**Author Analysis**

Loussac was not questioned in a follow-up testimony about this visit from Kermit on the morning of his death, helping him to the cab or his being too drunk to walk, and Loussac neglected to mention any of this. Wouldn't he have volunteered this important information if Kermit was too drunk to walk? Why didn't Moore follow-up with additional questioning of Loussac considering the conflicting testimony of Johnson?

### Major Phillip H. Hoff, Inf, ADC, Censor

**Q.** *"Will you state what you know about the facts and circumstances surrounding his death including the dates etc.?"*

**A.** *"Major Kermit Roosevelt was assigned as Assistant, Assistant Chief of Staff, G-2, Alaska Defence Command, by General Order number 90, dated May 28, 1943. His duties included procuring, compiling and recording information for the 'Alaska Digest.' Such duties necessitated pursuit of information work.*

*Lt. Josiah Collins, Jr., and I called at Major Roosevelt's quarters, NCO building #167, Apt "F", at approximately 7:15 PM Thursday, June 3, 1943. Finding he was not at his quarters and wishing him to contact us, a note was left requesting he get in touch with G-2. This note was addressed to Major Roosevelt and signed by me said: 'Please contact G-2, 6/4/43 AM.' Pfc Woyton, on duty at G-2 the night of June 3-4, received a phone call from an individual who only indentified himself as a Major, at 6:00 AM, the morning of June 4, 1943. At approximately 12:50 PM on June 4, 1943, Lt. Collins and I again visited Major Roosevelt's quarters. On opening the door to his room a cursory look indicated the Major had suffered a nasal or other hemorrhage and was lying on the bed unconscious. The dispensary was immediately phoned and medical assistance requested. On the arrival of Lt. Gordon D. Shoeck, MC, we, for the first time, entered the room. Closer examination and discovery of the pistol partially covered by the deceased's hands indicated suicide. In response to call, Major Meagher, Post Provost Marshall, took charge. In subsequent search no note or announcement of intentions was found.*

*I had never met or spoken to Major Roosevelt. I first saw what was subsequently identified for me as Major Roosevelt when Lt. Collins and I opened the door of his room.*

### Author Analysis

Major Hoff said he left a note for Kermit to contact the G-2 Intelligence Section. As Kermit worked on classified data, it is interesting to consider why the investigation did not ask Hoff, the post censor why he wanted to contact

Kermit. A perhaps more important question is why Kermit, with all of his past problems was even trusted with a security clearance. Hoff claimed that a Pfc. Woyton received a mysterious phone call the night of 3-4 from an unidentified Major. No mention is made in the inquiry (or in any record) if the Pfc. was ever questioned or if any effort was made to determine the nature of the call.

### 1ˢᵗ Lt. Josiah Collins, Jr., Assistant G-2, ADC

Q. *"Were you acquainted with him (Major Roosevelt) and if so, state if you observed any indication of mental unsoundness?"*

A. *"I didn't know the Major very well. I met him several months ago and have seen him several times since just to speak to and have had a few short conversations with him. Since his return from the States I have only seen him twice. I saw nothing that would indicate an unsound mind."*

Q. *"Did you have occasion to visit Major Roosevelt's quarters Thursday June 3, 1943?"*

A. *"Yes. Major Hoff was acting for Lt. Colonel Choinski and wanted to meet him, but Major Roosevelt had not been in all morning and Major Hoff wondered if he was ill and if he had gone to the hospital. Major Hoff and I called Thursday evening about 7:15 and found that he was not in. His roommate in the next room, Lt. Powell, stated he had only seen the Major once and that he would give Major Roosevelt our message, which was to call G-2. Major Hoff also left a card on Major Roosevelt's bed to that effect. I noticed a spot of smeared blood about 8 inches long and a small spot on the pillow which I thought to be blood from a nose bleed."*

Q. *"When was your next visit?"*

A. *"Friday, right after lunch, about 12:45 PM, June 4, 1943. Major Hoff and I opened the door and noticed the Major apparently sleeping and that he had been bleeding. The blinds were down and the light wasn't very good, but we could make out that there was blood on the pillow and that he was apparently unconscious. We notified the Hospital that Major Roosevelt had apparently suffered a nasal hemorrhage. The doctor, Lt. Skeoch, arrived with a Sgt. about 15 or 20 minutes later. He immediately walked in and we noticed Major Roosevelt had a .45 cal automatic pistol in his hands which was almost hidden by the manner*

189

*in which he was holding it. The gun had been fired and was cocked. We later found the empty shell on the floor. He held the gun in both hands, firmly gripped. His right hand on the grip, and the left on the barrel. He was lying on his back with his hands and the gun on his chest. The blood had run out of his mouth and down on the pillow to the floor forming a large pool which we had not noticed when we opened the door before. Major Roosevelt was in his pajamas but the bed clothes were not thrown over him but were back towards the foot. We then called the Provost Marshal. Lt. Skeoch stated that the Major had been dead several hours. We searched the room for evidence of a motive. No note was found that would give any such clue. We found one unopened letter from Mrs. Edith K. Roosevelt, Oyster Bay, postmarded May 23, 1943, and 3 or 4 small containers which from the markings appeared to be sleeping or insomnia tablets. We also found some blinders which are used for keeping light out of the eyes when trying to sleep. We didn't touch the body or gun until Major Meagher, the Post Provost Marshal arrived. All indications pointed to suicide."*

### Author Analysis

The foregoing monolog is an interesting and curiously lengthy response to the simple question of "When was your next visit?" Rather than answering a short direct question, this sounds more like a prepared report. If this was an extemporaneous rant, the investigating officer neglected to cross-examine with many important questions and simply released the witness. For example, how did the witness know the gun was fired? Just because it was cocked? Why did Hoff and Collins not notice the large pool of blood on the floor when they initially entered the room? If Kermit's death was a suicide, why did he bother to dress in pajamas?

According to the report, Lt. Josiah Collins and Major Hoff were the first to discover Kermit's body, at approximately 12:50 according to Hoff and 12.45 according to Collins. Collins said he and Hoff searched the room for evidence of a motive:

*"No note was found that would give any clue. We found one unopened letter from Mrs. Edith K. Roosevelt, Oyster Bay, postmarked May 23, 1943,*

*and 3 or 4 small containers which from the markings appeared to be sleeping or insomnia tablet."*

A similar statement under oath was made by the Post Provost Marshal, Major Edmund A. Meagher: *"No note of his intentions was found."*

However, Captain Charles B. Ely claimed he did find a *"...handwritten document found in the possession of Major Kermit Roosevelt following his death."* Text of the note was as follows:

Respectfully request that charges
be preferred against me and a
court martial instituted in order
to clarify ~~the~~ my position with
regard to ~~my~~ the curtailment of my
regard to sick leave
~~being curtailed two week~~ immediately
my being/ordered back to
Barnes General Hospital where
I was informed that I
Was virtually under arrest.

(The strikethrough text is the author's way to indicate words that were crossed out in the text.)

The concern expressed in this statement is stale evidence and is in regard to his stay in the hospital weeks before his death and is unlikely a suicide note but rather a weeks old note that he sent to Washington. Why would Kermit leave a suicide note requesting a court martial? Why also would he request a court martial when Loussac claimed, *"He seemed to be quite happy over a new assignment he expected."* However, this may have been the military's excuse to imply Kermit's insanity and official justification for his suicide. The note was excluded from the official inquiry documents.

On the day of his death, a detailed Inventory of Effects was compiled listing many dozens of items ranging from books to cigars to clothing but no suicide note is mentioned.

In regard to a motive for suicide, the Provost Marshal's death notice claimed, *"No note of his intentions was found."*

On June 17 the Deputy Commander of Headquarters Alaska Defense Command in Seattle sent the note to Major General H. B. Lewis in the War Department, Washington stating in his letter:

> *"An examination of the effects brought to light the enclosed rough notes which appear important as they indicate a possible reason for his suicide.*
> *"I did not have these included in the effects because I know the War Department has been interested in this case from the beginning and more or less personally chaperoned him and ordered him back to Alaska over the objection of the Commanding General, Alaska Defense Command. In order, therefore, to avoid any unpleasant comment, I am forwarding them to you for such disposition as appears appropriate."*

The question must be raised; if Collins and Hoff searched the room for evidence and found none, how did the note from Kermit surface? Was it discovered later when his belongings were being inventoried prior to being sent to his next of kin? If so, this is a peculiar and un-dramatic way to express one's plan to suicide. Particularly when the alleged motive is old information and preceded a period of contentment and mental stability as indicated by his later discussions with Loussac.

Additionally, what Collins said they discovered in Kermit's room was a few bottles of sedatives, 1st Lt. Gordon D. Skeoch who assisted the Provost Marshal in searching Kermit's room said they found *"...no notes or evidence of any kind."* In response to a question of finding any alcohol or drugs, besides the sedatives, Skeoch said they found *"... 2 or 3 empty bottles* (of alcohol) *in the room..."* which Collins and Hoff did not mention, or find.

### 2nd Lt. Guy H. Johnson
Q. *"Did you live in the same quarters with him?"*
A. *"Yes. In the same quarters in the next room."*
Q. *"How often did you see Major Roosevelt in the week preceding his death?"*
A. *"About every morning – just to say hello however."*

Q. *"Did you notice anything that would indicate an unsound mind or abnormal mental condition?"*
A. *"No sir. I noticed nothing out of the way."*
Q. *"Did you see him the morning of Friday, June 4$^{th}$?"*
A. *"Yes sir. Just to say hello."*
Q. *"What time?"*
A. *"About 7:15. I met him in the aisle on his way to the toilet."*
Q. *"Did he appear to be intoxicated?"*
A. *"No sir and I would have been close enough to him to smell whiskey if he had had any."*
Q. *"What about his physical condition?"*
A. *"Apparently all right. He walked to the bathroom and appeared to be steady*
*and his movements positive."*
Q. *"Where did you go after you left Friday morning?"*
A. *"I went to work and didn't come back until after lunch at 12.45. I didn't notice anything then but went back later between 2:30 & 3:00 PM – his door was open, the body gone, and while I was there a 1$^{st}$ Lt. and a T/5/G came in and gathered up his personal belongings."*

**Author Analysis**

The sanitizing of Kermit's room appears to have occurred very fast following the discovery of his body. This testimony appears to conflict with the accounts of his being drunk and the autopsy finding of 2.50mgm per cc of alcohol in his blood or any unsound mind. Additionally, Johnson was not questioned as to the time he left for work in the morning and with his room next to Kermit's he was not asked if he heard any gunshot. In fact, no one ever mentioned hearing any gunshot and the report from a .45 is very loud. Wouldn't someone in or around a multiunit billet have heard a gunshot?

**Captain James Edgar Nichols, in charge of Officer's Ward in post hospital –**

Q. *"Did you have a chance to observe his mental condition and if so did you*
*notice anything out of the ordinary?"*
A. *"His mental condition was good."*
Q. *"Did you notice anything at any time that would indicate an unsound mind or abnormal mental condition?"*

A. *"No Sir. However, I haven't seen him since his last treatment* (for malaria) *the_31st of May."*

**Author Analysis**

Yet again, testimony that indicated Kermit was of sound mind.

### Colonel Luther R. Moore, Surgeon

Q. *"How well did you know him?"*

A. *"I was associated with him daily for several months last year."*

Q. *"I will ask you to state the circumstances of your association with him, especially as to any indication of the soundness or unsoundness of mind."*

A. *"From September 18, 1942 to January 25, 1943, Major Kermit Roosevelt lived in Apartment H, Building 167, which was directly above Apartment D in which I was living. During this period our contact was daily, meeting in the hallway and at intervals visiting in each others rooms. Major Roosevelt was cheerful as a rule but it was noticeable that he appeared to be absent minded and was to be seen gazing as in study or walking slowly as if in concentrated thought at frequent intervals. His manner was that of a gentleman, solicitous of his fellow man's well being, but paradoxically he frequently came home late at night and almost invariably would make a great deal of noise in his room before retiring. The noises consisted of whistling, humming tunes, moving the bed and chairs, dropping shoes, and similar activities. This was annoying to other officers in the apartment, and as senior officer in the building I spoke to Major Roosevelt on two occasions regarding the noise made in his room late in the evening and depriving other occupants of their rest. The officer, Major H. G. Hahn, living directly under Major Roosevelt's room, was markedly disturbed and lost his rest continually during this period. Major Roosevelt registered sincere surprise when informed that he was making an undue amount of noise and stated that he was careful to move quietly and did procure a rug for his floor. The noise continued unchanged and it was apparent that he had little conception of its reality and the question of eccentricity or mental failure to grasp the significance was in the balance.*

*In contact with Major Roosevelt in his staff work I had
occasion to note delay and lack of decision in his action on
matters pertaining mutually to our sections.*

*I do not consider Major Roosevelt's actions as those of
average normal mental function during this period.*

*I have not seen Major Roosevelt drunk or under the
influence of narcotics at any time and have had no occasion
to give any consideration to drinking as a cause for his
actions.*

## Author Analysis

Although Moore provides the most critical testimony in
regard to Kermit's state of mind, his criticism raises
questions:  Kermit may have been a noisy neighbor.  Living
in the confined space of a military billet which are
generally not designed as plush, comfortable quarters
could magnify the idiosyncrasies of an adjoining neighbor.
Moore's claim that "*...apparent that he had little conception
of its reality...*" is questionable considering Kermit exerted
the effort to procure a rug to muffle any sounds.  Also
questionable is Moore's claim to "*had occasion to note
delay and lack of decision in his action on matters
pertaining mutually to our sections.*"  Kermit was assigned
to G2, the Intelligence Section and was working on the
Alaska Digest which was a classified, secret project.
Moore, as a surgeon in the post hospital would have no
cause to be working on matters pertaining mutually to
their sections; there is little probability these matters
existed.

### Lt. Col. Herbert G. Hahn, Infantry

Q. *"How well did you know him?"*

A. *"Only casually."*

Q. *"Did you know him well enough to be able to express
an opinion as to his mental stability?"*

A. *"I believe so.  In my opinion, I believed him to* (be)
*slightly unbalanced mentally.  I base this opinion on his
past actions as follows: He was absentminded and
forgetful; lacked coordination of movement and always
appeared to be lost in deep meditation when walking.  Even
though he passed quite near one, he would rarely speak –
not, as I have always believed, from a desire of not wanting
to speak, but rather from a point of view of not having
realized that he had passed you by.  Major Roosevelt*

occupied the small room in apartment H, NCO building #167, which was directly over the small room occupied by myself in apartment D of the same building. His usual habit was to return to his quarters each evening between the hours of 11:30 PM and 2:00 AM of the following morning. Upon entering his room, he would drag his chair roughly across the floor, open and close his desk drawers with a bang, slide shoes, etc, across the floor and make an unusual number of trips from his room to the bathroom and kitchen stopping halfway between, return to his room and do the same thing over and over again nightly. No matter what time he returned home, he never retired under less than forty-five minutes to an hour. Naturally, this action on his part disturbed my sleep and I – as well as other officers in the quarters – spoke to him about his actions requesting him to be a little more quiet. He appeared to be very sorry about this, apologized and stated that he would be more careful in the future. Then on the next night and subsequent nights – it would be a repetition of former nights over and over again. He also lacked rhythm in his movements because he would tap on the floor with his feet while humming and whistling, the latter being out of rhythm with the former, always denying that he ever tapped on the floor, hummed or whistled – and all of which led me to believe that he was totally unaware of the fact that he was in reality doing just those things particularly during the early hours of the morning and all of which made it extremely uncomfortable for the person occupying quarters directly beneath him and which, had he of been in full possession of his faculties, would have never happened I am sure.

Q. "Did he use intoxicating liquors or narcotics to excess to your knowledge?"

A. "Not to my knowledge."

Q. "Anything else you would care to add that would throw light on this matter?"

A. "Nothing except his taking his own life came as a surprise to myself."

**Author Analysis**

The only other testimony that corroborates Moore is Hahn's testimony which also has holes in it and to some may be considered comical. He states he knows Kermit only casually yet he claims Kermit was slightly unbalanced mentally. He bases his unqualified medical opinion on "*He*

*was absentminded and forgetful; lacked coordination of
movement and always appeared to be lost in deep
meditation when walking."* Absentminded and forgetful
sounds like numerous people in society (including the
author) who are not unbalanced mentally. Perhaps his
lack of coordination of movement and his appearance of
being lost in deep meditation when walking resulted from
his gastronomical problems and suffering from numerous
other painful ailments acquired over the years.

> *"Even though he passed quite near one, he would
> rarely speak – not, as I have always believed, from a
> desire of not wanting to speak, but rather from a
> point of view of not having realized that he had
> passed you by."*

This statement sounds clearly that it was coached
beforehand: *"… he would rarely speak – not, as I have
always believed, from a desire of not wanting to speak, but
rather…"* Well, what/who enlightened him and changed
his mind as he had always believed? Could it have been
Moore prior to the testimony? Moore testified on June 7,
Hahn on June 8, and the similarity of their complaints
indicates that they may have discussed their testimony
before hand.

Hahn's claim: *He also lacked rhythm in his movements
because he would tap on the floor with his feet while
humming and whistling, the latter being out of rhythm with
the former…"* is somewhat silly. Does lack of syncopation
between foot tapping and humming indicate mental
instability? Perhaps Kermit was aware that he was living
with two petty whiners and complainers and decided to
give them the business. It's hard to understand how
Hahn, an Infantry Major could be so petty and
presumptuous to claim that these annoyances were
indicative of insanity. It is interesting to consider how
Hahn would react if he were assigned to a combat infantry
unit under hostile fire.

### 1st Lt. Gordon D. Skeoch, Chief of Out Patients post hospital

This line of questioning was in regard to the high
alcohol level detected during the autopsy.

Q. *"Does the fact that the blood alcohol test was taken at approximately 2:30 PM have any bearing on the case in the elapsed time conditions in the blood could have changed?"*

A. *"No sir, it would change the condition of the blood very little, but if it did*
*change slightly it would go down and not up."*

Q. *"If he had been intoxicated at 1:30 AM could that alcohol have shown in the alcohol test you made the same afternoon?"*

A. *"Yes sir, it could last that long but to have such a high alcohol level would definitely indicate that he had been drinking more recently."*

## Author Analysis

How could he have been drinking more recently if Lt. Johnson said he passed him in the aisle on his way to the toilet at approximately 7:15 AM and didn't smell any alcohol or consider Kermit drunk? Unless he consumed a large amount of alcohol after 7:15 before committing suicide. However, others searched his room and only one claimed to find empty bottles (the others didn't), and besides, the official report said he shot himself around 8 AM. Would he chug that much alcohol in 45 minutes?

### T4/G Simeon Oliver

Q. *"Did you ever observe any action of his that would indicate mental instability or an unsound mental condition?"*

A. *"He seemed perfectly sound to me."*

### Pvt. Landen H. Bentley

Bently, an orderly assigned to the billet Kermit lived in was interviewed. He testified that the day before Kermit's death he and a Lt. Saxell assisted Kermit to his room:

Q. *"Did you see him and talk to him the day before?"*

A. *"Yes Sir, a few times."*

Q. *"What was the nature of your conversation?"*

A. *"Well Sir, I was sweeping out and I heard somebody coming through the door. I thought it was the laundry coming in for it sounded like someone throwing something. So I just kept on working. I finished the apartment I was working on and looked to the foot of the stairs and saw Major Roosevelt lying there."*

Q. *"What time was that?"*

A. *"About 2:30 or 3:00 PM, June 3, 1943. Lt. Saxell was in his room and I asked him to give me a hand to get Major Roosevelt up to his bed. We did that and that was the last I saw him."*

Q. *"Was he intoxicated or ill?"*

A. *"He seemed to be intoxicated."*

Q. *"What time do you usually clean his apartment?"*

A. *"I usually get to that end of the building between 2:30 & 3:00 PM."*

**Author Analysis**

A few issues come to mind: Bentley testified that he talked to Kermit a few times that day. However, he was questioned only on his claim to have helped Kermit to his room when *"He seemed to be intoxicated."* What about the other conversations and what was his condition then and at what time? Saxell supposedly helped Bentley to get Kermit to his room, however, there is no testimony from Saxell; he never corroborated Bentley's testimony. Perhaps rather than intoxication Kermit had a malaria attack if Bentley's testimony is true. Bentley was questioned about his orderly duties:

Additionally, his cleaning schedule for Kermit's building implies that he cleans other apartments earlier in the day and Kermit's later but he was not questioned if he heard any gunshots the following day.

**Major Edmund A. Meagher, Post Provost Marshal**

Q. *"Will you state what was found upon your arrival at NCO building #167 including any facts as to the conditions, time of day, etc?"*

A. *"I arrived at 1:25 PM and found Major Hoff and 1st Lt. Gordon Skeoch, MC inside the room. On a bed on the left side of the room was the body of Major Roosevelt dressed in pajamas. A .45 cal Model 1911 Colt Automatic pistol, serial no 95112, lay on his chest, with the muzzle pointed towards his face. The right thumb was near the trigger and the fingers of the right hand grasped the butt of the piece. The fingers of the left hand were over the barrel and slide. The piece was cocked with safety off and magazine in. An empty shell lay on the floor under the bureau about 7ft away. There was dried blood on two pillows, the mattress and the floor. The Major's body was cold and rigor mortis had started. The Major had a bullet hole in the roof of his*

*mouth, rather far back. Lt. Gordon Skeoch recovered the
bullet from the upper pillow while I was present and gave it
to me.*

*I did not observe any indication that a struggle had
taken place in the room. The Major's money, wrist watch,
and other valuables were undisturbed. I searched for a
farewell note but was unable to discover any. I did find an
unopened letter from Mrs. Edith Roosevelt, Oyster Bay, New
York, postmarked May 27, 1943. In a bureau drawer I
found a note written on a slip of paper which read 'MAJOR
ROOSEVELT Please contact G-2- 6/4/A.M. MAJOR P H
HOFF.'*

*I have no knowledge that Major Roosevelt had any
enemies. I have not been able to find anyone who might
have heard him express any intention to do away with
himself.*

*I have never seen the Major drunk or do any drinking on
any of the occasions that I have been out with him or in his
quarters."*

Q. *"In your contacts with Major Roosevelt at any time
previous to his death did you observe any indications of an
unsound mental condition?"*

A. *"No. Major Roosevelt had an excellent memory,
never failed to inquire after the health of my family, and
always acted normal in my presence."*

Q. *"Is there anything else you would like to add that
would throw light upon the matter?"*

A. *"No nothing sir, except heresay. I haven't been able
to uncover any evidence of foul play during the course of my
investigation. It is my opinion that Major Roosevelt's death
was due to suicide. I didn't break the clip out of the gun
because I did not wish to disturb any fingerprints. I
fastened the safety catch on the pistol, wrapped it in a towel
and delivered it to Lt. Col R. G. Williams, Hq ADC. I
examined the walls for bullet holes and found none."*

**Author Analysis**

Despite the care Meagher exercised in handling the
gun, no fingerprints were reported taken, no ballistics on
the bullet or any forensic analysis of the scene. Interesting
that he looked for bullet holes in the wall despite finding a
bullet beneath Kermit's head. Was he just trying to rule
out a gun fight? If so, why after finding Kermit with the
pistol in his hands and presumably a suicide would he

look for additional bullets? Lt. Col R. G. Williams, Hq ADC who supposedly received the pistol was never called to testify about what he did with the gun. His comment of "heresay" in response to the question of: "Is there anything else you would like to add that would throw light upon the matter" was not questioned.

### Lt. Col Walter F. Choinski, G-2

Q. *"What were his duties in connection with his office?"*

A. *"He was in charge of the revision of the ALASKA DIGEST, which is a compendium on the economic, geographic and political aspects of Alaska. This compendium is prepared for the MIS of the War Department."*

Q. *"Do you know about his physical condition?"*

A. *"I have known him since December 1942 and knew that his physical condition wasn't the best. He was continuously ailing from sinus trouble as well as stomach trouble which later became so aggravated that he was hospitalized. Since his return to Alaska he had been taking treatmet for malaria."*

Q. *"Did he have any peculiarities that would indicate an unsound mind?"*

A. *"No, none whatsoever. I do think his mind wasn't entirely on his work. I believe he was so engrossed in getting to the Forward Echelon that he didn't give the office his full attention as he should have."*

Q. *"Do you know whether he used intoxicating liquor?"*

A. *"Yes, I am quite sure that during the week prior to his death he was under the influence of liquor on two occasions. I didn't observe it personally, but on May 31 Sgt. Oliver was working with Major Roosevelt and commented on the fact that the Major had been drinking and was in all probability under the influence of liquor. It was also reported that the Major was under the influence of liquor when he came to the main office for the key to the Quonset on May 30."*

### Author Analysis

Sgt. Oliver was not called to corroborate Choinski's claim of Kermit drinking on May 31 nor did Choinski state who reported Kermit was under the influence on May 30 nor was he asked.

### Major Sanford C. Monroe, Medical Corp.

Monroe, a doctor at the post hospital was asked to comment on the metal attitude of Kermit: *"He impressed me as one who was always mentally clear and alert but one whose reaction to medical advice was more of the type usually obtained from a child than from a person of his age and ability."*

Q. *"State whether there were any indications of an unsound mind or abnormal mental conditions."*

A. *"Nothing more than an abnormal desire to be closer to combat conditions.*

Q. *"State the term used for such mental conditions as he might have had.*

A. *"This abnormal desire might possibly lead to an acute mental depression but it was not obvious when last seen."*

Q. *"Would you say that since the autopsy showed 2.5 milligrams alcohol at the time of death that his condition would be such that he could not exercise ordinary judgment or control of his conduct?"*

A. *"Yes."*

### Author Analysis

The doctor's claim Kermit's display of *"abnormal desire to be closer to combat conditions"* could *"...possibly lead to an acute mental depression..."* is questionable. His desire to engage in combat was no different than the rest of his brothers and the ex-President of the United States, Theodore Roosevelt.

### Summary

The foregoing details of Kermit's death and the War Department's treatment of his case before and after he died indicate one of two possibilities, either the Army was extraordinarily inept, superficial and hasty in their treatment of Kermit or the facts surrounding the cause of his death indicate something much more sinister. Either way, the claim that he was grasping the pistol, post mortem as stated in the official reports is highly improbable and immediately raises suspicions. Other issues also raise troubling questions that undermines the government's claim, for example the inept investigation where testimony sometimes conflicted and no follow-up questioning occurring; the official conclusion justifying the suicide motive as resulting from a mental disturbance with no expert evaluation and most witnesses claiming otherwise. No ballistics on the weapon or the bullet, no fingerprint analysis, no one hearing the gunshot, no forensic study of the death scene and the autopsy claim of a high instance of alcohol in the blood when the testimony and time line render this improbable, unless there was a surreptitious entry of alcohol into Kermit's body. Additionally, there is no reasonable explanation for the discovery of the bullet on or underneath his pillow. All of these issues render the official cause of Kermit's death very implausible, similar to the peculiarities of the official wartime death of the tough General George H. Patton by a mere fender bender.

The details surrounding the death of President John F. Kennedy also have raised many questions over the years. Many discount the claims of conspiracy, and yet, many of the details remain unanswered with the official investigation leaving many aspects of his death still wrapped in mystery.

The present day expertise of the Army's Criminal Investigation Command certainly exceeds the meager analytical capabilities of the wartime U.S. Army in 1943. This present day Federal organization (known as the CID for Criminal Investigation Division) was only formed in 1971 and provides a professional crime investigation service with extensive forensic capabilities. During World War II investigations of crimes within the military were a local command function conducted by generally inept Military Police within the Office of the Provost Marshal which could account for the shoddy investigation of Kermit's death.

Granted, forensic science has greatly improved in recent years, particularly with the development of DNA analysis. However, following the Saint Valentine's Day Massacre in 1929, forensic scientist and army officer, Colonel Calvin Hooker Goddard and Philip Gravelle, provided invaluable evidence in solving the crime by analyzing the spent bullets and cartridge casings used in the crime.

Goddard applied the same technology in upholding the convictions in the 1920, Sacco and Vanzetti case. In 1932 the Federal Bureau of Investigation crime laboratory was created, and naturally fingerprint analysis has been around since the latter 19th Century. Clearly, death of the ex-President's son and cousin to the sitting President would warrant an exhaustive, detailed investigation applying the latest scientific techniques.

The record indicates FDR painstakingly attempted to quiet Kermit and failed. Both he and the War Department certainly had motives to suppress Kermit and raises the question and brings into the realm of possibility of official involvement in Kermit's death. Aside from the probability of him causing great public embarrassment to the President and thereby a major propaganda tool for the enemy, as a Major in the U. S. Army he had access to classified material and besides, his philandering with a mysterious woman added to him being a significant security threat. FDR struggled with the dilemma of how to contain him. He first considered sending Kermit to Africa, then Hawaii and eventually exiled him to Alaska. But Kermit's ongoing physical ailments brought him back to the states and his request for a Court Martial while at the Barnes Hospital to determine the basis for his spurious Seattle incarceration if held would have certainly become a public scandal for the Roosevelt Administration. Additionally, Kermit's potential as a relative of the President, could have been a major propaganda tool for the enemy.

The War Department's effort to suppress any details of his death for so many years also raises intriguing questions. The only persons who were informed of his suicide were his wife and brother, Ted Jr. The obituary in the New York Times for June 6, 1943 stated the place of death was not revealed nor the cause, although *"it was believed his death was due to natural causes."* On June 26th, 1943 a note in regard to Kermit's file from a Colonel Easterbrook stated: *"Have an immstakable* (sic) *flag placed on the top of the 'Major Kermit Roosevelt' file that no information is given out without the personal OK of the executor or myself."* Classifying his personnel records for sixteen years following his death is not unusual. However, even into the 1970s the government discouraged the release of any information on Kermit. Government records show that in March, 1969 on behalf of a General Theodore J. Conway, Commander in Chief of the U. S. Strike

Command, a Major Rose at the Army War College requested information on *"How he died."* The general was to reference this in a speech concerning the Kermit Roosevelt Fund.

The response from the World War II office of the General Services Administration was: *"Advised Maj. Rose – 'Died as a result of self inflicted gunshot wound' also told Maj. Rose to tell Gen. Conway that this information was not to be released."* In February, 1972 the Dictionary of American Biography, under the auspices of the American Council of Learned Societies requested similar information from the Office of the Chief of Military History in Washington DC. The response was: *"The requested information may be furnished only upon receipt of an authorization signed by the decedent's next of kin."* Perhaps this was policy based upon sensitivity towards Kermit's family. However, by 2010 Kermit's wife, his siblings and his children were all deceased with only his grand and great grandchildren surviving. The author still experienced difficulty with the National Archives in gaining access to his records despite the National Archives web site listing Kermit's files as being open and available as a "Person of Prominence." Despite repeated attempts over a nine-month period the National Archives denied access and only released the file on Kermit's death following the intercession of Congressman John Hall.

After sixty-seven years, any questions of his death beyond the official version are mere speculation and will no doubt forevermore remain as such. However, a careful review of the official documentation pertaining to his death, although not concrete proof, does contain significant instances of gross oversight and improbable official conclusions that indicate the strong possibility of foul play and a government cover-up. This, coupled with a strong motive to silence him by the government raises doubt as to how his life ended leaving the reader to be the jury.

Notes-
01 Ref. Mornings on Horseback, David McCullough
02 Ref. Edith Kermit Roosevelt Portrait of a First Lady,
   Sylvia Jukes Morris
03 Ref. The Roosevelts, An American Saga, Peter Collier
   with David Horowitz, page 383
04 Time, April 25, 1938

# EPILOGUE;
# KERMIT ROOSEVELT LIVES ON

*Some die shouting in gas or fire;*
*Some die silent, by shell and shot.*
*Some die desperate, caught on the wire;*
*Some die suddenly. This will not.*

*"A Death Bed" by Rudyard Kipling*

In accordance with Theodore Roosevelt's sage advice: "Where a tree falls, there let it lay," Kermit was buried in the Fort Richardson National Cemetery in Alaska. In his memory, his wife Belle financed and dedicated the stone entrance gate to the facility and in an effort to keep his memory alive, established the Kermit Roosevelt Memorial Fund. The fund supported an annual international lecture event between American and British senior military leaders called the Kermit Roosevelt Exchange Lecture Series which still continues to this day. In a letter to General George C. Marshall in June, 1944, one year following his death Belle proposed:

> *"My husband, Kermit Roosevelt, ... attempted to carry out in his own life his conviction that the development of a closer relationship between individual English and Americans, and a better understanding between the military forces of the United States and the United Kingdom would contribute in large measure to the preservation of world peace. In view of this conviction of his, it seems appropriate to set up this Memorial"*

Following his death, Belle received a message from General Dwight Eisenhower: *"Heartfelt sympathy very depressed."* In World War I Kermit was awarded the British Military Cross and the Montenegran War Cross for his military exploits.

In World War II, Kermit's last military efficiency report dated January 10, 1943, only five months before his death, characterizes Major Roosevelt as *"A very intelligent, affable, kindly and loyal officer whose patriotism impels him to offer his services to his country as a member of the fighting forces...."*

Although Kermit lived a life of tragedy with much pain and strife, his overriding obsession in the twentieth century's two greatest wars was his duty to serve and defend his country.

Toward this end, he lost his life in a very violent and suspicious manner, which the Army classified as *"Death was in the line of duty and was not the result of Officer's own misconduct."* Besides his military service, his all but forgotten legacy includes his participation in the introduction to science of previously little known species of animals and his charting of vaguely understood territory in South America with his father and in Asia with his brother. On maps of Amazonia today, a river bears the name: "Rio Kermit."

The South American expedition introduced six new species of mammals to science. The James Simpson-Roosevelts Asiatic Expedition of 1925 enabled expedition member, George K. Cherrie, the group's ornithologist, to collect many birds in the high mountains of Asia besides the rare mammals collected by Kermit and Theodore Jr.

The William V. Kelly-Roosevelts Asiatic Expedition of the Field Museum of 1928-29, organized and led by Kermit and his brother, contributed many previously unknown and unstudied species to science. They ranged from squirrels and rare bats to larger mammals including the Roosevelt's Barking Deer.

A zoological publication by the Field Museum following the expedition commented: *"...the crowning exploit of the Kelley-Roosevelts Expedition was the trailing and shooting of a giant panda by the brothers Theodore and Kermit Roosevelt."*

Kermit was a major influence in rebuilding the American shipping industry following the First World War. The towns of Kermit, Texas, and Kermit, West Virginia, are named after him and the USS Kermit Roosevelt, a Luzon class repair ship, was also named to honor him. His intellectual brilliance included authorship of multiple books, numerous articles and speeches and skill in speaking many languages, among them Swahili, Arabic, Portuguese, Hindustani, Spanish, French and German.

❖

The death of Kermit Roosevelt in 1943 was not the end of his family's devotion to patriotic duty and the pursuit of high adventure. Kermit's eldest son, Kermit Jr., known to the family as Kim, was to lead an equally swashbuckling and even more internationally significant life than any of his father's past exploits. Kim's impact on the world scene in 1953 has had lasting effects that have rocked the United States, the Middle East and the major oil-consuming nations to the present day. However, his clandestine escapades in Iran are not commonly known to the public, and he has also been lost in the shadow of his family's fame for many decades.

At the time of his exploits, Kim's actions elicited words of praise from a very select group of world figures: Mohammed Reza Pahlavi, the Shah of Iran: *"I owe my throne to God, my people, my army and you!"*[1] Winston Churchill: *"Young man, if I had been but a few years younger, I would have loved nothing better than to have served under your command in this great venture!"*[2] Kim Philby, British double agent who later defected to the U.S.S.R., found Kim Roosevelt to be:

*"a courteous, soft-spoken Easterner with impeccable social connections, well-educated rather than intellectual, pleasant and unassuming as host and guest. An equally nice wife. In fact, the last person you would expect to be up to the neck in dirty tricks"*[3]

*The Adventure Continues-*

Immediately following in the smoldering ashes of the Second World War, western democracies began facing another world conflict. During the late 1940s and the early 1950s the United States and her allies became locked in a bitter Cold War with the Soviet Union and began a policy of Communist containment. The Soviets had recently acquired the Atomic Bomb, blockaded Berlin, and began a policy of supporting subversion and revolutionary unrest in many countries around the globe. Communist China and North Korea began a bloody conflict against United Nations

*Serene demeanor of Kermit Roosevelt Jr. (Kim), belies his clandestine
activities as a master spy who overthrew the Iranian Government of
Mohammad Mosaddegh.*

forces with the United States leading multinational troops
on the Korean Peninsula. Even into the 21st Century these
tensions have not been resolved. The shadowy intelligence
organizations of many nations began in full-swing around
the world, pursuing classified information and

undermining adversaries whenever and wherever possible in this new Cold War.

As the United States began struggling with this growing threat, Kim, a World War II veteran of the O.S.S., forerunner of the Central Intelligence Agency, became a mid-level operative in that super-secret organization as his influence in Washington power circles began to grow.

Kim was a mild-mannered, studious-appearing Harvard graduate in his mid 30s, a very unlikely appearing spy master to conduct the CIA's major coup in the Middle-East. This clandestine operation arguably became the most preeminent and successful of the CIA throughout the coming years of its subversion and nation toppling around the world. In 1953 as Kim was conducting intelligence operations as chief of the Near East and Asia Division of the CIA, Iran was locked in a bitter strife with the British; the issues were colonial control, communist expansion and oil.

The nation of Iran, the modern descendent of the great Persian Empire struggled throughout the 19th and early 20th Centuries with pressure from both Russia, desirous of expanding its influence upon a weakened state within its perceived grasp, and Britain, who saw a potential threat to the northeast flank of its prime colonial possession, India. Tensions in the entire region rose precipitously in the early 20th Century as oil became a critical commodity of the industrialized nations, and Iran had a superabundant*[28] supply.

For many decades the shaky stability of the country roiled in turmoil. In the latter 19th Century, as the Iranian people began to develop an independent state of mind, Nasir al-Din Shah began to barter-away various business, mineral and agricultural concessions to European nations. Dissatisfied with miserable living conditions, a broken economy and a corrupt monarchy, the Iranians sued for popular control of the government and the creation of a Majlis, or parliament.

Political and social stress continued for many years between the Majlis, the monarchists and the Muslim

---

28 *Even in the 21st Century, Iran is the second largest producer of oil in the Organization of Petroleum Exporting Countries.

clerics. Clashes between secular reformers and the mullahs, which continue to the present day, along with strife between the regional and tribal factions only added to undermine the social fabric of Iran. However, in these turbulent early years of the 20<sup>th</sup> Century, the thirst for democracy gained strong traction with the people as Britain and Russia began carving-up the country.

In 1908 the British discovered rich oil reserves in Iran, the first find in the Persian Gulf. The Anglo-Persian Oil Company*[29] was formed with Britain managing the entire enterprise and garnering all of the profits. For decades, the Iranian workers at the oil fields were forced to work in sub-standard conditions and live in a shanty-town as the British managers and technicians and their families lived in the comfort of a gated community. Winston Churchill referred to the operation as *"a prize from fairyland beyond our wildest dreams."*[4]

In 1921, as the Iranian people continued to live in misery, a strong military leader with an equally independent personality rose to power. Reza Khan was a fearless soldier and able leader who managed to displace the reigning Shah as he became war minister. In 1923 he aspired to the office of prime minister and in 1925 deposed the reigning Shah, Ahmad Mirza, naming himself Reza Shah Pahlevi, the beginning of the Pahlevi dynasty in Iran.

Reza Shah was a ruthless reformer who ruled with an iron hand. Although resentful and resistive of colonial influences imposed by the British but unable to eliminate their power and influence within Iran, he grudgingly maintained a mutually accepting relationship until World War II. In 1941, Iran maintained a neutral posture in the conflict but Reza Shah clearly was sympathetic to the Nazis. Concerned with the potential for a NAZI invasion, both Britain and the USSR invaded Iran and began occupying large regions of the country. Under pressure from the Allies, he abdicated thereby placing his eldest son, Mohammad Reza on the Peacock Throne.

Throughout the 1940s and into the 1950s, Mohammad Reza became increasingly involved in the political affairs of the country with a policy of transforming Iran into a

---

29 *Renamed the Anglo-Iranian Oil Company in 1935 and then the British Petroleum Company (BP) in 1954.

modern world power; interfering with the parliament and resisting the power and influence of the prime ministers. Many reforms were instituted including recognition of Israel and efforts to increase the secularization of the country resulting in friction with the Islamic majority. He maintained an iron fisted control of the populace, banned the Communist Party and suppressed political dissent. He later created SAVAK, the hated national intelligence organization.

In early 1950, General Haj-Ali Razmara, the Shah's handpicked choice, was elevated to prime minister. In less than a year he was assassinated, which added to the growing national unrest. The population began clamoring for nationalization of Iran's oil production; national strikes and rioting ensued that laid the groundwork for a populist leader to emerge and a sensitive, melodramatic politician stepped forward.

*Mohammad Mosaddegh, duly elected Prime Minister of Iran who was ousted by a coup d'état masterminded by CIA operative, Kim Roosevelt in 1953.*

Mohammad Mossadeg was an erudite lawyer and patriotic activist with a dour demeanor and an articulate, passionate manner of speech. He developed a reputation over many years as a sincere, honest leader while gaining a popular, national following. While a representative in the Majlis he passionately opposed the foreign influence in Iran and particularly Britain's control of the nation's oil industry.

In 1951 he was elected to the office of Prime Minister of Iran with an overwhelming majority of the Majlis as he argued strenuously against the British Government and for the nationalization of the Iranian oil industry while appealing to both the United States and the world community for support. Just days prior to his gaining office, the Majlis voted to nationalize the nation's oil industry. However, great concern existed within Washington and Whitehall - the British for continued control of their oil monopoly and in Washington worry over Mossadeg's relationship with the outlawed communist party in Iran. A secret CIA report₅ stated:

> "By the end of 1952, it had become clear that the Mossadeg government in Iran was incapable of reaching an oil settlement with interested Western countries; was reaching a dangerous and advanced stage of illegal, deficit financing; was disregarding the Iranian constitution in prolonging Premier Mohammed Mossadeg's desire for personal power; was governed by irresponsible policies based on emotion; had weakened the Shah and the Iranian Army to a dangerous degree; and had cooperated closely with the Tudeh (Communist) Party of Iran."

In retaliation for the loss of their critical resource, the British dispatched warships to the coast of Iran – a military invasion was considered as they pursued an international boycott of Iranian oil exports. The British Government lobbied for U. S. involvement; however, President Harry Truman, in the twilight of his administration, ruled out any American interference.

However, the newly inaugurated Eisenhower Administration harbored no such trepidation. Saddled with the inheritance of a heated Cold War and the ongoing

Korean War, Eisenhower worried over the possibility of a Communist takeover in Iran under the Mossadeg regime. Although even before Eisenhower gave his tacit approval for a covert action to unseat the troublesome Mossadeg, the CIA along with the British were scheming to remove him. When meeting with the powerful Dulles brothers in early 1953, John Foster, serving as Secretary of State and Allan who was Director of the Central Intelligence Agency, British spymaster Sir John Sinclair suggested Kim Roosevelt be assigned to prepare and implement a plan to depose Mossadeg and elevate the compliant Shah. Actually, the British approached Kim in November 1952 with a desire to topple Mossadeg.

The resourceful Kim Roosevelt was already prepared with a plan which he named Operation AJAX, after one of the hero's of Homer's "The Iliad," and the Trojan War. Author Tom Weiner in his Legacy of Ashes the History of the CIA notes:[6]

*"Roosevelt ran the show with flair. He had been working for two years on political, propaganda, and paramilitary operations to fight off a feared Soviet invasion in Iran. CIA officers already had enough cash and guns stashed away to support ten thousand tribal warriors for six months."*

The ambitious scheme included organizing military and popular support and Iran's Muslim clergy; elevating an individual to replace Mossadeg; gaining the Shah's support and restoring him to a position of overall authority. The plan would rely on groups of thugs to incite street protests and riots and large infusions of money which the CIA had available in ample amounts. Kim expected to secretly smuggle himself and a colleague across the Iranian border to orchestrate the operation. On July 19, 1953, he succeeded.

The extremely sensitive nature of his mission coupled with his famous name and previous trips to Tehran now required his presence in Iran to be unpublicized and undetected. The staples of spy-craft - establishing safe-houses and traveling under false identity were not new to Kermit Roosevelt – he was an old hand at subterfuge. On a recent trip to Tehran, he and his cohorts attempted to secure a high-ranking Soviet diplomat interested in defecting. In true James Bond fashion, they planned to clandestinely pickup the man in front of the Soviet Embassy. Kim, packing a pistol and a tear gas pencil, waited patiently in a parked car in front of the embassy gate but in a moment's notice, the diplomat's burly driver suspected the ruse and manhandled the diplomat back into the limousine and sped back into the embassy compound, denying Kim the prize. The diplomat was never seen again.

On this trip, he would use a pseudonym, James F. Lochridge, and travel by car from Baghdad across the desert to Iran. On leaving his initial starting point he reminisced: *"... I remembered what my father wrote of his arrival in East Africa with his father, T.R., in 1909 on The African Game Trails trip. 'It was a great adventure, and allthe world was young!'*

He traversed the Iraq-Iran frontier and entered the country, noting the almost comical circumstances:

> *"...we encountered an unusually listless, stupid and semiliterate immigration-customs fellow at Khanequin. In those days U. S. passports carried, as they do not now, some brief description of any notable features of the holder. With encouragement and help from me, the guard laboriously transcribed my name as 'Mr. Scar on Right Forehead.' This I found a good omen."[7]*

For his first weeks undercover in Iran, Kim lay ensconced in a walled compound in the mountain home of a fellow spook. He surreptitiously organized his resources and began to manipulate events from his comfortable, swimming pool equipped hideout. He began orchestrating behind the scenes: street rioting, bribery, spreading money around to key individuals and pressuring the mullahs. Through his British contacts, he was aided by three Iranian members of a wealthy and influential family, the Rashidian brothers. Using their influence and contacts, he was able to slip bribes to key members of the military, the Iranian press, certain legislators within the government and other well-placed members of Iranian society. *"They bought information with cookie tins filled with cash. Their circle even included the Shah's chief manservant. It would prove a catalyst in the coup."*[8]

As security concerns mounted, he moved to a CIA "safe house" in Tehran, addressing paperwork and receiving briefings from his local henchmen. The agreed upon replacement for Mossadeg, General Fazlollag Zahedi, a war veteran and anti-communist, was safely ensconced in a mountain hideout outside Tehran. So far, all details of the operation were setting-up as planned.

An essential part of the operation required the cooperation and support of the Shah. Not personally courageous by nature, he was acutely aware of the turbulent past of his country and fearful for his future. Consequently, he maintained a distant and guarded attitude toward any notion of participating in a coup against Mossadeg. His ambivalence became a stumbling-block to the operation. To quell the Shah's fears, his strong-willed and courageous sister, Princess Ashraf, was flown to Tehran to overcome his apprehensions and gain his involvement. When this effort failed, the CIA even enlisted the former commander of the Imperial Iranian Gendarmerie,*[30] General H. Norman Schwarzkopf.*[31]

After speaking with the Shah and failing to allay his fears, Schwarzkopf convinced Kim that the only possible way to sway the Shah into cooperating was if Kim spoke to the monarch himself. If a meeting were held, however, Kim's undercover involvement would be disclosed. Schwarzkopf emphasized: *"And if this undertaking fails – we'll all be in such hot soup that I really don't think disclosure of your name could make much difference."*[9] Realizing there was no other way Kim decided to work out a clandestine, personal meeting.

He would continue to maintain his anonymity to all Persians except for the Shah, General Zahedi and the general's associate, Mustapha Vaysi. Even his British contacts were unaware of his true identity. Despite his precautions, as a relief to the enormous tensions

---

30 *Iranian paramilitary police force trained and commanded by Schwarzkopf.

31 *West Point graduate and first Superintendent of the New Jersey State Police, Schwarzkopf is the father of four-star general Norman Schwarzkopf, commander of Operation Desert Storm.

associated with his mission, he did take an unnecessary risk:

*"In the meantime I was entertaining myself in a mildly dangerous way by playing tennis, either at the Turkish Embassy court or on those of the French Institute. I played with a girl in the U. S. Embassy staff against one of our own officers and his wife. The danger came not from the game but from a habit I had then, and still have, of saying, 'Oh Roosevelt' when I missed a shot. I did my best to pass myself off as a black hearted reactionary Republican to whom "Roosevelt" meaning FDR, was a heartfelt obscenity."*[10]

The meeting was arranged with the Shah through an intermediary saying *"...that and American authorized to speak for Eisenhower and Churchill desired a secret audience."*[11] Kim arrived on the palace grounds after midnight huddled under a blanket in the back seat of a common black sedan.

As Kim approached the palace steps the Shah appeared from the shadows commenting *"Good evening, Mr. Roosevelt. I cannot say that I expected to see you, but this is a pleasure."* Kim replied, *"Good evening, Your Majesty. It is a long time since we met each other, and I am glad you recognize me. It may make establishing my credentials a bit easier."*[12]

The U. S. President would shortly confirm the meeting by a phrase he would utter in a broadcasted San Francisco speech as Churchill signaled his agreement via a BBC broadcast the next night. Rather than saying *"It is now midnight,"* the announcer would comment *"It is now*-pause-*exactly midnight."*[13]

A second meeting was held the following night. Zahedi was agreed upon as the replacement for Mossadegh. The Shah would symbolically flee to the Caspian as Mohammed had from Mecca to Medina in 622 AD, after he signed a set of royal decrees delegitimizing Mossadegh and appointing Zahedi. If their plans went awry, the Shah and Queen Soraya would actually abscond to Baghdad in his private plane.

As Kim was organizing his resources and scheming details of the coup, the police were tipped-off about unusual goings-on at his safe-house and conducted a raid: *"The gates were forced open. Cars swept in, disgorging armed men who made a very thorough search of the house and grounds."*14

Nothing was uncovered and Kim was absent but the surveillance of the location forced Kim into securing an unlikely venue for his meetings – a Hillman Minx taxi – a bug proof and suitably portable location.

The time for action had arrived. Gaining support of the Mullahs was essential and large sums of cash were the inducement. Receipt of the questionably legal decrees signed by the Shah deposing Mossadegh and appointing Zahedi as prime minister were secured and were delivered. If rejected they were to be enforced even under gunpoint. The newspapers stepped-up a campaign of spreading propaganda. Organizing a select group of military commanders, loyal to the Shah who would lead the rank and file in revolt was arranged for the night of August 14.

However, Mossadegh got advanced warning of the coup and deployed troops and tanks around his home. The Shah's officers were seized when they attempted to arrest him and the operation appeared a colossal failure. Zahedi was sequestered in a hideout as the Shah fled the country. Mossadegh announced to the country of the failed coup.

In the absence of any information to Washington for a number of days, Under Secretary of State General Walter Bedell Smith sent a message to Kim, *"Give up and get out."*

However, within hours the conditions on the ground changed and Kim messaged back: *"Yours of 18 August received. Happy to report R. N. Ziegler (the pseudonym for Zahedi) safely installed and KGSAVOY (the cryptonym for the Shah) will be returning to Teheran in triumph shortly. Love and kisses from all the team."*15

In the interim, Kim, with the aid of CIA bribe money, frantically organized his street goons and began provoking demonstrations and riots throughout the streets of Tehran as Iranian Army officers loyal to the Shah began to mobilize outlying troops. Hundreds died in the street fighting that ensued.

In the vanguard of the chaos were a gang of famous Iranian weightlifters, the Zurkhaneh giants who made a showing in the streets and motivated the crowds as *"... these huge figures started marching westward, shouting and twirling more like dervishes than what they actually were."*[16]

Simultaneous to the mayhem and unrestrained violence in the streets, Tabriz radio was broadcasting dissension to the masses and strong support for the Shah.

Throughout the mass confusion Kim remained ensconced in the American Embassy compound. When realizing the tide had turned, he entered the street and forced his way through the mobs to liberate Zahedi from his hiding place. From the shoulders of his numerous supporters, the general mounted a column of tanks and proceeded to Mossadeg's residence. Kim later commented:

*"As I learned later but did not know then, they didn't reach old Mossy's house until he had already fled – over the garden wall and into a house from which he somehow managed to vanish. It was not until several days later that he called into the police station – hoping for help perhaps – and gave himself up."*[17]

On August 22, 1953, the Shah returned to Tehran as the new, supreme leader of Iran as Mossadeg was being incarcerated. He was to spend three-years in house arrest then exiled to remain within the confines of his home village there dying in 1967. The once democratically governed country whose prime minister was elected by popular vote now became a monarchy.

Kim slipped out of Iran posing as Mr. "Scar on Right Forehead" on a military air transport service plane as unknown and mysteriously as he entered weeks before.

In the ensuing years the Shah ruled the country with an iron hand through the army and the hated SAVAK secret police organization. His efforts to modernize and secularize the country angered many in the country's Islamic majority. The United States subsidized the regime with military support and enormous amounts of cash. In return, Iran provided a reliable ally in the region along with very generous oil concessions for the U. S. and Great Britain.

By 1979, suffering under the severe repression of the Shah's rule and the stress of his lightning fast modernization program, the people rose in revolt toppling the Pahlevi monarchy and forcing the Shah into exile. In November, 1979 Iranian students stormed the American Embassy in Tehran and held the 52 American diplomats hostage for 444 days creating a major crisis for the United States. This event, and President Jimmy Carter's failed attempts to liberate the Americans, are considered one of the major reasons for his loss to Ronald Reagan in the 1980 election and the Republicans winning control of the Senate for the first time in decades.

The deposed Shah died in Egypt in July 1980 from non-Hodgkin lymphoma as the Iranian Revolution elevated Ayatollah Khomeini as Supreme Leader of the country.

Upon his journey home, Kim met with Winston Churchill in London to relate his story. When he debriefed President Eisenhower and the Secretary of Defense in Washington, he stated:

*"If we, the CIA, are ever going to try something like this again, we must be absolutely sure that people and army want what we want. "If not, you had better give the job to the Marines!"*

He later commented,

*"Within weeks I was offered command of a Guatemalan undertaking already in preparation. A quick check suggested that my requirements were not likely to be met. I declined the offer. Later, I resigned from the CIA – before the Bay of Pigs disaster underlined the validity of my warning."*[18]

On March 17, 2000, then Secretary of State, Madeleine K. Albright gave a speech on American-Iranian relations. She remarked:

*"In 1953 the United States played a significant role in orchestrating the overthrow of Iran's popular Prime Minister, Mohammed Massadegh. The Eisenhower Administration believed its actions were justified for strategic reasons; but the coup was clearly a setback*

221

*for Iran's political development. And it is easy to see now why many Iranians continue to resent this intervention by America in their internal affairs."*

To this day, the Iranian people harbor a resentment for the United States originating with the overthrow of their government in 1953. Following the revolution in 1979, this isolated country has become one of the greatest threats to the State of Israel and the stability of the Middle-east region. The Iranian Government has been providing arms and technology to America's enemies in both the Iraq War and the outlawed jihadist group, Hamas. The regime under Mahmoud Ahmadinejad has been actively pursuing a nuclear arms program in contradiction to the United Nations and the Western World and remains today one of the greatest threats to world peace. The legacy of Kim Roosevelt's 1953 Iranian coup d'etat has had an enormous and lasting impact on the Middle-East and the world.

Despite TR's legendary patriotism and well-publicized adventures, Kermit and his son equaled and perhaps exceeded their famous forebear's "strenuous life" and thirst

*United States Navy repair ship named after Kermit Roosevelt. Commissioned in 1945, the vessel also saw service in the Korean War.*

for action.  Kermit by his heroism in the Great War; his peripatetic wanderings in search of rare and exotic species and failed, but gallant effort to serve under arms in the Second World War.  And Kim, in a later era continued in the family tradition in a manner that not only is remarkable for its audacity, but for its importance and lasting influence on international relations and the world's economy to the present day.  Unfortunately, both of these extraordinary individuals have today, been lost in the shadow of their family's fame.

Notes:

1.  Counter Coup – The Struggle for the Control of Iran by Kermit Roosevelt, page 199
2.  Ibid., page 207
3.  Ibid., page 110
4.  The World Crisis 1911-1914 by Winston Churchill, page 134; Charles Scribner's Sons
5.  CIA Clandestine Service History, "Overthrow of Premier Mossadeq of Iran, Novermber 1952-August 1953," March 1954 by Dr. Donald Wilber.
6.  Legacy of Ashes the History of the CIA by Tom Weiner, page 83; Doubleday, 2007
7.  Counter Coup – The Struggle for the Control of Iran by Kermit Roosevelt, page 139
8.  Legacy of Ashes the History of the CIA by Tom Weiner, page 84; Doubleday, 2007
9.  Counter Coup – The Struggle for the Control of Iran by Kermit Roosevelt, page 148
10. Ibid., page 154
11. Ibid.
12. Ibid., page 156
13. Ibid., page 157
14. Ibid., page 161
15. Ibid., page 190
16. Ibid., page 186
17. Ibid., page 193
18. Ibid., page 210

# ADDITIONAL READING

Published Material

Collier, Peter with David Horowitz, *The Roosevelts: An American Saga:* Simon & Schuster, 1994.

Donn, Linda, *The Roosevelt Cousins: Growing Up Together, 1882-1924:* Alfred A. Knopf, 2001.

Kinzer, Stephen, *All the Shah's Men: An American Coup and the Roots of Middle East Terror:* John Wiley & Sons, Inc., 2003, 2008.

Millard, Candice, *The River of Doubt: Theodore Roosevelt's Darkest Journey:* Broadway Books, 2005.

Miller, Nathan, *The Roosevelt Chronicles: The story of a great American family:* Doubleday & Company, Inc., 1979.

Morris, Sylvia Jukes, *Edith Kermit Roosevelt: Portrait of a First Lady:* Coward, McCann & Geoghegan, Inc., 1980.

Ornig, Joseph R., *My Last Chance to Be a Boy:* Stackpole Books, 1994.

Persico, Joseph E. *Roosevelt's Secret War:* Random House, 2001.

Renenhan Jr., Edward J., *The Lion's Pride: Theodore Roosevelt and His Family in Peace and War:* Oxford University Press, 1999.

Roosevelt, Kermit, *War in the Garden of Eden:* The Echo Library, 2007.

Roosevelt, Kermit, *The Long Trail:* Charles Scribner's Sons, 1912, 1920.

Roosevelt, Kermit, *Counter Coup: The Struggle for the Control of Iran:* McGraw-Hill Book Company, 1979.

Roosevelt, Mrs. Theodore Roosevelt, Jr., *Day Before Yesterday: The Reminiscences of Mrs. Theodore Roosevelt, Jr.:* Doubleday & Company, Inc., 1959.

Roosevelt, Mrs. Theodore Roosevelt, Sr., Mrs. Kermit Roosevelt, Richard Derby, Kermit Roosevelt, *Cleared for Strange Ports:* Charles Scribner's Sons, 1924, 1927.

Roosevelt, Theodore, *Through the Brazilian Wilderness:* Charles Scribner's Sons, 1922.

Roosevelt. Theodore, *African Game Trails:* Charles
 Scribner's Sons, 1926.
Roosevelt, Theodore and Kermit, *East of the Sun and West
 of the Moon:* Charles Scribner's Sons, 1926.
Roosevelt, Theodore and Kermit, *Trailing the Giant Panda:*
 Charles Scribner's Sons, 1929.
Weiner, Tim, *Legacy of Ashes: The History of the CIA:*
 Doubleday, 2007.

Non-published Material

The Belle and Kermit Roosevelt Papers reside in the Library
 of Congress Manuscript Division in Washington D.C.
 and contain approximately 56,900 items. The files
 span the years 1725 to 1975, with the bulk of the
 material dating from 1900 to 1964. The collection
 includes diaries, family correspondence, subject files,
 business papers and miscellaneous items.

The Franklin D. Roosevelt Presidential Library and
 Museum in Hyde Park, New York contain many letters
 and other pieces of correspondence before and during
 World War II between the War Department, the White
 House and Roosevelt family members and friends.

The National Archives National Military Personnel Records
 Center in St. Louis, Missouri contain Kermit Roosevelt's
 military records for World War I and World War II. Also
 at this location relating to his death is the coroner's
 report, autopsy report, death certificate, medical
 records, report of the Fort Richardson military
 command's investigation into his death with witness
 testimony and much correspondence between various
 military officers, the War Department and the White
 House.

The Explorer's Club, the American Museum of Natural
 History in New York and the Smithsonian Institute in
 Washington D.C. contain much detailed information
 pertaining to Kermit's many exploratory and hunting
 trips.

# INDEX

43758030R00144